THE OFFICIAL FILTHY RICH HANDBOOK

by Christopher Tennant

Contributing Writers
Sarah Horne and Marnie Hanel

Project Editor
Laura Yorke

Workman Publishing
New York

Published simultaneously in Canada by Thomas Allen & Son Limited.

Library of Congress Cataloging-in-Publication Data is available.

ISBN-13: 978-0-7611-4703-9

Cover illustration by Bob Hambly

Cover design by Paul Hanson and
Francesca Messina

A version of "The Lush Life," p. 226, originally appeared in *Radar* magazine.
Reprinted with permission.

Workman books are available at special discounts when purchased in bulk for premiums and sales promotions as well as for fund-raising or educational use. Special editions or book excerpts also can be created to specification. For details, contact the Special Sales Director at the address below.

Workman Publishing Company, Inc.
225 Varick Street
New York, NY 10014-4381
www.workman.com

Printed in the United States of America

First printing May 2008
10 9 8 7 6 5 4 3 2 1

For Zoë

CONTENTS

"The rules are... there are no rules."

—ARISTOTLE ONASSIS

INTRODUCTION

WELCOME TO THE CLUB

REMEMBER WHEN HAVING A COUPLE MILlion dollars meant something?

Neither do we.

Particularly when we recall (with just the slightest of tingles) that over 30,000 Americans are now sitting on at least thirty times that.

This crew includes every entry on the Forbes 400 (who, at last count, were worth a combined $1.54 trillion, more than all the money held in commercial U.S. banks) right on down to that guy back in B-school who first told you what a hedge fund was.

They're not all famous, or even well known, but these 30,000 do have much in common. Relative to the average citizen, they can travel where they want, live where they want, do what they want, and even screw who they want—both for business and for pleasure. Their money allows them to be truly free, and isn't that what our forefathers were getting at?

But, as we've been told so many times, freedom has its price. In the case of the aforementioned 30,000, it's the tyranny of too many options. St. Barts or St. Moritz? Gulfstream or Boeing? Where to build your private golf course—or did you want a polo field? With all those wealth managers incessantly ringing you up, should you consider counter-surveillance measures?

We're exhausted just thinking about it.

We call this tippity-top tier the Filthy Rich. As you'll soon learn, you don't need to earn or inherit more money than you already have to join their ranks. You just need to try a little harder.

Maybe a lot harder.

—Christopher Tennant

THE PLUTOCRAT PRIMER

"There are people who have money and people who are rich."
—COCO CHANEL

ARRIVISTE (AR•RI•VISTE n.): *derived from the past participle form of the French* arriver *(to reach or arrive). One that has recently or suddenly risen to an unaccustomed position of wealth or power and has not yet gained the prestige, dignity, or manner associated with it.*

At some point or another, everyone's an arriviste. Perhaps your great-great-grandfather was a tinned-bean mogul who paid your great-grandfather's way into Yale with a generous donation to the library and a case of bootleg whiskey. In that scenario, you've had a three-generation headstart insinuating yourself into the American upperclass and have the tragic family history to prove it. But, let's be honest. You probably became a so-called "high net-worth individual" within your own lifetime (or even last week)—proving that, yes, our fabled meritocracy still allows for the making of ungodly sums of money.

Whether or not you are ever accepted by your peers will be influenced by a number of factors. But before we get ahead of ourselves, a pertinent question: Who are your peers? And why are they all so leathery looking?

Should you, like several hundred of your fellow countrymen each year, suddenly find yourself in eight-figure territory, don't be surprised if you feel like you've landed on Planet Bizarro—populated by a highly sophisticated, if wildly eccentric, race of beings with their own peculiar culture and customs. That ruddy faced fellow in the faded cords and cardigan? He only looks like a math teacher. Recognizing the sum of his parts will be half the battle.

KA-CHING!

THE RAIDER

OLD SCHOOL

"Want a friend? Buy a dog"

MADE FORTUNE: In private equity

NET WORTH: $7 billion

DAD WAS: Head of the men's department at Bloomingdale's

EDUCATION: City College; Harvard Business School

NICKNAME: Pump 'n Dump

CONFIDANTE: His lawyer at Skadden Arps

SOUL MATES: Miss Latvia 2005; his staff publicist ("to keep me out of the press")

COLLECTS: Vendettas; black-suited bodyguards (most recently, Yuri and Ramen, ex-Mossad agents plucked from Bibi Netanyahu's detail)

PASSIONS: Nondisclosure agreements; personal hygiene; getting daughter into Brown

PET PEEVE: Alimony

FONDEST MEMORY: His first defamation suit

BIG DREAM: To have all five ex-wives apologize to him in print

BÊTE NOIRES: The *New York Post*'s Page Six; microbes; "pansies"

PATRON SAINTS: Ron Perelman; Kirk Kerkorian

Yankees cap and Blinde wraparound sunglasses: *Helps him blend in*

Turnbull & Asser button-down

Organic kosher box lunch: *"Eating in restaurants is like eating from the sewer"*

Armani single-breasted blazer

Sure-Lock II handheld bug detector: *Won't talk business unless the room's been swept*

Travel-size bottle of Purell: *For deal closings; other occasions he's forced to shake hands*

.22-caliber Beretta: *A P.I. pal pulled strings to get him a carry permit*

BlackBerry. On speed dial: *the White House; the Likud; banker in Zurich; G550 pilot (on 24-hour standby);* Vanity Fair *editor Graydon Carter; daughter's college coach*

Ralph Lauren "vintage"

Ostrich-skin Lucchese cowboy boots

THE HEDGER

NEW SCHOOL

"It's not enough to succeed. Others must fail"

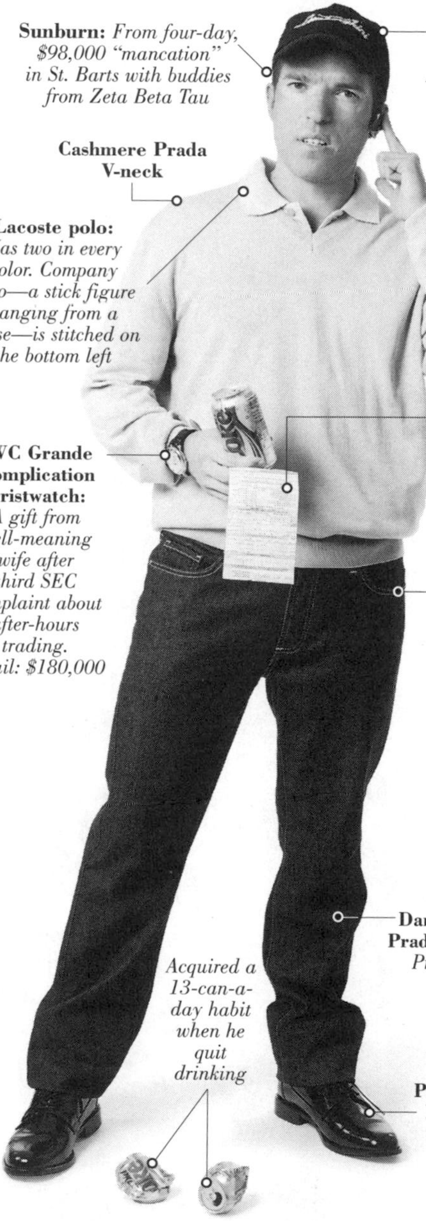

Sunburn: *From four-day, $98,000 "mancation" in St. Barts with buddies from Zeta Beta Tau*

Cashmere Prada V-neck

Lacoste polo: *Has two in every color. Company logo—a stick figure hanging from a noose—is stitched on the bottom left*

IWC Grande Complication wristwatch: *A gift from well-meaning wife after third SEC complaint about after-hours trading. Retail: $180,000*

Lamborghini baseball cap: *Knows it's tacky; doesn't care. Came with the Murciélago*

Traffic court summons: *Opened up his Murciélago on the Merritt in a bid to impress Veronica*

Listerine Breath Strips; golf tee from Round Hill Country Club: *He's on the waiting list*

Keys to SoHo bachelor pad: *He keeps "forgetting" to sell it*

Dark blue Prada jeans: *Pressed*

Acquired a 13-can-a-day habit when he quit drinking

Paul Smith lace-ups

MADE FORTUNE: Unloading Google at $498; used proceeds to start hedge fund, Hangman Capital™

NET WORTH: $2.4 billion

DAD WAS: A pharmacist/bookie

EDUCATION: UPenn; Goldman Sachs

NICKNAMES: 2 and 40; $498; Jerkoff *(sotto voce)*

CONFIDANTE: Thelma, his 65-year-old assistant

SOUL MATE: Veronica, his 25-year-old art advisor at Gagosian Gallery

COLLECTS: Overpriced contemporary art; Lamborghinis

PASSIONS: Getting an "in" at the Greenwich Planning and Zoning Department; heli-skiing

PET PEEVE: Hamptons traffic

FONDEST MEMORY: Outbidding Paul Tudor Jones at the Greenwich Country Day School fund-raiser

BIG DREAM: To take the pot in the World Amateur Poker Series

BÊTE NOIRES: Chumps; the AG's office

PATRON SAINTS: ESL Investments honcho Eddie Lampert; SAC Capital's Stevie Cohen

THE DYNASSEUR

OLD SCHOOL

"Noblesse oblige"

MADE FORTUNE: When Mummy passed away

NET WORTH: One-sixth share of $4 billion trust

GRANDDAD WAS: An illiterate German peasant with a head for business

EDUCATION: Four years at Princeton; one semester at Cambridge (considers it his alma mater)

NICKNAMES: Chappy; Junior

CONFIDANTE: Lifelong chauffeur, Rodney

SOUL MATE: Charlotte, a Suffolk-born, Sotheby's-bred expert in Eastern Han period Chinese porcelain

COLLECTS: Gutenberg Bibles; 17th-century Italian firearms

PASSIONS: Buffing the family name through good works; Napoléon

PET PEEVES: Rudeness; "the smoking of drugs"

FONDEST MEMORY: Donating his Ortelius maps to the Yale library

BIG DREAM: For men to start wearing hats again

BÊTE NOIRE: Scheming cousin

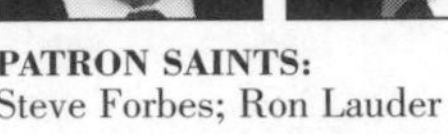

PATRON SAINTS: Steve Forbes; Ron Lauder

Bespoke suit from Jermyn Street, London: *Has 43 others just like it*

Charvet custom shirt

Monogrammed Irish linen handkerchief: *"A true gentleman never leaves the house without one"*

Red Hermès tie: *Dancing clowns are his favorite pattern*

Wall Street Journal: *The best philanthropy coverage in town*

Burberry trench

Hermès briefcase: *Dyed to match his shoes*

Vertu limited edition cell phone. On speed dial: *Julian Niccolini at the Four Seasons; socialite daughter's office at MoMA; antiquities department at Sotheby's*

John Lobb custom brogues: *$4,200, but they last forever*

Trademarks and brands appear solely for purposes of parody. The products pictured are not necessarily those of the owners of the marks/brands used.

THE WASTREL

NEW SCHOOL

"What day is it?"

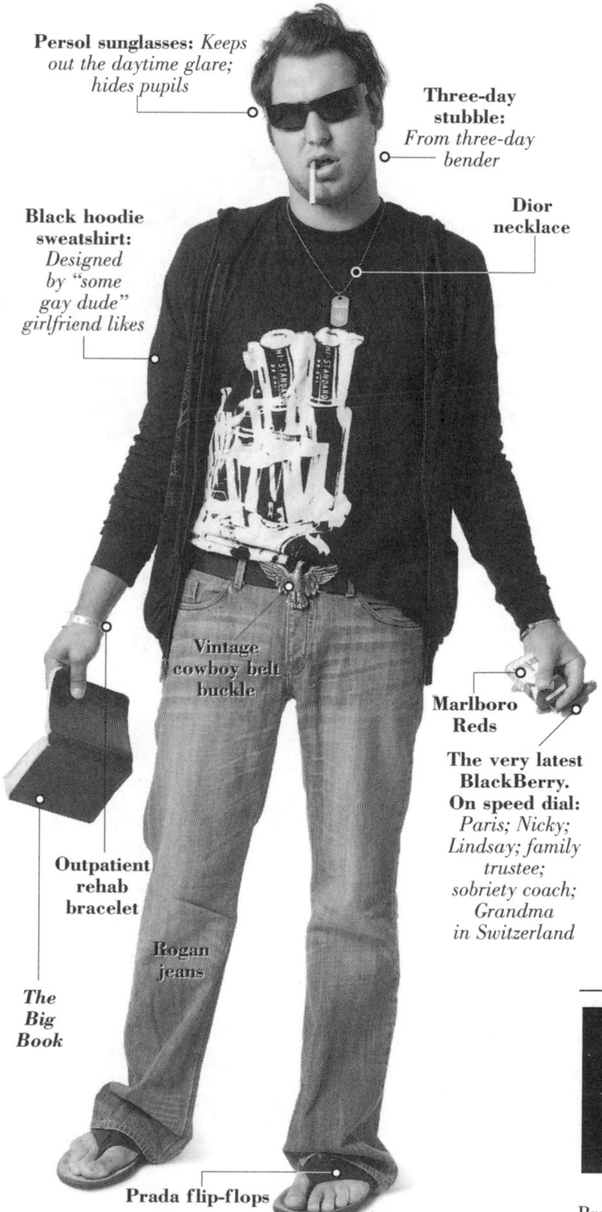

Persol sunglasses: *Keeps out the daytime glare; hides pupils*

Three-day stubble: *From three-day bender*

Dior necklace

Black hoodie sweatshirt: *Designed by "some gay dude" girlfriend likes*

Vintage cowboy belt buckle

Marlboro Reds

The very latest BlackBerry. On speed dial: *Paris; Nicky; Lindsay; family trustee; sobriety coach; Grandma in Switzerland*

Outpatient rehab bracelet

Rogan jeans

The Big Book

Prada flip-flops

MADE FORTUNE: Convincing Grandma he needed $5 million cash to start a hip-hop label

NET WORTH: $400 million if he makes it to 25

GRANDDAD WAS: A Texas wildcatter; Greek shipping tycoon

EDUCATION: Two semesters at Crossroads in L.A.; one semester at Beverly High; 28 days at Promises Malibu

NICKNAME: Bloater

CONFIDANTE: The junkie Venezuelan juice heir he met at Hazelden

SOUL MATE: Jasmine, his personal shopper at Fred Segal

COLLECTS: Own press clippings; racist jokes

PASSIONS: *US Weekly;* freebasing

PET PEEVES: Stepdads; fat chicks

FONDEST MEMORY: Crashing Prince Harry's 21st

BIG DREAM: A threesome on P. Diddy's yacht

BÊTE NOIRES: Valley trash; TMZ

PATRON SAINTS: Brandon Davis; Stavros Niarchos

THE TECHNOCRAT

OLD SCHOOL

"The geek shall inherit the earth"

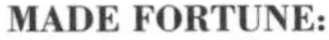

MADE FORTUNE: "Fundamentally altering the course of human existence"

NET WORTH: $18 billion

DAD WAS: An engineer

EDUCATION: Expelled from MIT for equipment theft; two years puttering in his parents' garage

NICKNAMES: God; Satan (both *sotto voce*)

CONFIDANTE: Warren Buffett

SOUL MATE: His wife, Laurie, a Montessori kindergarten teacher

COLLECTS: Submersibles; heavily guarded foreign compounds

PASSIONS: Jamming with Mick and Keith; planned obsolescence

PET PEEVES: Politics; antitrust legislation

FONDEST MEMORY: Hacking into the DMV in junior high

BIG DREAMS: To find a cure for Asperger's; win the Nobel Peace Prize

BÊTE NOIRES: Other technocrats; the U.S. Attorney General's Office

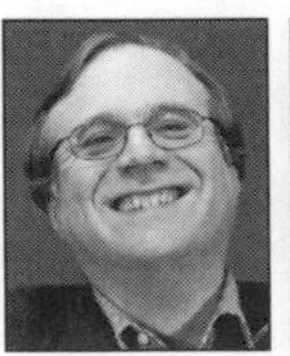

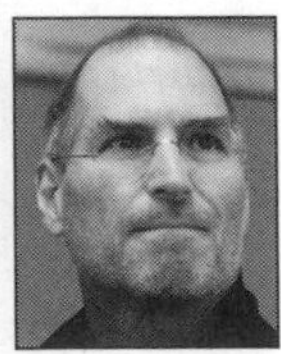

PATRON SAINTS: Microsoft cofounder Paul Allen; Apple's Steve Jobs

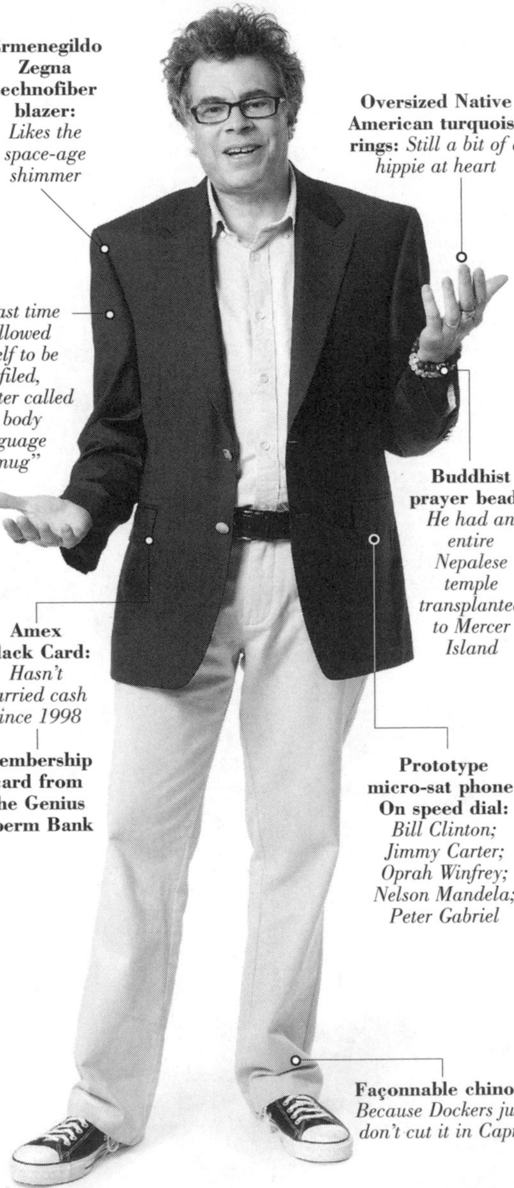

Ermenegildo Zegna technofiber blazer: *Likes the space-age shimmer*

The last time he allowed himself to be profiled, the writer called his body language "smug"

Amex Black Card: *Hasn't carried cash since 1998*

Membership card from the Genius Sperm Bank

Oversized Native American turquoise rings: *Still a bit of a hippie at heart*

Buddhist prayer beads: *He had an entire Nepalese temple transplanted to Mercer Island*

Prototype micro-sat phone. On speed dial: *Bill Clinton; Jimmy Carter; Oprah Winfrey; Nelson Mandela; Peter Gabriel*

Façonnable chinos: *Because Dockers just don't cut it in Capri*

Trademarks and brands appear solely for purposes of parody. The products pictured are not necessarily those of the owners of the marks/brands used.

THE NERDLING

NEW SCHOOL

"Acha, amoowa nocka!"
(Ewokese for "Okay, you have a deal!")

Robert Marc specs: *Prescription's too thick to wear contacts (he's legally blind). His publicist picked them out*

Fifth-generation iPhone: *"A gift from Steve." (You can touch it if you sign an NDA)*
On speed dial: *Randi, his girlfriend since eighth grade;* World of Warcraft *player support; Mom and Chuck*

"Goatse.cx": *You really don't want to know*

Auto-start control for Lexus hybrid: *A gift from M&A team at Goldman Sachs*

Jack Spade manbag with "¡I PARTY IBIZA!" patch: *Rented a villa next to Jade Jagger's last summer. Nicole Richie called him a "dork loser"*

Fair trade-approved Edun jeans: *A gift from "The Bon-ster"*

Beat-up New Balances: *Muddied from afternoon of intraoffice Ultimate Frisbee (team name: Optimus Prime)*

MADE FORTUNE: Overnight

NET WORTH: $800 million on paper

DAD WAS: A substitute physics teacher

EDUCATION: One semester at Caltech

NICKNAME: Obi-Wan

CONFIDANTE: Eurethra Antwerp, a dominatrix on *Second Life*

SOUL MATE: Julie, his VP of Executive Dream Coordination and Actualization

COLLECTS: Life-size *Matrix* figurines; vintage console video games; photos of 18-year-old Asian girls he meets on Facebook

PASSIONS: Social networking; Web 3.0

PET PEEVES: Messy code; condescending venture capitalists

FONDEST MEMORY: Turning down Google

BIG DREAM: To speak Mandarin

BÊTE NOIRES: Larry Page and Sergey Brin; the jock who pantsed him on the quad freshman year

PATRON SAINTS: Facebook's Mark Zuckerberg; YouTube's Chad Hurley

THE SHOWMAN

OLD SCHOOL

"Knock 'em dead!"

MADE FORTUNE: In strip malls; megahotels; casinos; syndicated television

NET WORTH: $3.7 billion

DAD WAS: The Vacuum King of Toledo

EDUCATION: Honorary degree from Stanford

NICKNAME: Buster

CONFIDANTE: Luscious from the Spearmint Rhino

SOUL MATE: Second wife, Bunny

COLLECTS: Vintage Disney animation cells; Picassos, Renoirs, Cézannes, Van Goghs . . .

PASSION: Developing a reality TV series with a trademarkable catchphrase

PET PEEVE: Cynicism

FONDEST MEMORY: Watching Liza and Siegfried perform at his 60th

BIG DREAMS: Table 1 at Per Se on permanent hold; a gold-plated Boeing 767

BÊTE NOIRES: "Low-class people"; labor unions

PATRON SAINTS: Donald Trump; casino kingpin Steve Wynn

Doc swears eye lift will eventually settle

"Supporting the troops is good business"

Off-the-rack double-breasted Brioni suit: *"When you can afford the best, why settle for less?"*

Motorola StarTAC. On speed dial: *Candy Spelling; Vegas mayor Oscar Goodman; Andrew Lloyd Webber; Michael Jackson; Elizabeth Taylor; David Gest; Elton John; his Eurocopter pilot*

Patek Philippe watch, a gift from Nancy Reagan: *"We've had Mandela, the Dalai Lama, Mother Teresa, Gorbachev, and every president since Nixon stay with us"*

THE IMPRESARIO

NEW SCHOOL

"Money ain't a thang... it's everythang"

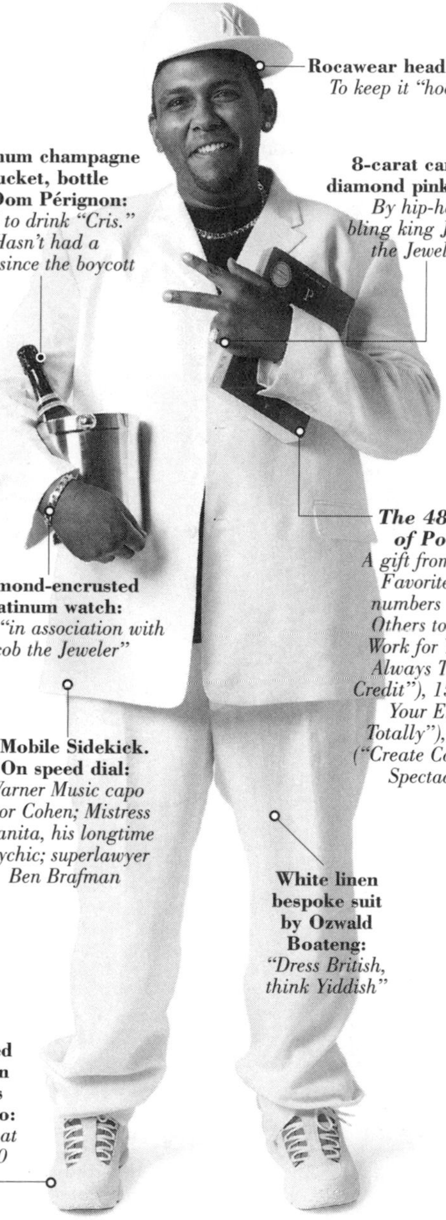

Rocawear headband: *To keep it "hood"*

Platinum champagne bucket, bottle of Dom Pérignon: *Used to drink "Cris." Hasn't had a drop since the boycott*

8-carat canary diamond pinky ring: *By hip-hop bling king Jacob the Jeweler*

The 48 Laws of Power: *A gift from Kanye. Favorite laws: numbers 7 ("Get Others to Do the Work for You, but Always Take the Credit"), 15 ("Crush Your Enemy Totally"), and 37 ("Create Compelling Spectacles")*

Diamond-encrusted platinum watch: *By self "in association with Jacob the Jeweler"*

T-Mobile Sidekick. On speed dial: *Warner Music capo Lyor Cohen; Mistress Juanita, his longtime psychic; superlawyer Ben Brafman*

White linen bespoke suit by Ozwald Boateng: *"Dress British, think Yiddish"*

Limited edition Nikes by Nigo: *A steal at $4,000*

MADE FORTUNE: When he sold his label to Universal

NET WORTH: $650 million cash; $300 million song catalog

DAD WAS: In and out of jail

EDUCATION: Dropped out of Morehouse to promote concerts full-time; half a year answering phones at Jive

NICKNAME: Changes by the hour

CONFIDANTE: Grandma, who raised him

SOUL MATE: Loud-mouthed ex-model

COLLECTS: Publishing rights to his artists' recordings; *Scarface*-iana

PASSION: His sportswear/soul food/auto body franchise

PET PEEVE: The gay rumors

FONDEST MEMORIES: The early '90s, "when it was still about the music"; poaching his vegan chef from Katie Couric

BIG DREAM: To take himself public

BÊTE NOIRES: *XXL*; his "baby mama"

PATRON SAINTS: Russell Simmons; P. Diddy

THE SPECULATOR

"Money's just a way of keepin' score"

MADE FORTUNE: Betting against the big boys

NET WORTH: $14.6 billion as of 7 A.M. this morning

DAD WAS: A field rep for State Farm

EDUCATION: University of Nowhere at Tumbleweed; two semesters at Wharton

NICKNAMES: T-Bone; Ace; Oakie

CONFIDANTE: Buddy, his ancient black Lab

SOUL MATE: Fourth wife, Li-Ho ("Lilly") Quan

COLLECTS: Undervalued industries; toy trains

PASSIONS: Base metals; extra-lean "black and blue" sirloin

PET PEEVES: Pretentiousness; laziness; overpaying; restaurants that serve "those goddamn tiny portions"

FONDEST MEMORY: Collapsing the peso

BIG DREAM: To play shortstop for the Cubs

BÊTE NOIRES: "Moron" analysts; "extortionist" ex-wives

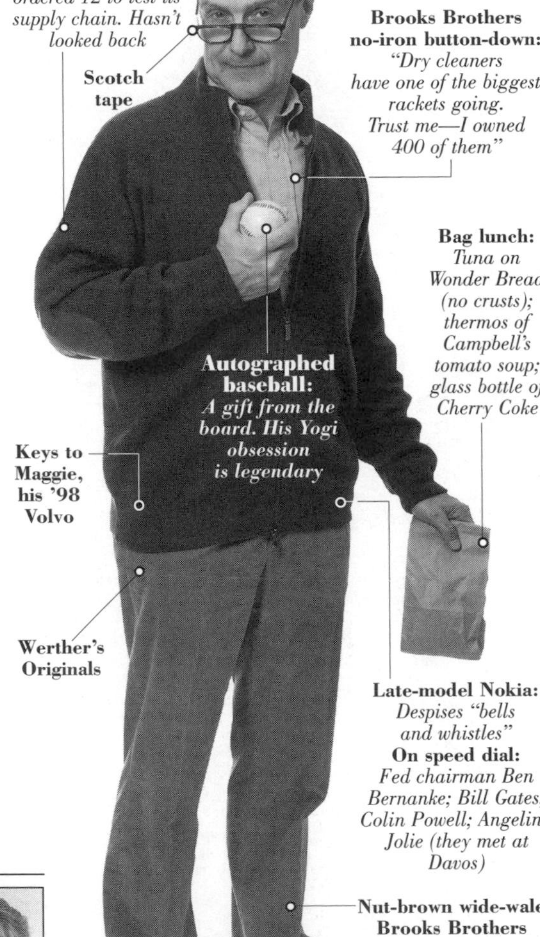

PATRON SAINTS: Warren Buffett; George Soros

THE THRILLIONAIRE

"I can do that"

Australian cowboy hat: *Still waiting for the bison burger craze to hit. Keeps a herd of 1,400 on his ranch*

Salt-and-pepper hair: *Stopped dying it after a particularly heavy peyote trip*

Daily cocktail of Lithium, Prozac, and Wellbutrin: *Saved his life and got him off the sauce.Helps with anger management*

Leather satchel: *Contains NSA briefing on alien life forms; dog-eared issue of* Popular Science*; half-smoked joint. Ties his own flies. Strictly catch-and-release*

Sat phone. On speed dial: *Stephen Hawking; Charlie Rose; ghostwriter at* Fortune*; his Navajo spirit guide;* New York Times *publisher Arthur Sulzberger Jr. ("for feedback on my op-eds")*

Piercing blue eyes: *Landed him on* People's *"50 Most Eligible Bachelors" list in '86, '88, and '94*

His third memoir, *I Ain't Done Yet!* *Every visitor gets an autographed copy*

MADE FORTUNE: Selling satellite dishes

NET WORTH: $8 billion

DAD WAS: M.I.A.

EDUCATION: Dropped out of high school to deal pot full-time; served (as a cook) in 'Nam; two years of community college

NICKNAMES: Tex; the Comeback Kid

CONFIDANTE: Fat Carl, his Cherokee estate manager in Big Sky

SOUL MATE: His first wife, Rhonda (he's on his seventh)

COLLECTS: Shark teeth; gold bars salvaged from Spanish galleons; Marchetti fighter jets

PASSIONS: Motown; hot-air ballooning; shareholders' rights

PET PEEVES: Republicanism; the word "no"

FONDEST MEMORIES: Buying his first cable network; sticking it to Murdoch

BIG DREAM: To be president of the moon

BÊTE NOIRE: That Russian son-of-a-bitch trying to beat his world record

PATRON SAINTS: Ted Turner; Richard Branson

THE MOGULESS

"You go, girl!" ™

MADE FORTUNE: Off strength of own charisma

NET WORTH: $1.8 billion

DAD WAS: A high school principal

EDUCATION: Barnard

NICKNAME: Everywoman; Ms. Perfect *(sotto voce)*

CONFIDANTE: Staff diarist

SOUL MATE: Bland public-television producer and all-around yes-man

COLLECTS: Dappled gray horses; seating charts; favors

PASSIONS: Garden mazes; thank-you notes; bringing Rainer Maria Rilke's *Letters to a Young Poet* to the Broadway stage

PET PEEVE: Tardiness

FONDEST MEMORY: Getting picked up for syndication

BIG DREAM: To give the Third World access to free health care and spa treatments (all women need a little "me time")

BÊTE NOIRE: Rachel Ray

PATRON SAINTS: Oprah Winfrey; Martha Stewart

Personal trainer's bestselling fitness book: *Her blurb is on the back*

Monogrammed silver Vertu. On speed dial: *Endeavor agent Ari Emanuel;* Beloved *author Toni Morrison; Ellen DeGeneres; Deepak Chopra; Tom Cruise*

Green tea: *Drinks a pot a day to flush out toxins*

Birkin bag: *Photocopied packet of today's press mentions; bag of raw almonds; slice of Parmesan; six sliced grapes*

Daily affirmation calendar: *"There's No 'I' in Synergy"*

Eponymous magazine with self on cover

Escada pencil skirt

Serious gams: *Daily hour on the elliptical isn't for nothing*

Trademarks and brands appear solely for purposes of parody. The products pictured are not necessarily those of the owners of the marks/brands used.

THE OPERATOR

"Let them hate so long as they fear"

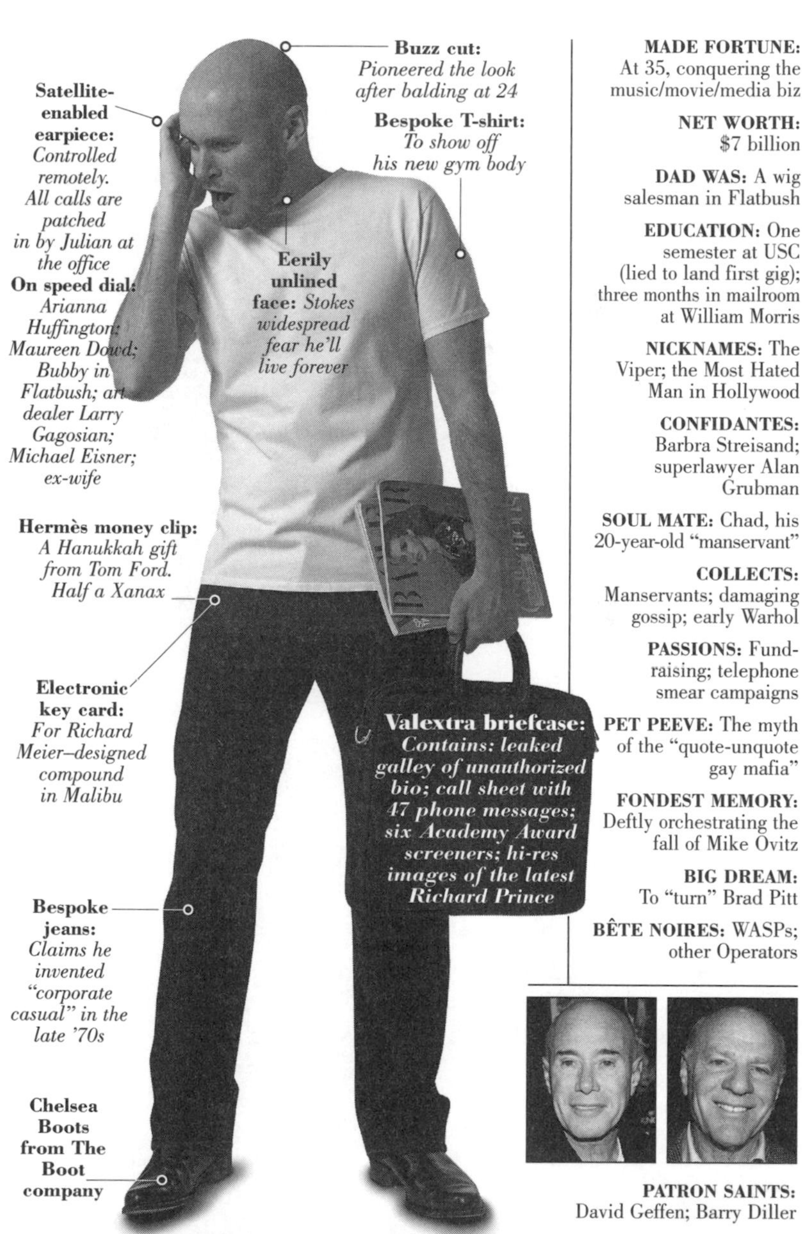

MADE FORTUNE: At 35, conquering the music/movie/media biz

NET WORTH: $7 billion

DAD WAS: A wig salesman in Flatbush

EDUCATION: One semester at USC (lied to land first gig); three months in mailroom at William Morris

NICKNAMES: The Viper; the Most Hated Man in Hollywood

CONFIDANTES: Barbra Streisand; superlawyer Alan Grubman

SOUL MATE: Chad, his 20-year-old "manservant"

COLLECTS: Manservants; damaging gossip; early Warhol

PASSIONS: Fund-raising; telephone smear campaigns

PET PEEVE: The myth of the "quote-unquote gay mafia"

FONDEST MEMORY: Deftly orchestrating the fall of Mike Ovitz

BIG DREAM: To "turn" Brad Pitt

BÊTE NOIRES: WASPs; other Operators

PATRON SAINTS: David Geffen; Barry Diller

THE A-LISTER

HIM

"Truth is what is true to you"
—L. RON HUBBARD

MADE FORTUNE: Reprising lead role in action/comedy franchise

NET WORTH: $700 million

DAD WAS: Salt of the earth; alcoholic

EDUCATION: Palukaville High; "mind-blowing" 12-week Scientology immersion course at the Gold Base

NICKNAME: Checks into hotels as "Edward Penishands"

CONFIDANTES: Mom; his church-appointed minder

SOUL MATE: Studio-sanctioned eye candy

COLLECTS: Frank Lloyd Wright houses; People's Choice Awards

PASSIONS: Vintage Indian motorcycles; ridding self of "body thetans"

PET PEEVE: U.S. libel laws

FONDEST MEMORY: Reaching OT-VII

BIG DREAM: To write, direct, produce, and star in the definitive L. Ron Hubbard biopic

BÊTE NOIRE: French paparazzi

PATRON SAINTS: Tom Cruise; John Travolta

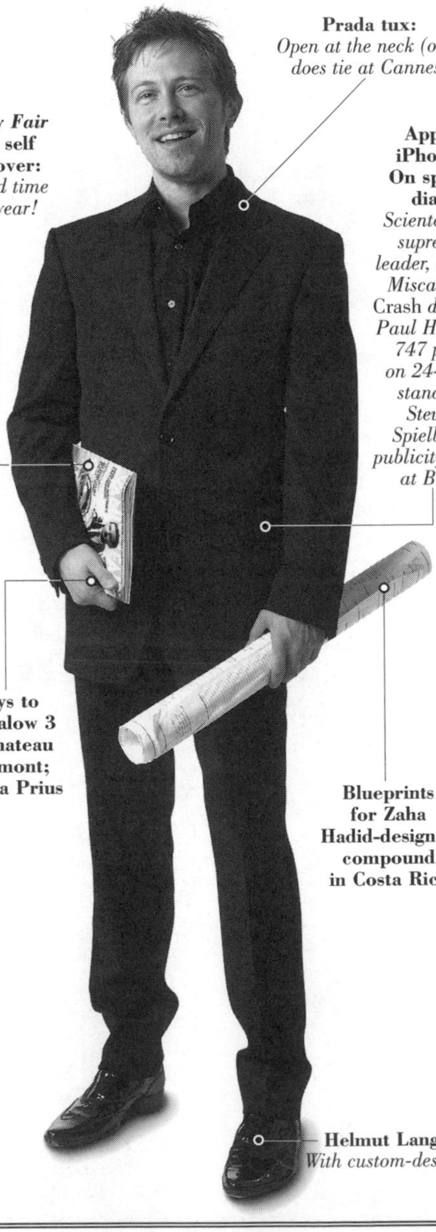

Prada tux: *Open at the neck (only does tie at Cannes)*

***Vanity Fair* with self on cover:** *Second time this year!*

Apple iPhone. On speed dial: *Scientology supreme leader, David Miscavige;* Crash *director Paul Haggis; 747 pilot on 24-hour standby; Steven Spielberg; publicity team at BWR*

Keys to bungalow 3 at Chateau Marmont; Toyota Prius

Blueprints for Zaha Hadid-designed compound in Costa Rica

Helmut Lang boots: *With custom-designed lifts*

Trademarks and brands appear solely for purposes of parody. The products pictured are not necessarily those of the owners of the marks/brands used.

THE A-LISTER

HER

"At the end of the day, it's about the work"

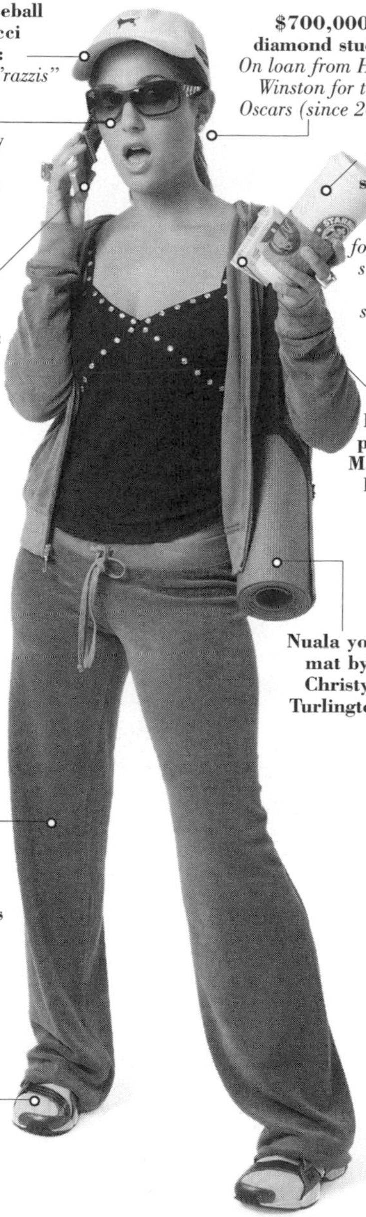

Black Dog baseball cap and Gucci sunglasses: *To throw off the "razzis"*

$700,000 diamond studs: *On loan from Harry Winston for the Oscars (since 2004)*

Surgically refined ski jump

Vanilla soy chai latté: *Drinks four a day since she quit smoking*

Dolce & Gabbana gold-plated Motorola: *A baby shower gift from Domenico and Stefano*

On speed dial: *nanny 1; nanny 2; stylist L'Wren Scott; concierge desk at Beverly Hills Hotel; maître d' at the Ivy; Harvey Weinstein*

Half a pack of Marlboro Lights

Nuala yoga mat by Christy Turlington

Stella McCartney for Adidas cashmere sweats

Hogan trainers

MADE FORTUNE: On syndication; shilling for Hitachi in Asia

NET WORTH: $320 million

DAD WAS: Distant

EDUCATION: Fresno School of the Performing Arts

NICKNAMES: America's Sweetheart; Ice Queen *(sotto voce)*

CONFIDANTE: Her hairstylist Ludovic

SOUL MATE: Actor or musician of lesser standing, dubious sexuality

COLLECTS: Heartbreak

PASSIONS: Bikram yoga; saving the world, one orphan at a time

PET PEEVE: "Misogynist directors"

FONDEST MEMORY: Summer stock with Dame Judi Dench

BIG DREAMS: To win Best Actress; live in London and have play-group with Madonna and Gwyneth

BÊTE NOIRE: Trailer-dwelling mother who sold her baby pictures to the *Daily Mail*

PATRON SAINTS: Renée Zellweger; Jennifer Aniston

THE GRANDE DAME

OLD SCHOOL

"In my day, there was something called class"

MADE FORTUNE: When she married into the Dodge family

NET WORTH: $580 million from third husband; $40 million in Lowell, Massachusetts, real estate from Granddaddy's textile empire

DAD WAS: A gentleman pecan farmer

EDUCATION: Two years at Sweet Briar College

NICKNAME: Cookie

CONFIDANTES: Her five Jack Russell terriers

SOUL MATE: Her walker, Reinaldo

COLLECTS: Blackamoor cameos; South American orchids; working farms

PASSIONS: Competitive bridge; the anorexic diet she's been on since age eight; saving Venice

PET PEEVE: Rubbery lobster salad

FONDEST MEMORY: Her two-day affair with Ari Onassis in 1962

BIG DREAM: To be acknowledged for her decades of selfless toil

BÊTE NOIRE: Her "degenerate" son

PATRON SAINTS: Annette de la Renta; Lynn Wyatt

Frozen forehead: *"How Mummy braved the world without Botox I'll never understand"*

Bottle-blonde helmet hair: *Has blowouts every morning at 7; sleeps sitting up*

Venetian red lipstick: *Her signature shade*

Bulgari diamond-and-sapphire brooch: *Mortimer's last gift before the aneurysm*

Christian Lacroix knit suit

Motorola RAZR, programmed by her PA. On speed dial: *Bergdorf's; Dominick Dunne; Annette de la Renta; florist Robert Isabel; Carolina Herrera; Henry Kissinger; the maître d' at Swifty's*

Kelly bag: *One of five*

Trademarks and brands appear solely for purposes of parody. The products pictured are not necessarily those of the owners of the marks/brands used.

THE HEIRESS

NEW SCHOOL

"What more can I give?"

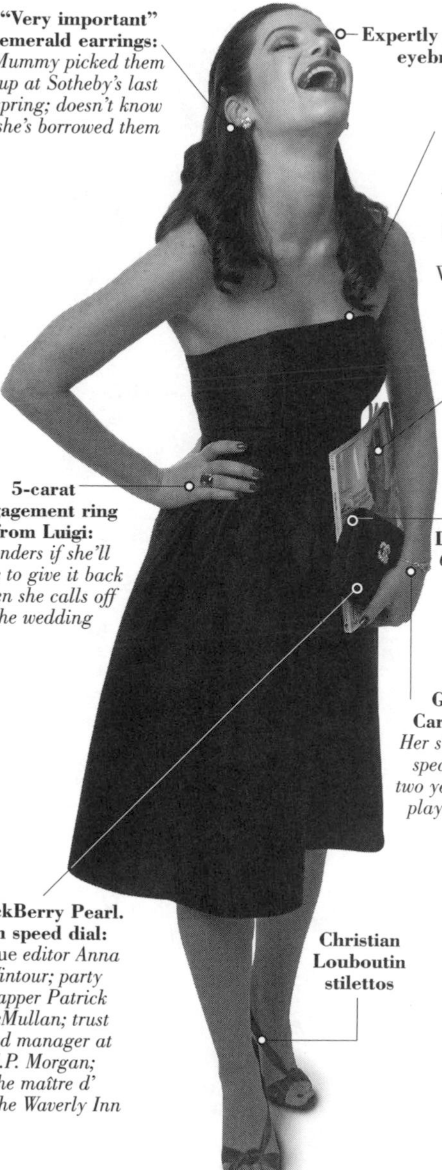

"Very important" emerald earrings: *Mummy picked them up at Sotheby's last spring; doesn't know she's borrowed them*

Expertly plucked eyebrows

Oscar de la Renta sample tag: *A loan from the designer. Since her mini-profile in* Women's Wear, *every day's like Christmas*

Her spread in last month's *Tatler*

5-carat engagement ring from Luigi: *Wonders if she'll have to give it back when she calls off the wedding*

Judith Leiber clutch: *Contains: four carb-free Larabars; $1,200 cash*

Grammy's Cartier watch: *Her sister wouldn't speak to her for two years (Grammy played favorites)*

BlackBerry Pearl. On speed dial: Vogue *editor Anna Wintour; party snapper Patrick McMullan; trust fund manager at J.P. Morgan; the maître d' at The Waverly Inn*

Christian Louboutin stilettos

MADE FORTUNE: When she turned 21

NET WORTH: $80 million in tightly controlled trust

DAD WAS: A mere shadow of his father

EDUCATION: Spence in Manhattan; Le Rosey in Switzerland; four blacked-out years at Trinity

NICKNAME: Naughty

CONFIDANTE: Gay best friend, Lyle

SOUL MATE: Luigi, her foppish South American banker fiancé

COLLECTS: Invitations; free clothes

PASSION: Giving back

PET PEEVES: Being called a "socialite"; being seated in the second row at couture shows (behind Mummy)

FONDEST MEMORY: Seventh grade, "when we were all friends and nobody cared about this crap"

BIG DREAMS: To launch her own handbag line; be taken seriously

BÊTE NOIRE: Her coat-tail-riding cousin

PATRON SAINTS: Lauren Bush; Lydia Hearst

THE HEIRHEAD

NO SCHOOL

"If only people could see the real *me"*

MADE FORTUNE: Playing role of debauched spoiled brat

NET WORTH: Share of $140 million family trust (plus sex-tape residuals)

DAD WAS: A well-known '70s lothario

EDUCATION: Expelled from Deerfield; bribed younger sister to take GED

NICKNAMES: Celebutard; Heir Mattress

CONFIDANTE: Mr. Sparkles, her pygmy house cat

SOUL MATE: *Girls Gone Wild* mogul Joe Francis

COLLECTS: Minor STDs; parking tickets

PASSIONS: "Feminitism"; exotic marsupials

PET PEEVES: Ugly girls; "mean people"

FONDEST MEMORY: Back-to-back spreads in *Vanity Fair* and *Maxim*

BIG DREAM: To find a European prince and live happily ever after on the pages of *Hello!*

BÊTE NOIRE: The Heiress (see p. 17)

PATRON SAINTS: Paris Hilton; Kimberly Stewart

Trademarks and brands appear solely for purposes of parody. The products pictured are not necessarily those of the owners of the marks/brands used.

COMMON ROGUES & REMORAS

Imposters and Parasites to Know and Avoid

THE STRIP MINER

Gold-digging personal trainer, exotic dancer, masseuse, or flight attendant who attaches herself to men of means for financial succor

HOSTS Old fools, late bloomers, pro athletes, serial philanderers, and widowers who hate their children

FEEDING GROUNDS Gentlemen's clubs in Nevada, Florida, Texas, and New York; back-page advertisements in city magazines

IDENTIFYING TRAITS Prescription drug abuse; kleptomania; tribal-themed lower-back tattoos; visible roots; stretch marks

THE POWER WALKER

A sophisticated and impeccably groomed homosexual who cultivates subservient friendships with bored, self-obsessed rich women in exchange for social entrée, free meals, and Gulfstream rides

HOSTS Lonely, polished women whose husbands never socialize; unpolished second or third wives in need of a Henry Higgins

FEEDING GROUNDS Major charity events across the country

IDENTIFYING TRAITS Acid wit; encyclopedic gossip recall; face work. Mature specimens may have hearing aids

THE ARISTOWHAT?

Despite cut-glass accent and aggressive name-dropping, this Count of No Account responds to questions about his regal bearing with a stream of mumbles

HOSTS American Anglophiles and hard-partying nouveau richerie in Palm Beach, Gstaad, and Manhattan's Upper East Side

FEEDING GROUNDS Private clubs; other people's yachts

IDENTIFYING TRAITS Never paying for anything—ever; threadbare double-breasted Savile Row blazers with gold buttons; monogrammed slippers; protruding gut; gin blossoms

THE MONOGRAMMED COASTER

Nothing says "class" like this drunken relic of depleted WASP fortune

HOSTS Impressionable and insecure Catholics and Jews in Nantucket; Northeast Harbor, Maine; and Grosse Pointe, Michigan

FEEDING GROUNDS The Northeast Corridor; any town where there's an annual regatta

IDENTIFYING TRAITS Johnny Walker breath; air of assumed privilege; J. Press khakis; open-necked Brooks Brothers shirts; Gucci loafers; sun damage

PANTHEON OF THE GODS

Tycoons Who Set the Gold Standard

JOHN JACOB ASTOR

(1763–1848)

HANDICAPPED BY A THICK provincial German accent and a habit of licking peas off his knife, America's first slumlord began his New World career cleaning beaver pelts. At his death, Astor's American Fur Company dominated the international trade in animal skins (and, it was rumored, Turkish opium) and controlled enormous swaths of low-end Manhattan real estate. Setting the bar for generations of immigrant tycoons to come, he never stopped overseeing the daily minutiae of his rental accounts, despite being the richest man in America.

JEAN PAUL GETTY

(1892–1976)

THE MOST REVERED INDUSTRIALIST OF his day, this privileged son of a Minneapolis lawyer used his father's millions to jump-start history's first ten-figure fortune. Having cornered the world oil market (and over 200 other basic industries) at an early age, he retreated to his 16th-century English estate, Sutton Place, in the 1950s to live out his days in pampered eccentricity. A notorious cheapskate, he installed a pay phone for overnight guests and, in 1973, balked at paying his grandson's ransom until his Italian kidnappers mailed the boy's ear to a newspaper. Author of the first billionaire memoir, *How to Be Rich*, he is said to have never carried more than $25 in his wallet.

DORIS DUKE

(1912–1993)

THE ONLY CHILD OF A TOBACCO KINGpin, Duke inherited $100 million (over a billion in today's dollars) at age 12. Raised by a phalanx of neurotic maids who kept photo albums of her clothes to help coordinate her outfits, she spent her adult life amassing collections—rare orchids, Islamic art, sprawling estates—and caring for animals. A bit of a dupe in her old age, she adopted (though later disinherited) a 35-year-old Hare Krishna she met at a dance class and left her $1.3 billion fortune in the hands of her Rasputin-like, illiterate Irish butler, Bernard Lafferty. Her dying wish was that her ashes be fed to the sharks off the coast of her seaside Hawaiian lair, Shangri La. Her dog received $100,000.

MARJORIE MERRIWEATHER POST

(1887–1973)

WITH A FORTUNE ESTIMATED at $250 million, Post—a Midwestern cereal heiress and the founder of General Foods—lived like a queen. (Her schnauzer slept on a bed formerly owned by the Belgian royal family.) A shrewd businesswoman, she built a series of wildly ostentatious homes, including the 118-room Palm Beach estate Mar-a-Lago (since converted into a private country club by new-money menace Donald Trump), which she filled with her world-class collections of fine Sèvres porcelain, Fabergé eggs, and other priceless bric-a-brac. When her third husband, Joseph Davies, was appointed ambassador to Moscow in 1937, Post—one of the 20th century's most celebrated hostesses—brought along two tons of food and 40 freezers to fuel their lavish soirées.

ARISTOTLE ONASSIS

(1906–1975)

HISTORY'S MOST INFAMOUS Greek shipping magnate shocked the world when he married America's sainted first widow, Jackie Kennedy, but few who knew him were surprised. Despite his reptilian looks, little Ari knew how to charm. Whether holding court at El Morocco or hosting million-dollar blowouts on his private island fortress, Scorpios, his playboy persona was writ large. The guest log on his yacht, the *Christina O*, reads like a history of the 20th century: Marilyn Monroe, Grace Kelly, Winston Churchill, and Frank Sinatra were all wined and dined on its decks.

ADNAN KHASHOGGI

(b. 1935)

WITH FRIENDS IN ALL THE RIGHT places, this shadowy Saudi Arabian arms dealer significantly upped the ante on '80s excess, most notably with a series of legendary parties he threw at his Marbella compound, aboard his $70 million mega-yacht, and on his various tricked-out jumbo jets. The hard-partying Casanova has confessed to spending ever $500,000 on prostitutes in a single year, but that was pocket change compared to his 1980 divorce settlement, believed to be the largest in history. With clients like defense contractors Northrop, Lockheed, and Raytheon, he knows world leaders are just a sat phone call away from his hideouts in Kenya and Monte Carlo, leading conspiracy theorists to link him to just about every major world catastrophe of the past 50 years.

RONALD PERELMAN

(b. 1943)

KNOWN AS MUCH FOR HIS DISASTROUS personal life as his varied business holdings, this cartoonishly confident, cigar-chomping dynamo is a man of outsized appetites. Born into privilege, he bought his first company as a freshman at UPenn and has gone on to invest in everything from makeup (Revlon) to cars (Hummer) to comic books (Marvel). A gossip-column staple to this day, his ugly divorce from his fifth wife, actress Ellen Barkin (who auctioned off $20 million worth of jewels he had given her as an act of very public revenge), provided months of dinner-party fodder.

LARRY ELLISON

(b. 1944)

SINCE TURNING A $2,000 investment into a $26 billion software empire, Silicon Valley's prickliest mogul has given the robber barons a run for their money, funneling the fruits of his labors into an ever-expanding portfolio of extreme toys and compounds. Recent projects include the 454-foot, 82-room gigayacht, *Rising Sun;* a 40-acre Japanese imperial village he's building in the redwood-covered hills above his Oracle offices; a World Cup sailing team; and buying up large tracts of the Malibu coastline.

MARRYING INTO IT

For Richer and for Richer

HAVEN'T PATENTED A NEW OPERATING SYSTEM LATELY? FEAR NOT: THERE ARE PLENTY of ways to make a fortune that don't involve working, particularly if you're the romantic type. Just take a few cues from the following . . .

PORFIRIO RUBIROSA

(1909–1965)

"Work? It's impossible for me to work. I just don't have the time."

THE FAMOUSLY OVER-ENDOWED DOMINICAN playboy married twice for great wealth, to tobacco heiress Doris Duke in 1947 and to Barbara Hutton (of the Woolworth department store fortune) in 1953. Though both marriages were brief, he reaped dividends for life. Along with generous cash settlements, he scored a coffee plantation, polo ponies, vintage airplanes, and a mansion in Paris.

CAROLINE DE OTERO

(1868–1965)

"I wasn't meant to be domesticated."

BORN TO GYPSY PEASANTS IN RURAL SPAIN, Otero was transformed, Pygmalion style, into an "Andalusian aristocrat"-cum-Flamenco-dancing sensation by an enterprising American businessman. Enamored gazillionaires like William Vanderbilt and Prince Albert of Monaco courted her with their vast riches, but she begged off, putting lie to the notion that gold-digging divas always want a ring. Otero died at 96—whilst cooking rabbit stew—with checks still coming in regularly from her admirers.

CLAUS VON BÜLOW

(b. 1926)

"I can live by [Sunny's] standards of living. If there were thirty gardeners before, there can be thirty gardeners now."

WHEN BILLIONAIRE J. PAUL GETTY'S EXECUTIVE assistant married American heiress Martha "Sunny" Crawford, the cunning Danish social climber adapted effortlessly to the high life, jaunting between her grand Fifth Avenue apartment and her family's majestic estate, Clarendon Court, in Newport. But when his roving eye led him into a torrid affair with soap actress Alexandra Isles, the union soured. In 1980, when Sunny slipped into an irreversible coma after a night of too much eggnog (and an overdose of insulin), her family cried foul. The ensuing trials, culminating in von Bülow's dramatic acquittal, were truly cinematic spectacles. In *Reversal of Fortune,* Jeremy Irons and Glenn Close gave the couple the ultimate Hollywood treatment. Now in her seventies, Sunny von Bülow remains comatose at New York's Columbia-Presbyterian Hospital.

BARBARA "BABE" PALEY

(1915–1978)

"One can never be too rich or too thin."

THE HYPERSOCIAL DAUGHTER OF A BOSTON surgeon, Babe married well both times: first, to Standard Oil heir Stanley Mortimer Jr. in 1940, while she was biding her time at *Vogue,* and then, seven years later, to CBS founder Bill Paley, five days after his divorce from newspaper heiress Dorothy Hearst. Where Mortimer and Paley had dough, Babe had Brahmin respectability, making for two mutually beneficial mergers.

ZSA ZSA GABOR

(b. 1917)

"I am a marvelous housekeeper. Every time I leave a man I keep his house."

EVERYONE'S FAVORITE HUNGARIAN BEAUTY queen was born with an eye for power. Following her starter marriage—and a dalliance with Kemal Atatürk—she wed hotel magnate Conrad Hilton. Though the marriage hit the skids when Hilton cut her allowance, Gabor earned a hotel discount for life and quickly moved on to husband number three (only six more strategic alliances to go!).

BARBARA AMIEL

(b. 1940)

"It's about time we dismissed those words like 'meal ticket' and 'gold digger.'"

WITH A STAUNCHLY MIDDLE-CLASS UPbringing under her belt, Amiel rose to prominence in London as a bomb-flinging right-wing journalist, famously authoring a 1986 article, "Why Women Marry Up." In 1992 she took her own advice, marrying ill-fated media magnate Conrad Black. Prior to Black's conviction on fraud charges, the couple attended a ball at Kensington Palace dressed, appropriately enough, as Cardinal Richelieu and Marie Antoinette.

CAROLYNE ROEHM

(b. 1951)

"I have never asked [Henry] what he's worth, and I never will."

WHEN CAROLYNE ROEHM (NÉE JANE SMITH) wed financier Henry Kravis, society rags breathlessly crowned her "the czarina of Nouvelle Society," and their over-the-top lifestyle, lampooned in Tom Wolfe's *The Bonfire of the Vanities,* was the talk of the town. She had rare coins cooked into her holiday cakes and threatened to stiff caterers if the sorbet didn't gel quite right. During the marriage, Kravis sank $20 million into Roehm's fashion business, picking up where her former Svengali, Oscar de la Renta, left off. Now a merry divorcée, Roehm has set up shop as a lifestyle guru at the Connecticut spread she got in the split.

TOO COOL FOR SCHOOL

Filthy Rich Dropouts

Several factors determine success. A college diploma doesn't happen to be one of them.

Steve Jobs
Apple and Pixar Studios founder
Estimated Net Worth:
$5.7 billion
Dropped Out Of:
Reed College

Bill Gates
Microsoft cofounder
Estimated Net Worth:
$59 billion
Dropped Out Of:
Harvard

Donald Newhouse
Condé Nast scion
Estimated Net Worth:
$8.5 billion
Dropped Out Of:
Syracuse University

Paul Allen
Microsoft cofounder
Estimated Net Worth:
$18 billion
Dropped Out Of:
Washington State University

David Geffen
DreamWorks SKG cofounder
Estimated Net Worth:
$6.5 billion
Dropped Out Of:
University of Texas at Austin

Sheldon Adelson
Casino kingpin
Estimated Net Worth:
$26.5 billion
Dropped Out Of:
City College of New York

Larry Ellison
Oracle founder
Estimated Net Worth:
$26 billion
Dropped Out Of:
University of Illinois at Urbana-Champaign

Ralph Lauren
Polo Ralph Lauren founder
Estimated Net Worth:
$4.7 billion
Dropped Out Of:
City College of New York

CHAPTER TWO / HOMING PATTERNS

WHERE TO LIVE

"In my Father's house are many mansions."
—JOHN 14:2

MERELY HAVING LOTS OF MONEY WON'T earn you a place in the Club. You must also mingle with its members. And what better way to announce yourself than to move in next door?

There are enough Filthy Rich havens to suit every taste and eccentricity, so a bit of introspection is called for. Are you a Francophilic fashion victim with bottle-blonde helmet hair and a gift for extreme hosting? Say howdy to River Oaks! Or maybe you're the self-made-mogul type, anxious to show the world how far you've come through your jaunty affinity for platinum-plated bathroom fixtures. Say whassup to Saddle River!

While the majority of your compatriots—like the 89 American billionaires who pay California taxes—tend to cluster on the coasts, there are hundreds of other gilded ghettos in the flyover states for you to choose from. Well, not hundreds, really. More like six. Some, like Chicago's Near North Side, are better known than others, but do be mindful of where you snub. Today's McMansion-clotted nightmare could be tomorrow's Greenwich, Connecticut. (Though we wouldn't bet the trust on it.)

Of course, before making any rash moves, you need to consider where it is you're currently living, take a long, hard look in the mirror, and ask yourself: Is my neighborhood *really* as Filthy Rich as local realtors always say it is? If you even have to think about the answer (or there's a Wal-Mart within walking distance), call Sotheby's Great Estates immediately and start packing.

But first, let's decide where you're actually headed.

BACKDOOR FRIENDS ARE BEST

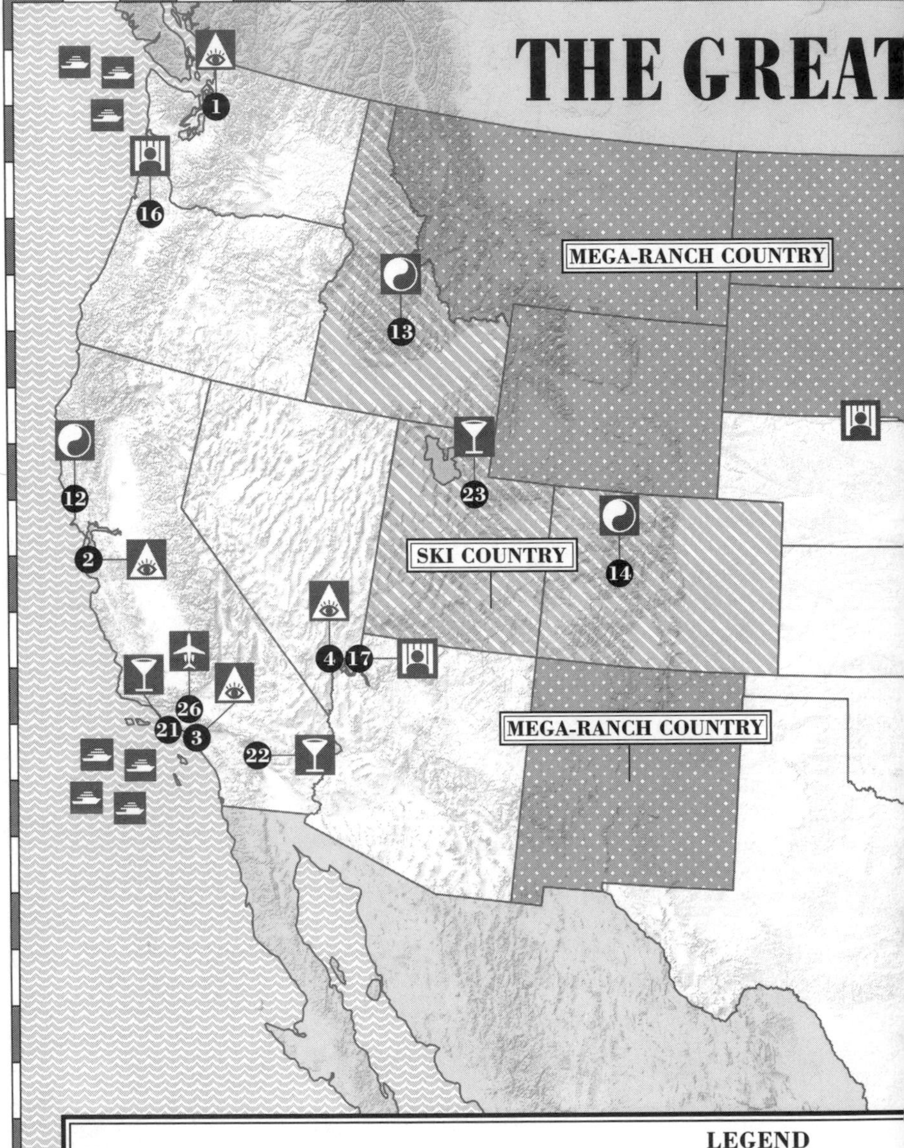

LEGEND

POWER SPOTS

1. Bill's Place, Mercer Island, WA
2. Google Gulch, Mountain View, CA
3. The Industry, Los Angeles, CA
4. Wynn City, Las Vegas, NV
5. Oil Country, Houston, TX
6. Buffett's Place, Omaha, NE
7. Wal-Mart World, Bentonville, AR
8. "The Merc," Chicago, IL
9. 1600, Washington, DC
10. Rap City, Alpine, NJ
11. "The Street," New York, NY

ANNUAL RETREATS

12. Bohemian Grove, Monte Rio, CA
13. Allen & Co. Sun Valley Conference, Sun Valley, ID
14. Forstmann Little, Aspen, CO
15. Renaissance Weekend, Charleston, SC

WHITE COLLAR PRISONS

16. Sheridan, Sheridan, OR
17. Nellis Federal Prison Camp, Nellis, NV

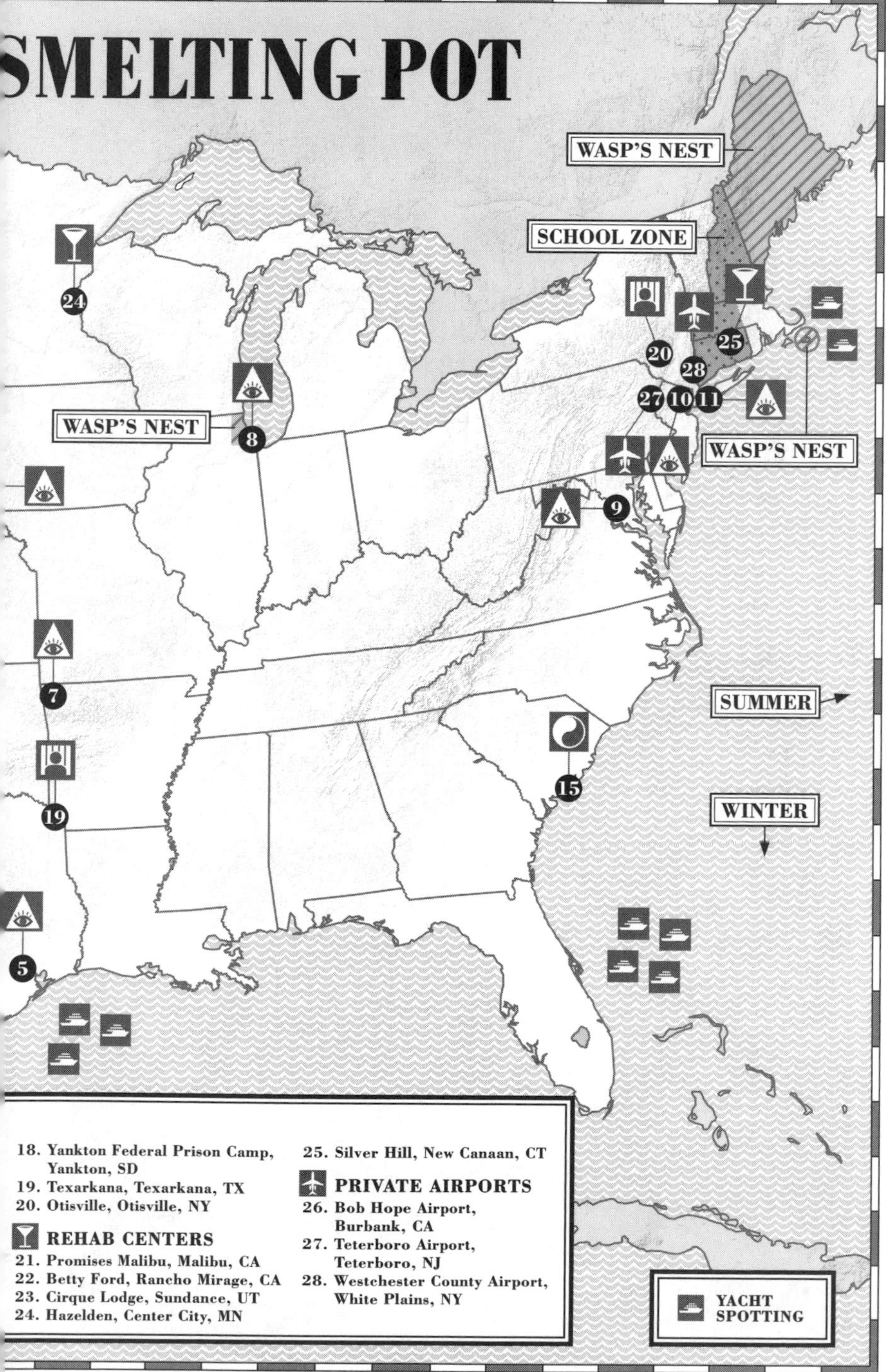
SMELTING POT
WASP'S NEST
SCHOOL ZONE
WASP'S NEST
WASP'S NEST
SUMMER
WINTER
18. Yankton Federal Prison Camp, Yankton, SD
19. Texarkana, Texarkana, TX
20. Otisville, Otisville, NY
REHAB CENTERS
21. Promises Malibu, Malibu, CA
22. Betty Ford, Rancho Mirage, CA
23. Cirque Lodge, Sundance, UT
24. Hazelden, Center City, MN
25. Silver Hill, New Canaan, CT
PRIVATE AIRPORTS
26. Bob Hope Airport, Burbank, CA
27. Teterboro Airport, Teterboro, NJ
28. Westchester County Airport, White Plains, NY
YACHT SPOTTING

PRICE UPON REQUEST

A Discriminating Guide to Filthy Rich Enclaves

BUCKHEAD, Atlanta

CHOCKABLOCK WITH ANTEBELLUM mansions, the confederate splendor of Old Buckhead, nestled politely between Peachtree Road and Northside Drive, is known as the "Golden Fingerbowl." Georgia's wealthiest neighborhood (Tom Wolfe's *A Man in Full* is set here), it's also one of the country's ten richest. In the "Beverly Hills of the South," shoppers spend over $1 billion annually at Phipps Plaza and Lenox Square, Buckhead's answer to Rodeo. **FAMOUS NEIGHBORS:** Top brass at Coca-Cola and CNN; Doug Ellis, CEO of textile giant Southern Mills; Home Depot honcho Arthur Blank; occasionally, Elton John

$14.8 MILLION BUYS YOU: A 17-acre estate on Glen Devon Drive with six-bedroom main house, two lakes, horse paddocks and stables, two terrariums, and guesthouse

BEACON HILL, Boston

DEVELOPED IN THE 1790S ON farmland settled by Boston's first resident, this square-mile warren of Federal-style row houses, lopsided cobblestone streets, and sloping brick sidewalks overlooking the Public Garden has been preferred by native Brahmins and their imitators since the days of John Hancock. Absurdly picturesque Louisburg Square is still the Hill's grandest address (though anything on the south side, where

WHISTLIN' DIXIE
Buckhead

streets are wide and more sanely laid out, will do).
FAMOUS NEIGHBORS: Folkster Carly Simon; Senator John Kerry and his ketchup queen, Teresa Heinz; Staples founder Tom Stemberg; Fidelity Investments guru Ed Johnson
$16.5 MILLION BUYS YOU: A recently renovated 9,000-square-foot, five-bedroom, five-floor 1833 townhouse on the corner of Mt. Vernon Place, with elevator, fitness center, and professional-grade spa

WESTON, Boston

THE BAY STATE'S WEALTHIEST SUBURB was only recently rolling fields. Now it's the only place convenient to town where you can still snag serious acreage. It may not be the most Brahmin of settings, but Beantown's newish wave of serious money has spent the last decade laying formidable roots in its densely wooded confines. So what if the wives aren't Colonial Dames material: They're too busy filling their 30-car garages.
FAMOUS NEIGHBORS: Hedge-funder James Pallotta; Atlanta Hawks owner Steve Belkin; various real estate zillionaires; Patriots, Red Sox, and Celtics
$6.5 MILLION BUYS YOU: A 9,300-square-foot contemporary colonial with wine cellar, yoga studio, and paneled library on three acres

PALM SPRINGS, California

THIS DESERT OASIS MADE FAMOUS by Sinatra was *the* weekend playground for 1960s American royalty—Howard Hughes, Ron and Nancy Reagan, Johnny Carson, you name it. Today, it's known mostly for its Republican leanings, midcentury modern houses, and hospicelike role amongst the shuffleboard set.

PROPER BOSTONIAN
Beacon Hill

FAMOUS NEIGHBORS: Duffer Arnold Palmer; Microsofty Bill Gates; ex-Chrysler boss Lee Iacocca
$5 MILLION BUYS YOU: An 8,300-square-foot villa with guesthouse, tennis court, and oval pool fed by a waterfall

LAKE FOREST, Chicago

WHILE CASH-RICH COMMODITIES traders flock to glitzier suburbs like Glencoe, genteel types like Marshall Field V and his old-money pals still call bucolic Lake Forest home, presiding over their sprawling faux-Tudor and Italianate estates with aristocratic indifference. Lakefront lots remain the choicest.
FAMOUS NEIGHBORS: The Palmers of Drake Hotel fame; the Swift and Ryerson meatpacking clans; fool-pitying '80s icon Mr. T
$11 MILLION BUYS YOU: A 14,000-square-foot, six-bedroom 1917 Italianate villa designed by David Adler for the Pike family with the "grandest gardens on Lake Michigan"

NEAR NORTH SIDE, Chicago

MODERN-DAY INDUSTRIALISTS IN THE city that meatpacking built still hunker down in the grand, chimneyed mansions on Astor Street and beaux arts mini-scrapers skirting East Lake Shore Drive. If it's good enough for Oprah, it's good enough for you.

FAMOUS NEIGHBORS: The Pritzkers (Hyatt Hotels); the Crowns (General Dynamics); Ron Gidwitz (Helene Curtis); Oprah Winfrey (Harpo Productions)

$9.2 MILLION BUYS YOU: A three-bedroom condo with custom everything on the 11th floor of 209 East Lake Shore Drive

GREENWICH, Connecticut

LIKE "HARVARD" AND "HERMÈS," the "Greenwich" brand stands for something in the minds of the Filthy Rich. So it should come as no surprise that this former seat of Protestant power has had a bit of a renaissance lately. ("Of the $1.2 trillion currently invested in hedge funds worldwide, approximately one-tenth, or $120 billion, is now managed out of Greenwich," is how *Vanity Fair* put it.) Predictably, many of its bluer-nosed residents have their Talbot's Intimates in a twist over the influx of fast-talking traders building 40,000-square-foot monoliths on their winding country roads. But such is progress. Construction cranes notwithstanding, Round Hill Road and the gated grandeur of Belle Haven overlooking Long Island Sound are still the primo perches.

FAMOUS NEIGHBORS: The Forbes family; ex-IBM CEO Louis Gerstner Jr.; Eddie Lampert; hedge fund hitters Stevie Cohen and Paul Tudor Jones II

$19 MILLION BUYS YOU: A Conyers Farm fieldstone estate with pool and tennis court, excessive wood paneling, turrets, and eight-foot fireplace

HIGHLAND PARK, Dallas

ARCADIAN HIGHLAND PARK IS AWASH in 1920s white-pillared brick mansions perched at the end of stately lanes. Beverly Drive, Armstrong Parkway, and Lakeside Drive are its most revered stretches. The perfect neighborhood to start your *Dynasty*.

FAMOUS NEIGHBORS: Dallas Cowboys owner Jerry Jones; megabuilder Trammell Crow; Dallas Mavericks owner Ross Perot Jr.; private equity rainmaker Tom Hicks

$6 MILLION BUYS YOU: An 8,664-square-foot, four-bedroom, seven-and-a-half-bathroom 1989 McMansion with circular driveway on Highland Drive

BLOOMFIELD HILLS, Detroit

IN THE GO-TO TOWN FOR "ARRIVED" Motor City magnates since the 1930s, the best houses are on Rathmor Road by the Bloomfield Hills Country Club and pretty much any patch of grass formerly attached to the original Ford and Dodge estates.

FAMOUS NEIGHBORS: Auto heir William Ford Sr.; shopping mall moguls Alfred, Robert, and William Taubman; J. T. Battenberg III, vice president of General Motors' Delphi division; windshield tycoon William Davidson

$6 MILLION BUYS YOU: A 9,500-square-foot Tudor contemporary on Hidden Ridge (a short putt from the BHCC)

RIVER OAKS, Houston

MOCK CHÂTEAUS DATING FROM THE Jazz Age set the over-the-top tone in this petro-powered suburban fantasia. A French baronial manor on Willowick, Knollwood, or Inverness is *de rigueur* for Texas-born oil barons, while Lazy Lane draws the flashier "foreign types."

FAMOUS NEIGHBORS: Disgraced oilman Oscar Wyatt and his socialite wife, Lynn; couture queen Becca Cason Thrash and her husband, John Thrash; financier Fayez Sarofim; megadeveloper Gerald Hines; tort tycoon Joe Jamail

$14.5 MILLION BUYS YOU: Unfinished four-bedroom, eight-bathroom, 17,000-square-foot neoclassical estate on two gated acres just off the 15th tee at the River Oaks Country Club.

BEL AIR, Los Angeles

LOOKS CAN BE DECEIVING IN THIS faux-gated community girding Sunset Boulevard, where the higher up you go, the *cheaper* the houses get. Farther down, $30 million estates sit as little as five feet away from the curb, betraying none of the sprawling excess that lies behind their blandly painted, reinforced-steel gates.

FAMOUS NEIGHBORS: Nicolas Cage; Clint Eastwood; Nancy Reagan

$11.5 MILLION BUYS YOU: A gated, Frank Lloyd Wright–inspired estate with 30-foot glass walls overlooking the city, drug-lord-level video surveillance system, 40-foot ceilings, and remote-controlled everything

CALIFORNIA DREAMIN'
Bel Air

HOLMBY HILLS, Los Angeles

KNOWN FOR ITS EUCALYPTUS TREES and Hollywood Regency–style estates, this sliver of serenity above the sleaze of West Hollywood comprises one-third of L.A.'s infamous "golden triangle," along with Bel Air and Beverly Hills. Its large lots with set-back houses and mature, paparazzi-proof hedges have drawn generations of industry heavyweights (Walt Disney, Gary Cooper, and Humphrey Bogart all lived here). Which isn't to say it's pure class: Hugh Hefner's porno palace, the Playboy Mansion, is on Charing Cross Road.

FAMOUS NEIGHBORS: Department store doyenne Betsy Bloomingdale; Revlon chief Ron Perelman; Hard Rock Cafe founder Peter Morton

$24 MILLION BUYS YOU: A 10,000-square-foot Tuscan-style palazzo with Olympic-sized swimming pool and 30,000-bottle wine cellar

MALIBU, Los Angeles

ON THIS 27-MILE STRIP OF BEACH hugging the Pacific Coast Highway (PCH), the sand castles of Hollywood's heaviest are so tightly packed, they can look downright modest. Successive industry invasions have managed to sterilize this legendarily dippy surfer's colony of any boho appeal. And good riddance! In the coming years, expect übernerd land baron Larry Ellison to finish the job.

FAMOUS NEIGHBORS: PCH menace Mel Gibson; DreamWorks cofounder Jeffrey Katzenberg; Grammy-winning warbler Bob Dylan; head-shaving hedonist Britney Spears; former *Friend* Courtney Cox Arquette; movie maestro Steven Spielberg; shadowy Israeli financier Vivi Nevo; Imagine Entertainment maven Brian Grazer

$28.5 MILLION BUYS YOU: A mid-century modern "cottage" on Broad Beach Road with 123 feet of oceanfront and a private sand volleyball court on a highly coveted triple lot

LOCUST VALLEY, New York

ENCOMPASSING MILL NECK, LATTINGTOWN, Matinecock, and Oyster Bay, Locust Valley is the nexus of Long Island's storied gold coast. The descendants of robber barons (Phippses, Rockefellers, Roosevelts) rub Paul Stuart–clad shoulders with new-money arrivals flush with Wall Street bonus money. A home on Feeks Lane, Horse Shoe, Piping Rock, or Duck Pond roads confers the ultimate in social clout.

FAMOUS NEIGHBORS: Lazard Frères & Co. chairman Michel David-Weill; publishing scion Nelson Doubleday Jr.; William T. Comfort of Citicorp Venture Capital

$18 MILLION BUYS YOU: A waterfront Mediterranean-style manse with massive indoor solarium and swimming complex

CALI' CARTEL
Malibu Colony

TRIBECA, Manhattan

FOR A BRIEF TIME IN THE LATE '80s, the "Triangle Below Canal" was the city's southern frontier—a desolate haven for arty types fleeing a newly mallified SoHo. With several million square feet of vacant, unfinished industrial space, cavernous, dirt-cheap lofts could be had. Then came the stroller brigade. Its yuppification complete, TriBeCa is now the Filthy Richest neighborhood on the island, with zero properties available for under a million. Unless you're in MoMA, artists need not apply.

FAMOUS NEIGHBORS: Local booster Robert De Niro; Oscar-winner Meryl Streep; kooky playwright Edward Albee; high-strung songbird Mariah Carey; creepy thespian Harvey Keitel; supermodel Gisele Bündchen

$7.75 MILLION BUYS YOU: A 5,000-square-foot, four-bedroom loft on Franklin Street. Includes 360-degree city views, sunny library, and limited access to groceries.

UPPER EAST SIDE, Manhattan

TO ADEQUATELY HOUSE THE LEGIONS of Filthy Rich who flock to Manhattan every year would require an endless supply of $10 million co-ops (with views of Central Park) and limestone townhouses abutting Madison Avenue. Sadly, it's an island. Such is the competition for prime apartments in "good buildings" that prices have risen well beyond reason for what might be a simple, 2,000-square-foot ho-hummer. Even its museums, libraries, and embassies—many of which were converted from private mansions in the threadbare 1970s—are tumbling back into the hands of the international overclass. Hedge fund mogul Bruce Kovner had

TOM WOLFE'S NEW YORK

Where East Is Eden

In a 1985 *Esquire* article, author Tom Wolfe published a list of Manhattan's "Good Buildings." "What drives people really wild . . . is the simple fact that *le monde* is sheerly divided into Good Buildings and those that, for whatever reason, are not Good," he coolly explained. According to Wolfe (who holds a doctorate in plutocrat studies), there wasn't a single Good Building on the Upper West Side–the fabled Dakota included. While many of the people who populated *le monde* Wolfe was referring to now sip their martinis through straws, one can't help noticing how little things have changed. Per Wolfe, you still need to head east to find the Good Buildings:

- **1 Beekman Place**
- **10 Gracie Square**
- **1 and 120 East End Avenue**
- **550, 555, 635, 640, 720, 730, 740, 765–75, 770, 778, and 812 Park Avenue**
- **810, 820, 825, 834, 953, 960, 998, 1020, 1030, and 1040 Fifth Avenue**
- **435 East 52nd Street (River House)**
- **4 and 131–135 East 66th Street**
- **2 East 70th Street**
- **4, 19, 36, 117, and 160 East 72nd Street**
- **50 East 77th Street**
- **21, 39, 66, and 79 East 79th Street**
- **25 Sutton Place North**
- **One Sutton Place South**

EAST SIDE STORY Wolfe

FAMOUS CO-OP REJECTS

Boldface Names Who Were Shown the Door

Securing the right to plunk down absurd sums of money—*in cash*—for an apartment that would go for a 50th of the price elsewhere is a lot more difficult than you'd think. This is particularly true if you earned said cash in some uncouth manner, like leveraged buyouts, or acting, or—God help you—rapping. (Former dictators and arms dealers may require additional letters of recommendation.) Every building is elitist in its own way but, as a rule, the power-mad sociopaths who dominate the co-op boards of Manhattan's white-glove buildings love nothing more than blackballing a boldfacer. How tough are they? Consider the following rejects:

1. The San Remo
146 Central Park West
MADONNA
Shape-shifting pop star

2. 927 Fifth Avenue
BARBRA STREISAND
Reclusive battle-ax

3. River House
435 East 52nd Street
THE AGA KHAN
Hard-partying Imam
GLORIA VANDERBILT
Jeans-designing heiress
JOAN CRAWFORD
Mommy dearest
DIANE KEATON
Oscar-winning actress
RICHARD NIXON
36th President

4. 88 Central Park West
SEAN LENNON
Beatles kid

5. 770 Park Avenue
MIKE WALLACE
60 Minutes *maestro*

6. 320 Central Park West
MARIAH CAREY
Wacky popstress

7. One Sutton Place South
J. SHELBY BRYAN
East Coast oilman
ARNOLD SCAASI
Society clothier

8. 825 Fifth Avenue
STEVE WYNN
Casino kingpin

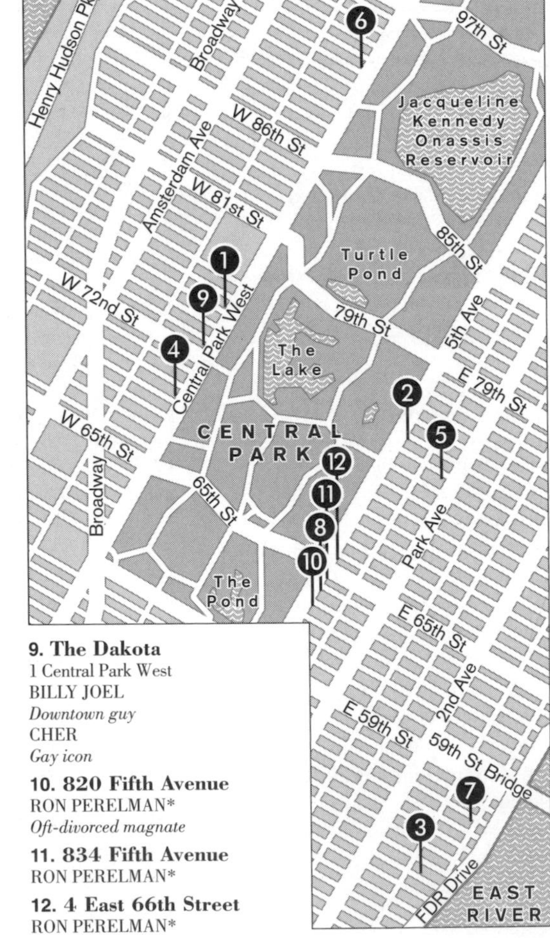

9. The Dakota
1 Central Park West
BILLY JOEL
Downtown guy
CHER
Gay icon

10. 820 Fifth Avenue
RON PERELMAN*
Oft-divorced magnate

11. 834 Fifth Avenue
RON PERELMAN*

12. 4 East 66th Street
RON PERELMAN*

**Quite possibly a record*

to plop down over $17.5 million for the International Center of Photography on Fifth Avenue and 94th just to have a decent place to sleep! Some claim the Upper East Side is dead, but if it's a trophy property you want, you still have to cross 59th Street.
FAMOUS NEIGHBORS: Aussie press lord Rupert Murdoch; cosmetics titan Leonard Lauder; lit couple Nora Ephron and Nick Pileggi; Lazard chairman and *New York* mag owner Bruce Wasserstein; Sony CEO Howard Stringer; real estate and media mogul Mort Zuckerman (to name but a few)
$48 MILLION BUYS YOU: A seven-story, 12,000-square-foot townhouse with limestone façade, sweeping central staircase, elevator, indoor pool, 150-person ballroom, and painstakingly restored original details, in the 70s off Madison

UPPER WEST SIDE, Manhattan

CENTRAL PARK WEST'S STORIED apartment blocks—the Dakota, the El Dorado, the Beresford, and the San Remo—serve as well-appointed hives for the city's buzz-generators and those whose distaste for Lilly Pulitzer puts them off the Upper East (or whose pedigrees simply aren't Park Avenue–worthy). Fetishized on film by Woody Allen, the Mild West's brownstone-lined streets are more family friendly—if considerably less fabulous—than those across the park. Here, Mom Jeans are worn with impunity. Farther south on Columbus Circle, the ultramod Time Warner Center and recently converted Plaza Hotel lure foreigners and Wall Street hot shots with something to prove.
FAMOUS NEIGHBORS: Dakota dweller Yoko Ono; U2 frontman Bono; megaproducer Scott Rudin; *Rolling Stone* and *US Weekly* founder Jann Wenner and his partner, Matt Nye; *Saturday Night Live* creator Lorne Michaels and his wife, Alice
$25.5 MILLION BUYS YOU: A grandly appointed two-bedroom beaux arts apartment on the second floor of the Dakota with its original period details and six fireplaces intact, overlooking Central Park

SADDLE RIVER, New Jersey

ONCE PRAISED FOR ITS "ABUNDANCE OF cream, berries, and pretty girls," this Bergen County hamlet of 3,000 has lately morphed into a Medici-esque showplace for elaborately gated, multiwinged bling palaces housing impresarios of all stripes. East Saddle River Road and Chestnut Ridge Road remain the toniest of the Old School addresses. Next door, woody Alpine has been giving it a run for its money.
FAMOUS NEIGHBORS: The emir of Kuwait; comic Chris Rock; rappers Ja Rule and Wyclef Jean; Def Jam founder Russell Simmons; Bad Boy mogul P. Diddy
$7.5 MILLION BUYS YOU: A 16,000-square-foot mock Tudor with eight bedrooms, 25-car garage, and tennis court

PARADISE VALLEY, Phoenix

THIS PATCH OF MOD MANSIONS, EACH fitted with the requisite infinity pool, sits nestled on the steppes of Camelback and Mummy mountains, framed by giant saguaro cacti. Unpretentious and sporty, its year-round residents tend toward WASPily low-key golf obsessives.
FAMOUS NEIGHBORS: Author Clive Cussler; Campbell Soup heir Bennett Dorrance; bungling former veep Dan Quayle
$25 MILLION BUYS YOU: A 10,000-square-foot adobe-style desert compound on North 64th Street with every conceivable amenity

PRESIDIO HEIGHTS, San Francisco

HIGH ATOP SAN FRANCISCO'S precipitous hills, Presidio Heights and neighboring Pacific Heights sprang up in the late 19th century with an influx of nouveau riche gold prospectors. Think vintage San Francisco, of the kind immortalized in *Guess Who's Coming to Dinner.*
FAMOUS NEIGHBORS: Levi's heiress Miriam Haas; Senator Dianne Feinstein; philanthropic bons vivants Ann and Gordon Getty; romance writer Danielle Steel; socialites Trevor and Alexis Traina; Democratic Party princess Nancy Pelosi; Metallica drummer Lars Ulrich; '80s heartthrob Don Johnson
$19.5 MILLION BUYS YOU: A Palladian, 22-room 1904 mansion with grand ballroom, eight bedrooms, and seriously manicured grounds

ROSS, California

WHERE GOLD RUSH MILLIONS MEET Tech Boom billions. With so much proprietary data floating around, it's no wonder *Town & Country* calls Marin County's filthy richest nabe "fiercely insular and obsessively private." The choicest domiciles are set deep into the canyons on Laurel Grove.
FAMOUS NEIGHBORS: *Rain Man* director Barry Levinson; NationsBanc chieftain Thom Weisel; former Levi Strauss COO Tom Tusher
$7 MILLION BUYS YOU: An ultramodern five-bedroom, seven-bath complex with indoor lap pool and stunning views of Mt. Tamalpais and the San Francisco skyline

MEDINA, Seattle

ON THE SHORES OF LAKE WASHINGTON directly opposite Seattle, Medina is America's premier technocrat haven. No

NERD NIRVANA
The Gates Estate

wonder. It's only minutes from the on-ramp to Highway 520, a straight shot to the Microsoft "campus." When it comes to home design, it's next-level tech or nothing—Bill and Melinda Gates set the bar with their $135 million, 55,000-square-foot, PC-enabled lair. Care to raise it?
FAMOUS NEIGHBORS: Software whiz-turned-space-tourist Charles Simonyi (aka Martha Stewart's boyfriend); Amazon ace Jeff Bezos; Microsoft CEO Steve Ballmer lives in neighboring Hunt's Point; Gates's old partner, plutocrat poster boy Paul Allen, is just a short hovercraft-ride away on Mercer Island.
$10.5 MILLION BUYS YOU: An evergreen-dotted compound with a 7,470-square-foot contemporary main house by architect Arthur Erickson, with six fireplaces, chef's kitchen, tennis courts, and reflecting pool

McLEAN, Virginia

SITUATED ON ROCKY CRAGS ABOVE the Potomac River, McLean has a wildness to it that disguises its

proximity to bureaucratic D.C. The CIA was born here, and its private estates still house senior politicos, lobbyists, and international potentates of various leanings. Chain Bridge Road, Crest Lane, and Kirby Road are the most coveted byways, with homes overlooking the river at a premium.
FAMOUS NEIGHBORS: Retired general Colin Powell; Saudi Arabian ambassador Prince Bandar bin Sultan bin Abdulaziz; conservative flamethrower Pat Buchanan; old-moneyed Virginian landowners; most of the U.S. Senate
$20.5 MILLION BUYS YOU: A 20,000-square-foot, seven-bedroom, nine-bath spec house under construction in The Reserve, a gated community on Founders Ridge Lane

WESTCHESTER COUNTY, New York

BEDFORD VILLAGE, BEDFORD HILLS, and Katonah offer English country living to nouveau Wall Street raiders and Welly-wearing blue bloods alike. Equestrian fashion reigns, as does grandly shabby classical architecture and a studied look of tasteful decay. Of the innumerable places in the world billionaire WASPloitationist Ralph Lauren could live, there's a reason he chose Bedford. Remote Hook and Upper Hook roads are the ritziest addresses.
FAMOUS NEIGHBORS: Polo pashas Ralph and Ricky Lauren; felonious lifestyle maven Martha Stewart; philanthropist George Soros; mega-author Michael Crichton; leverage buyout big shot Nelson Peltz
$14 MILLION BUYS YOU: A 31-acre 1936 estate with six-bedroom main house, five-bedroom carriage house, stable, barn, and various outbuildings overlooking the Beaver Dam River on Harris Road. Jodhpurs not included.

SEE ALSO . . .

ATHERTON, California
Live near: Google guy Eric Schmidt; Charles Schwab; Sequoia Capital boss Tom Stephenson; eBay cofounder Meg Whitman

BELLE MEAD, Tennessee
Live near: Al and Tipper Gore

CHEVY CHASE, Maryland
Live near: *Hardball* host Chris Matthews; various millionaire congressmen

MISSION HILLS, Kansas
Live near: Noir novelist James Ellroy; tax man Henry Block; Hallmark chairman Don Hall Jr.

NEW CANAAN, Connecticut
Live near: Late-nighter David Letterman; GE helmer Jeff Immelt; crooner Paul Simon; anchor Brian Williams

NEWTON, Massachusetts
Live near: Viacom chairman Sumner Redstone; playwright David Mamet; casino bigwig Sheldon Adelson

PALO ALTO, California
Live near: Facebooker Mark Zuckerberg; Googlers Sergey Brin and Larry Page; Steve Jobs

RANCHO SANTA FE, New Mexico
Live near: Corporate raider T. Boone Pickens; Match.com founder Gary Kremen; suds scion Joseph Coors

SAN JOSE, California
Live near: Apple cofounder Steve Wozniak; Yahoo! cofounder Jerry Yang

WESTPORT, Connecticut
Live near: Super-couple Paul Newman and Joanne Woodward; shock jock Don Imus

WOODSIDE, California
Live near: Oracle CEO Larry Ellison; rock fossil Neil Young; Dr. Carl Djerassi, inventor of "the Pill"

GILDED CAGES

WHILE MEDIEVAL LORDS had moats and drawbridges, today's plutocrats prefer minimalist, tinted-glass guard booths and the ex–Green Berets who man them. Though it all sounds a bit dystopian, tycoons from Rio to Riyadh—fueled by a shared need for privacy, security, and communal clay tennis courts—are leading America's retreat into gated communities.

The gilded cage was invented in Los Angeles in 1908, when an enterprising developer built Fremont Place in the Wilshire section of the city, complete with wrought-iron gate and 24-hour guard to keep bomb-throwing anarchists at bay. By 1929, another gated community had taken hold in Malibu, where landowner May Rindge allowed a select group of industry up-and-comers to rent bungalows on her property. Today, the Malibu Colony has its own police station and beach which, while public, is famously impossible to access without trespassing. (And you know how Mr. Geffen is about his peonies!) Like cults, skateboarding, and IV drug use, this L.A.-based fad has since trickled down to bougier burgs. Here, a glimpse inside five gilded cages that aren't just fancy subdivisions:

CONYERS FARM, Greenwich, Connecticut

FORMERLY A PRIVATE 2,000-ACRE estate in backcountry Greenwich, the land was purchased in 1981 by polo-loving land shark Peter Brant. Today, it's home to 96 gargantuan houses and the Greenwich Polo Club. Local residents include Brant and his supermodel wife, Stephanie Seymour; feel-good director Ron Howard; populist funnywoman Rosie O'Donnell; and schlock-TV titan Montel Williams. **$6.9 MILLION BUYS YOU:** A 10.5-acre "Georgian-inspired" estate with custom millwork, ten-foot ceilings, and canopied terrace

ALL CHIEFS
Indian Creek Island

TWINKLE, TWINKLE
Star Island

INDIAN CREEK, Miami

THIS 300-ACRE ISLAND ON THE BANKS of Biscayne Bay has its own police force and marine patrol. With just 40 homes, all shaded by dramatic banyan trees, its gated bridge is the first line of defense for the likes of Spanish pop legend Julio Iglesias, Archer Daniels Midland chairman Dwayne Andreas, and Saudi prince Turki bin Abdul Aziz Al Saud against the unmoneyed hordes.
$23.5 MILLION BUYS YOU: An 11,000-square-foot Spanish-style white stucco villa with seven bedrooms, nine bathrooms, marble floors, and bay frontage

STAR ISLAND, Miami

ONCE HOME TO HOWARD HUGHES, THIS artificial blip on Biscayne Bay takes its name literally. Part-time residents include P. Diddy, Gloria Estefan, Alex Rodriguez, Madonna, Sylvester Stallone, and Rosie O'Donnell. Lesser-known superstars, like billionaire pharmaceutical investor Dr. Phillip Frost, round out the list.
$35 MILLION BUYS YOU: A 20,000-square-foot party palace with indoor basketball court, 312 feet of water frontage, 20-person Jacuzzi, tennis court, and private dock

BEVERLY PARK, Los Angeles

A STONE'S THROW FROM RODEO, IT'S SO stuffed with folks like Viacom capo Sumner Redstone, fat-suit-loving funnyman Eddie Murphy, disgraced home run king Barry Bonds, country crooner Reba McEntire, musclehead actor Sly Stallone, and Oscar-winner Denzel Washington that it's been called a "Billionaire's Levittown."
$13.4 MILLION BUYS YOU: A 10,000-square-foot Provence-style villa designed by Richard Landry on a 3.5-acre peninsula, with infinity pool and attached guesthouse

BRENTWOOD COUNTRY ESTATES, Los Angeles

DEVELOPED BY PARIS HILTON'S UNCLE Barry, this 13-lot, heavily guarded enclave is where California governor Arnold Schwarzenegger and his wife, Maria Shriver, rest their heels. "Starter homes" are priced to move at $12 million apiece.
$27.9 MILLION BUYS YOU: A 16,000-square-foot mock-Spanish villa with mountain and ocean views, 6,500-square-foot covered loggia, and 20,000-bottle, climate-controlled wine cellar

THE HOLMBY HYATT
Chez Spelling

ERECTILE DYSFUNCTION

When it comes to telling the world you've made it, size matters. Build too big, however, and the neighbors start talking. A sampling of houses that, due to their sheer size and unapologetic vulgarity, ended up doubling as tourist attractions:

- Upon completion, **Aaron** and **Candy Spelling's** 123-room, 56,500-square-foot faux French château in Holmby Hills, Los Angeles, was dubbed the "Holmby Hyatt" by outraged locals. No street-corner star map is complete without it.

- Renco tycoon **Ira Rennert's** 100,000-square-foot Italianate monstrosity, Fair Field, in Sagaponack, New York, inspired neighborhood protests, as well as James Brady's novel *The House That Ate the Hamptons*.

- Explaining his rationale for building a 56-bedroom, 41-bathroom, 74,000-square-foot castle, **William Randolph Hearst** explained, "We are tired of camping out in San Simeon and I would like to build a little something." His "little something" went on to be front-page news around the globe and a central plot point in *Citizen Kane*.

- Whatever **Larry Ellison** has planned for the 12 adjacent beachfront properties he's purchased in Malibu, only time (and subpoenas) will tell.

EVERY MAN, A KING OF POP

Michael Jackson and the Neverland Revolution

It seems Wacko Jacko was on to something. These days even those who don't go the gilded cage route *(see p. 38)* are turning their homes into self-contained fantasias equipped with all the services and amenities of the outside world. Herewith, a few of the more extreme examples:

SPORTS FACILITIES
In Greenwich, Connecticut, hedge fund bigwig **Steve Cohen** has kitted out his 32,000-square-foot estate with a private ice-skating rink, indoor basketball court, hairdressing salon, and squash court.

INDOOR MALLS
A $75 million compound for sale in Corona del Mar, California, features a miniature indoor "Main Street" lined with a theater, greasy-spoon soda shop, bowling alley, jewelry store, car museum, and service station.

RECORDING STUDIOS
Microsoft cofounder and amateur axman **Paul Allen** has a state-of-the-art recording studio on his 464-foot yacht, his jumbo jet, and in each one of his estimated nine houses for impromptu jamming sessions.

SCHOOLS
Ann and **Gordon Getty**'s 30,000-square-foot Pacific Heights manse also has a recording studio (for Gordon), as well as a private Montessori school for the couple's grandkids and an elite selection of their equally privileged pals.

STOP, THIEF!

Filthy Rich Repros

When it comes to making an architectural statement, plutocrats love nothing more than plundering the past. Which would be fine, if they weren't always robbing the same houses.

"VERSAILLES ON THE POTOMAC"
Perp: Cocky Internet mogul **Michael Saylor,** best known for losing $6 billion in a single day in the 1999 market bust
Crime: Modeling his Great Falls, Virginia, mansion on both Versailles *and* the White House
Cost: $50 million in 1999

"VERSAILLES ON THE PACIFIC"
Perp: Tacky Texan **David Saperstein,** founder of Metro Networks, a traffic reports service
Crime: Building Fleur de Lys, a 45,000-square-foot replica of Versailles near Beverly Hills
Cost: $100 million in 2002. Later became the center of a billion-dollar divorce battle, the most expensive in U.S. history.

"GREENWICH MONTICELLO"
Perp: Billionaire financier **Paul Tudor Jones II.**
Crime: Aggressively dominating the landscape of Belle Haven—Greenwich, Connecticut's snootiest community—with a megamansion combining elements of Thomas Jefferson's Monticello *and* the University of Virginia
Cost: Built in 1998 for an estimated $60 million

RULES OF ENTITLEMENT

How to Name Your House

WHAT TO NAME YOUR HOUSE IS A DEEPLY PERSONAL DECISION, SO GIVE YOURSELF time. Live in it for a month or two and see what clicks. The only rule that's hard and fast concerns puns. Your house is not a boat, and under no circumstances should you name it like one (we're looking at you, Pond Memories). Double goes for names related to how you made your fortune. You might be the hottest divorce lawyer in America, but naming your home Exhibit A is a déclassé felony. So, is it a hall, a farm, a grove, or a manor? Is it a haven of some sort? Is it bigger than a bread box? Once you've figured that part out, just remember that "it" is a "she," and fill in the blank:

________ FARM

FOR A LOW-KEY GENTLEMAN-FARMER vibe, insert harmonious word of English-sounding origin, preferably with Mayflower connotations (e.g., Hammersmith Farm, the Bouvier-Auchincloss estate in Newport, Rhode Island, aka JFK's "summer White House"). Or simply pick your favorite tree (e.g., Linden Farm, ex–Simon & Schuster honcho Dick Snyder's Westchester sprawl). Native American modifiers also work, harkening back to idyllic precolonial days when your tennis court was a sacred burial ground (e.g., Cantitoe Farm, Martha Stewart's Bedford, New York, spread, named for the wife of local chief Katonah).

________ HALL

FOR A TRULY REGAL AIR, INSERT obscure surname of English-sounding origin or bland natural feature; promptly monogram said name on guest towels. In all cases, "Hall" is shorthand for "humongous," so use cautiously (e.g., Bassett Hall, John D. Rockefeller's 585-acre plantation in Virginia; Dunellen Hall, Leona Helmsley's Greenwich, Connecticut, castle; Meadow Brook Hall, Matilda Dodge's Detroit estate; and Toad Hall, art dealer Larry Gagosian's Southampton, Long Island, bachelor palace). "Manor" may also be substituted, though it's decidedly more gauche. "House," as in media baron Barry Diller's Swift House in Roxbury, Connecticut, also has the desired Oxfordshirian ring.

THE ________(S)

FOR A SOMEWHAT LESS UNDERSTATED mood with a hint at majesty, insert underwhelming description of your estate's most distinctive characteristic (e.g., The Breakers, the Vanderbilt family's Newport, Rhode Island, monolith, named for the foamy surf that breaks below its cliffs, or The Creeks, Ron Perelman's East Hampton, Long Island, property, named for its . . . creeks).

HAVEN/COURT

For a level of parvenu pomposity rarely observed in modern times, attach a syllable from your surname to one of the preceding suffixes. This works well if, like Oliver Belmont, the son of a Rothschild functionary who built Belcourt Castle in Newport, Rhode Island, you have a surname that's pleasing to the ear. Less so if it's Schnelsky. As with so many things, the Vanderbilts excelled here. Biltmore, George Washington Vanderbilt's French Renaissance–inspired château in Asheville, North Carolina, is the most enduring example. More than a hundred years old, it's still the country's largest privately owned house, at 175,000 square feet.

NOUVEAU NAMES

Not everyone respects tradition. In addition to the time-tested formulas above, there are also . . .

THE MAVERICKS
A certain kind of self-made billionaire ignores convention and goes with his gut. Standouts include Zorro, disgraced New York financier Jeffrey Epstein's 10,000-acre ranch outside Santa Fe; Sweet Potato, Ron Lauder's Bridgehampton, Long Island, fortress (the guesthouse is New Potato); Quelle Barn, director Steven Spielberg's awkwardly Anglo-Frenchified Georgica Pond, Long Island, pad; and Eothen, J. Crew CEO Mickey Drexler's Montauk, Long Island, estate, previously owned by Andy Warhol. (The extra "o" is for ostentatious.)

THE EXOTICS
Also known as the "pink flamingos"—as over-the-top as the Spanish colonial "villas" they denote. Renowned (and often copied) exotics include Shangri La, Mar-a-Lago, Valhalla, La Follia, Ponderosa, and Las Incas. The Palm Beach housing department seems to require all homes to have cheesy sounding foreign names, so reread *Don Quixote* and see what strikes you. If the Spanish thing isn't working, you have other options: For inspiration, consider Ca d' Zan, circus magnate John Ringling's Sarasota Bay estate; or Xanadu, Irénée du Pont's Cuban villa, which housed his menagerie of trained iguanas.

THE MAGNUMS
A fantastical French name adds Old World charm to your New World ambitions. Scrutinizing wine labels will come in handy: Le Colombier, Beaulieu, Le Trianon, Château de Cantenac, and so forth. Falaise, Harry F. Guggenheim's 26-room Sands Point, New York, estate, is a noted example.

THE ECCENTRICS
Perfect for those with *Wuthering Heights* aspirations, these monikers conjure stately disrepair, large hunting dogs, and the stench of wet wool. The works of Brontë, Jane Austen, and Shakespeare are rife with inspiration. Combermere Abbey, Shepherd Park, and Darcy Manor are common favorites. There's also Winterthur, Henry du Pont's 1,000-acre Wilmington, Delaware, compound, and Cold Comfort, Cordelia Scaife Duggan's Ligonier, Pennsylvania, pile.

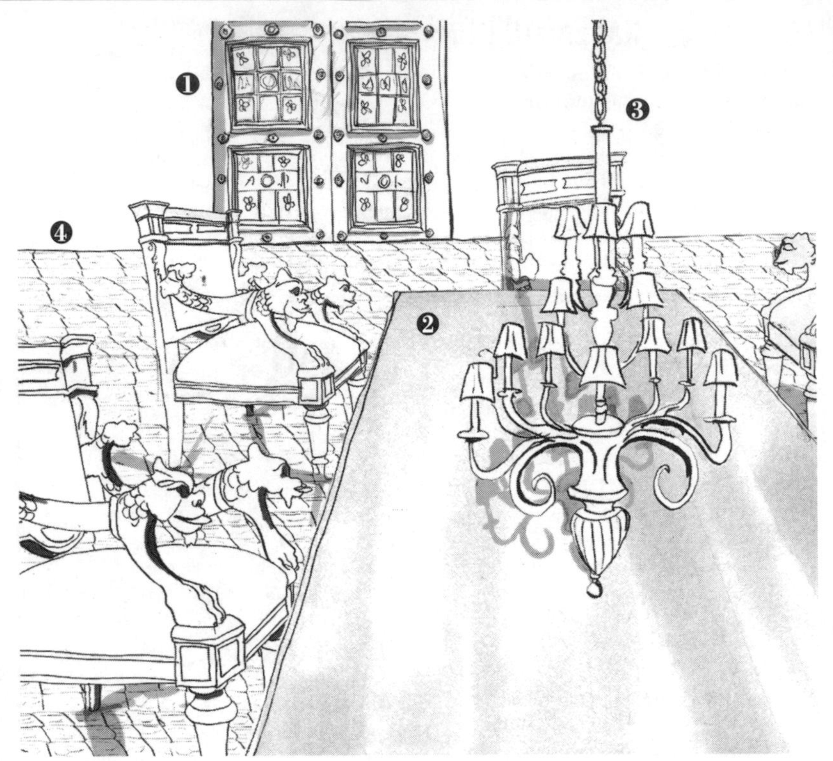

CHOOSING YOUR LOOK

Where Inspiration Meets Aspiration

HAUTE HACIENDA

NOTHING SAYS CULTURED LIKE IMPORTED MOORISH FLOOR TILES, CLAY CHIMINEAS, AND indoor-outdoor living spaces. Home is "unpretentious" and "cozy," with the "Spanish" in "Spanish Mission" loosely interpreted to mean "anything old and ethnic and conquistadory." **SUITABLE FOR: A-list Male; A-list Female** ***(see pp. 14–15)***

1. **Reclaimed door** from demolished Portuguese mosque

- **18th-century mantelpiece** salvaged from Guatemalan sugarcane plantation

2. One-ton **Venetian feasting table**

3. **Triple-tiered cast-iron chandelier/** medieval torture device

- Worm-eaten **ceiling beams** from Basque monastery

- Overstuffed light-green **velvet sofas from Axel Vervoordt**

4. **Forte dei Marmi floor tiles** with fossilized fern markings

- **Ceiling-mounted hi-def projection TV** from Academy Awards gift bag

LET THEM EAT CAKE

HERE, THE UNIVERSAL "MORE IS MORE" MANTRA OF CERTAIN NEW-MONEY MOGULS gets a full airing. Furnishings are bought at auction upon consultation with a Sotheby's expert, and Saudi sheiks, Russian oligarchs, and show-offs of all stripes will be bidding against you with glee. So what if none of you know your Louis XIV from your Louis XVI? The more gold leaf, the better. **SUITABLE FOR: The Raider; The Showman** ***(see pp. 2, 8)***

1. **Louis XIV chairs** upholstered in custom-dyed pink ostrich

- **Pillows** stitched from tattered remnants of 15th-century French tapestry

- **Ceiling frieze** reproduced from Versailles

2. **Ebony inlaid Louis XIV desk** strewn with various tortoiseshell knickknacks

- **Antique tomes** by the yard from the Strand book store in New York

3. Theatrical gold picture lights illuminating six **oversized Titians or Tintorettos**

4. Voluminous, **pale-yellow silk chintz-patterned curtains** tied back with oversized gold tasseled cords

FASCIST MODERN

AN ANTISEPTIC 3-D REPRESENTATION OF THE DISCIPLINE IT TAKES TO WIN. THOUGH THE uninitiated typically dismiss this look as "soulless" or "scary," devotees insist its trademark symmetry and lack of ornamentation actually have spiritual benefits, calming the mind and body after a long day of reaming out assistants. Maintaining its integrity takes vigilance, however. A cabinet left clumsily ajar can ruin the whole look. You might as well burn the place down. **SUITABLE FOR: The Technocrat; The Operator** ***(see pp. 6, 13)***

1. **Giant black-and-white canvas** by Franz Kline

- **Signed outtakes** from Mapplethorpe's bullwhip series
- **Custom, unadorned sectional** in "champagne" from Italian furniture house *del giorno*
- **Balinese orchids** on all flat surfaces
- **Universal remote control** lights, shades, stereo, heating, A/C, and retractable projection screen

2. **Poured concrete floor**

- **Knobless white lacquered doors**

3. **Giant gold Buddha's head** from Angkor Wat

WASP DECAY

IDEALLY, ONE WOULD INHERIT THIS LOOK. THE ALTERNATIVE IS TO HIRE AN OLD-GUARD designer who doesn't know any better. Stacks of books at conflicting angles, bad lighting, ratty Orientals, and elderly cocker spaniels complete the picture of a worldly Protestant at rest. An abundance of duck-print and petit-point pillows (rendering the couch impossible to sit on) discourages social-climbing cocktail guests from lingering. **SUITABLE FOR: The Dynasseur; The Grande Dame** ***(see pp. 4, 16)***

1. **Threadbare Aubusson carpet**

- **Three-foot-long photos** of Grandpa's Yale crew team
- **Early-1900s handmade model** of Grandpa's pond yacht

2. **Sun-damaged de Gournay wallpaper**

3. **Worn velvet Chesterfield sofa**

- **Monogrammed cheese knife,** tray of stale Carr's crackers, and sharp supermarket cheddar

4. **Circular Tiffany's tray** with 2-liter bottles each of Gordon's extra dry gin, Smirnoff vodka, Johnny Walker Black, and Cutty Sark, a kitchen knife, two rotten limes, and a stack of embroidered coasters

- **Woven basket** (by the fireplace) with Duraflame logs and stack of yellowed *Wall Street Journals*; *National Geographics* from 1996

WESTERN PATRIOT

WHEN IT COMES TO THRICE-DIVORCED BACHELORS PADS, NOTHING SAYS FILTHY RICH quite like dozens of dead animals and some old-fashioned jingoism. A sense of being at one with the land is conveyed in the scale of the furnishings and the floor-to-ceiling windows. Blazing fires and a multitude of "games" make this the preferred retreat for cronies. **SUITABLE FOR: The Hedger; The Thrillionaire** ***(see pp. 3, 11)***

1. **Whale-skin-covered bar stools**

- **Moose antler chandelier**

2. **Double-height fieldstone fireplace**

3. **World-class gun collection** (fully loaded)

- **Ralph Lauren Navajo blankets**

- **Poker table** for midnight games; $50,000 pots

4. **Series of framed letters** from Thomas Jefferson

- **Door** to walk-in humidor

INTERIOR DECORUM

Designer Dos and Don'ts

DO...

REALIZE THAT HE HATES your horrifically pedestrian taste. The sooner you internalize this and bow to his will, the sooner he will allow you to speak. Little by little, he will learn to trust you, and may even take a suggestion or two. But don't push. Repayment will come in the form of obsequious quotes about your breathtakingly cosmopolitan lifestyle and impeccable eye for antiques in the high-end shelter magazine of your choosing.

SUGGEST SOURCING TRIPS to places like Uzbekistan. Bonding aside, the cachet of traveling to remote locales to see if a certain type of marble tile will work in the children's nursery cannot be underestimated. "Mario and I spent all of yesterday scouring the markets in Tyrol for albino elk heads" is also the perfect excuse for ditching a snoozy black-tie gala.

DON'T...

FORGET THAT HE'S cosmically attached to you. (His tarot cards told him so!) Like your life coach, your Pilates instructor, and your divorce lawyer, your decorator should be kept on speed dial for daily, cameraphone-enabled consultations whilst shopping. Invite him to Gstaad, make him the godfather of your firstborn, set him up with your hairstylist. Eventually, you'll fire him for overbilling or for the next big name, but until then, he's family.

INTRODUCE HIM TO ANYONE, ever, as "the decorator." He is not staff, and he is not interested in mere "decoration." He is an artist designing the sets for the fairy tale that is your life. At dinner parties, smile adoringly and introduce him to guests as "Mario, the genius I've been telling you about!"

ARCHITECTURAL DIGRESS

To Shoot or Not to Shoot

Now that you've splurged on a name designer and ironed out the imperfections in the hand-painted wallpaper, should you let the camera crews in? If you're comfortable with images of your Schnabel-lined bathroom ending up on the Web, sure. Though, really, it depends on who's asking . . .

THE HOT NEW HOME SHOW

No. Never. Unless you're a lottery winner, quarterback, pop star under the age of 25, or other species of PlayStation-addicted parvenu.

THE LOCAL "LUXURY LIFESTYLE" MAG

A firm no—but thanks for asking! Save for an appearance on *MTV Cribs* there's nothing sadder. Though you'd hate to be banished from their party pages.

ARCHITECTURAL DIGEST* OR *WORLD OF INTERIORS

Yes and yes! Consider it a necessary evil that will keep your decorator in good standing. Allow the shoot, but insist on anonymity. The right people will know it's you.

THE FILTHY RICH·TION·ARY

The A to Zeds of Stylish Living

LIKE MOST PEOPLE WHO SPEND THEIR DAYS BILKING THE VERY RICH, SUPERSTAR decorators are acutely sensitive to the slightest change in status pressure. The reasons for this are twofold. First, while they'd sue you if you said so, the fluid pricing structure of the industry allows them to charge a massive premium on everything they purchase on your behalf. If you're the type of client who doesn't know what an Aubusson is, it stands to reason that your decorator might assume you're also the type who wouldn't notice if he charged you triple for one. The second reason is simpler. They love to gossip. What better way to ingratiate yourself to a new client than to tell her what a tacky moron whatshername is? To avoid getting ripped off (or worse, becoming whatshername), brush up on these classic terms.

-A-

Aga This 1,000-pound, $30,000-plus, cast-iron cooker is capable of heating a medium-sized manor. Its starring role in the kitchens of the English upper class is best reflected in the term "Aga Saga," dismissive shorthand for a cliché-laden novel set in the British countryside. Naturally, Martha Stewart swears by hers.

-B-

Baldwin, Billy *(1903–1984)* The petite, Baltimore-bred Baldwin was society's most adored and influential decorator of the 20th century, known for helping the merely rich look Filthy Rich with whimsical touches like velvet fainting couches. A favorite of Pauline de Rothschild, Diana Vreeland, Babe Paley, and Jackie O.

-C-

Chinoiserie A look heavy on red lacquer and cartoonish images of pagodas, latticework, and mythical beasts, Chinoiserie is what happened when haute 16th-century Paris went mad for Peking. Louis XIV was an early and ardent adopter, installing Chinoiserie-themed guest rooms in several of his palaces.

-D-

Draper, Dorothy *(1889–1969)* An Amazonian debutante from Tuxedo Park, New York, Draper had a hugely influential aesthetic as outsized and exuberant as her persona. The Breakers hotel in Palm Beach was signature Draper, awash in vaguely psychedelic florals, checkerboard floors, and laughably oversized chintz-covered wing chairs.

-E-

Eames, Charles
(1907–1978)
Charles Eames and his ambiguously named wife, Ray, revolutionized home décor in the 1950s by bringing bleeding-edge Finnish and Danish design to the U.S. market. Their Eames Lounge Chair, patented in 1956 and ubiquitous in chichi libraries, remains popular in spite of a brisk trade in cheaper knockoffs.

-F-

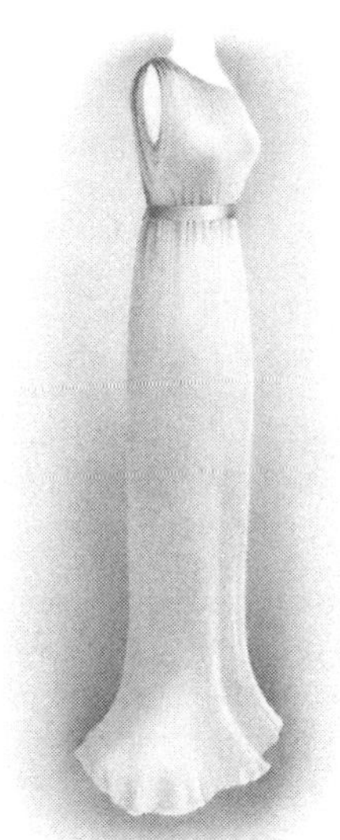

Fortuny, Mariano
(1871–1949) Fortuny's exotically opulent fabric designs, infused with nostalgia for Renaissance Italy and the Persian empire, earned the plutocrat seal of approval in 1927 when jet-setting interior decorator (and future wacky countess) Elsa McNeill stumbled upon them in Paris. McNeill knew every Upper East Side dowager worth a damn for the next 80 years would find them just smashing, and quickly struck an exclusive deal to sell them out of her shop on Madison Avenue. The secret techniques Fortuny used to perfect the look of "authentic antiquity" are still practiced today at the company's island workshop in the Adriatic.

-G-

Gwathmey, Charles
(b. 1938) As one half of the major New York architecture firm Gwathmey Siegel, he has earned a name for himself as the go-to guy for ultramodern billionaire compounds. Gwathmey's restrained, elegant fingerprints are all over the homes of Steven Spielberg, Ron Meyer, Michael Dell, Jerry Seinfeld, and P. Diddy.

-H-

Hicks, David
(1929–1998) This British design darling of the '60s and '70s jet set was renowned for his vivid textiles and daring juxtapositions of modern and traditional. When he married Pamela Mountbatten (daughter of the Earl of Mountbatten and viceroy of India), Hicks rocketed into the stratosphere of oxygen-thin British society, where he cultivated a royal following. Today, his graphic patterns and devotion to Lucite inspire fashion designers like Tory Burch and decorators like Jonathan Adler and Kelly Wearstler. He's the reason some tycoons think any old candelabra from the Portobello Road can be blended seamlessly into a "modern eclectic" roomscape.

-I-

Ikat The design world's current fabric flavor of the month. A handwoven silk textile from the islands of Indonesia, it was recently the subject of a Metropolitan Museum of Art exhibit. Park Avenue decorators caught on and now the geometrical, jewel-toned patterns are showing up on down-stuffed throw pillows in living rooms across the country.

-J-

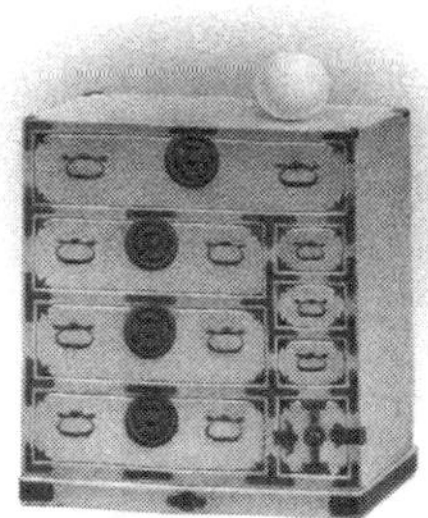

Japanese The new Chinese. Ever since those hulking wedding chests were reproduced en masse by Pottery Barn, they've lost their panache. Now it's all about Japanese Tansu chests. ("They have much better lines," your decorator, Mario, assures you.)

-K-

Knoll An American furniture house that holds patents for contemporary collections by Marcel Breuer, Mies van der Rohe, and Eero Saarinen. Recently, a dangerous proliferation of Knoll-designed housewares has led more than a few middlebrow designers to think they can throw down a Saarinen tulip chair and call it a day. Not to be confused with Knole, the 15th-century estate in Kent, England.

-L-

Lancaster, Nancy *(1897–1994)* A Southern belle (born into Virginia's colorful Langhorne clan), Lancaster married her way into the upper echelons of British society and eventually became more English than the English. Her love of gardening and interior design prompted her to found the influential firm Colefax and Fowler, where she took the posh yet ramshackle English country house look to new heights.

-M-

Meier, Richard *(b. 1934)* The Gettys, Martha Stewart, and Nicole Kidman have him on speed dial; you should, too. The modern era's reigning starchitect, he can make the simplest of materials stratospherically expensive. His sterile, white-on-white look is ideal for those who don't mind the notion of living without red wine, pets, children, or shoes.

-N-

Netto, David *(b. 1970)* It's Netto's fault that your child's nursery must now resemble the lobby of an Ian Schrager hotel. This oh-so-hip telegenic young designer makes spartan cribs, aloof baby rockers, and subdued changing tables. His mini-armoires are just the thing to store Maude's and Caspian's onesies from Lucy Sykes's baby line.

-O-

Obelisks Since the Brits first pillaged Egypt, no country house has been complete without a crumbling obelisk or other ancient treasure smuggled across borders under the cover of night, be it pre-Columbian, Etruscan, or Khmer.

-P-

Parish, Sister *(1910–1994)* The design firm founded in 1962 by Sister Parish and Albert Hadley is still a byword for genteel WASP fabulosity. Though Albert Hadley Inc. remains in operation, modern tycoons turn to Parish-Hadley alums Bunny Williams, Mario Buatta, or Mariette Himes Gomez for an updated take on the classic look.

-Q-

Queen As in, "Yes, Mario's a nasty old queen but he has terribly chic taste." See also: Queen Anne, a highly collectible period in colonial furniture and silver named for Britain's Queen Anne (1702–1714). Furniture made in this period marked a vast improvement over the rustic pieces from the time of William and Mary.

-R-

Rense, Paige *(b. 1929)* Long before Anna Wintour had sharpened her editing claws, Paige Rense (reigning editrix of *Architectural Digest* for over three decades) was terrifying editorial staffers and deciding the fates of designers on the rise. If you dream of seeing your equestrian estate in rural Virginia in *AD*'s pages, it's Rense you'll need to impress. (See "Architectural Digress," p. 49.)

-S-

Smith, Jeffery
(ageless) Who doesn't love a loggia? For those who wish resort architect Addison Mizner would rise from the dead and build them a palazzo, there's Jeffery Smith. "Grand scale" isn't a problem for Palm Beach's premier starchitect (his "La Reverie" is 67,000 square feet), who's been building for Beach royalty like cosmetics heir Leonard Lauder, Allen & Co. heiress Terry Allen Kramer, and the Donald's ex Ivana since the early '90s.

-T-

Toile de Jouy Few patterns scream "taste!" quite as loudly as toile de Jouy. First developed in the 1800s, it literally means "cloth from Jouy," a town in France. Traditional toile consists of a white background with an intricate pastoral scene (say, a band of merry minstrels) repeated in dark red, black, blue, or green. Though toile was once deployed sparingly, the WASP decor revival at the turn of the last century saw the rise of the all-toile room, in which every conceivable surface—walls, drapes, furnishings, and ceiling—is covered in the same idyllic pattern. This calculated bit of whimsy has been known to induce nausea.

-U-

Uzbekistan Every decade or so the style set christens a new It Destination for espresso-fueled sourcing trips. This minute it's Uzbekistan. By the time you flip this page, it may be Iceland. Treasure seekers jet to this Central Asian backwater (or send the decorator) for colorful Bukhara embroidery and Suzani rugs and textiles to give their homes a decadent opium den appeal.

-V-

Vervoordt, Axel
(b. 1947) This world-renowned Belgian antiques dealer sells *objets extraordinaire* and his own custom-designed furniture from his family castle near Antwerp. Select clients also take the living legend on for his envy-inducing interior design services.

-W-

Wright, Frank Lloyd
(1867–1959) Best known for the Guggenheim, Wright is the undisputed master of the modern home. His walls of glass and utilitarian ethos provided an alternative for titans bored with deciding between mock Tudors and neo-Georgians.

-X-

The "X" Factor
Why one designer becomes a surefire name drop while another sinks into obscurity. Hence, design mags will trumpet Rex von Whiffenpoof's use of paisley tufted ottomans as "the work of a true design visionary"; meanwhile, Twinkle Chatsworth has been using paisley tufted ottomans since 1984, and no one has a clue who she is.

-Y-

Yoga Studio Since Donna Karan built one (for private daily lessons with Rodney Yee), residential yoga retreats have become a must-have indulgence. Geodesic domes are the purest place for "practice," while bamboo flooring, picture windows with inspiring ocean views, and $40,000 Bose speaker systems (to better hear the chanting) are practically commonplace. An outdoor grass meditation mandala adds seasonal versatility.

-Z-

Zebra As traditionalists tire of mid-century modern, the Victorian obsession with taxidermy has taken hold again. Primo specimens come from Deyrolle's in Paris, where full-size zebras and rare albino peacocks make for a brisk trade.

THE GREAT OUTDOORS

Where Money Grows on Trees

SINCE THE HEADY DAYS OF MARIE ANTOINETTE AND HER PASTORAL VERSAILLES FOLLY (miniature dairy farm *inclus*), the super rich have flexed their muscles with extreme landscaping. Like the Gilded Age robber barons who bankrolled our nation's vast arboretums, today's billionaires also have a passion for nature's gifts. A few garden-variety fetishes to keep in mind:

PRIVET HEDGES

A PRIVILEGED LIFE UNFOLDS MOST beatifically behind an impenetrable green wall of utter privacy. An 8,000-square-foot palace visible from the road may be acceptable in subdivision circles, but in seriously exclusive enclaves like Palm Beach, it's better not to be seen *or* heard.

Ligustrum vulgare is the Latin name for the common English privet, but there's nothing vulgar about this hardy little shrub. Unfortunately, a hedge can take as long as 20 years (with proper twice-weekly grooming) to reach its mature height of 12 feet. Even a suitable six-foot privet can take 15 years to fill out. Which is troublesome, as the Filthy Rich do not take their hedge heights lightly.

GREEN MONSTERS
The Privets of Palm Beach

In Southampton, Long Island, for instance, privet norms are strictly adhered to, most adamantly by newcomers. One such neighbor even sued tobacco heiress Robin Duke, claiming she was not keeping her hedges pruned to the proper height, creating an unsightly discrepancy within the neighborhood. In court, Ms. Duke, baffled by the charges, quietly responded that her family had been part of the community for decades (since the privet was a seedling) and was fairly certain her hedge heights had always been in keeping with those of other longstanding residents. After hearing Ms. Duke's testimony, the plaintiff's lawyer was so mortified by his client's ignorance that he asked for her suit to be withdrawn.

So, what's an arriviste to do? After all, there's nothing more revealing than sparse three-foot shrubbery. You may as well throw in the monogrammed towel and erect a chain-link fence! Unless you can afford to buy a place with mature privets, or import some yourself for several hundred grand, perhaps it's best to choose an impossibly remote address where the neighbors can't judge you (unpaved road a plus).

SPLENDOR IN THE GRASS
A Champion Specimen

TROPHY TREES

IF YOU'RE BUILDING YOUR OWN UTOPIA, standard-issue "developer's trees" won't do. Connected landscape architects know where to find the ultimate mature trunks and how to safely transplant them (and their giant root balls) to your property. Oscar de la Renta even had some airlifted from the United States to his compound in the Dominican Republic. A single trophy tree can cost anywhere from $25,000 to

THE SECRET GARDENER

Not content to roll out some sod and call it a day, tycoons lacking the Martha Stewart touch have been known to spend up to $5 million an acre cultivating their outdoor spaces.

Today, those in the know turn to California-based landscape guru Robert Truskowski, whose discriminating global client roster (stretching from Quogue to Qatar) demands the pinnacle in grandiose gardening. Trained in Greenwich, Connecticut, under chintz-loving interior design icon Sister Parish, Truskowski employs a battalion of sixteen to help him shape every blade of zoysia grass on your River Oaks bowling green or Mustique yoga circle. No task is too daunting: Previous jobs include constructing a shark pool for a client's beach retreat on the Red Sea and a floating massage pavilion for a villa on the Côte d'Azur. Just don't ask for a price list.

HIGH SOCIETY
A Dream of a Tree House

$100,000, plus the considerable cost of transporting it on a flatbed truck (or boat or plane), with attendant arborist.

RARE ORCHIDS

THOUGH THEIR UBIQUITY IN W HOTEL lobbies suggests trouble ahead, rare orchids remain objects of obsession for collectors like L.A. mega-investor David Murdock (who has a staggering 30,000). The rarest subspecies (imported from Borneo) start at $1,000 per stem.

TREE HOUSES

STING HAS ONE, THANKS TO DESIGNER Roderick Wolgamott Romero, who creates "adult tree houses" that double as ecosculpture. One of his recent creations sparked controversy in Brentwood, California, when it turned out the aerie had a scandalously direct view of the neighboring plastic surgeon's hot tub. The chance to have a custom hideout built for you by Romero (care of the Neiman Marcus Christmas catalog) starts at $50,000.

EXTREME LAWN CARE

ONCE YOU HAVE THE JAPANESE PAGODA, the orchid greenhouse, and the white winter vegetable garden in place, someone needs to tend to them. Eighties villain Ivan Boesky is said to have employed swarms of gardeners to manicure his lawn with scissors, ensuring all the grass blades were kept at the same height. Long Island eccentric Adele Herter made her gardeners work through the night, replacing existing plantings with individual vases of cut flowers to amuse her houseguests in the morning with the miraculous change of color. For a modest five-acre estate, the annual cost of immaculate lawn care can easily spiral past the $500,000 mark.

THE THIN GREEN LINE

When Topiary Takes Over

Like all things quaintly English, experimenting with topiary (the traditional art of tree shaping) is quite fashionable these days. Heck, even Oprah rings up her dealer, "Topiary Joe," from time to time. If you must indulge, however, we urge you to use sparingly. We'd hate to see you end up like the following shrub junkies:

- **THOMAS BRAYTON, a Gilded Age cotton kingpin, went topiary mad at his Newport Estate (later dubbed "Green Animals"), hiring Portuguese garden guru Joseph Carreiro to create over 80 whimsical animals to amuse his daughter, Alice. The property, now owned by the Newport Preservation Society, is overrun with elephants, camels, giraffes, unicorns, teddy bears, and a giant Rhode Island rooster, all made of California yew and English boxwood.**

- **LORD BATH, one of the richest (and most far-out) men in England, has spent the last 30 years on a maze-building bender at his 16th-century ancestral seat in Wiltshire. His grounds at Longleat house a safari park and several of the modern era's more impressive living mazes—one of which, the world's longest, consists of 16,000 yew trees painstakingly sculpted into two miles of beguiling twists and turns.**

- **SARAH WINCHESTER, the bizarre widow of Oliver Winchester (of repeating rifle fame), created a menagerie of eerie topiaries at her San Jose, California, estate. When she wasn't holding séances to commune with the victims of her husband's invention, she was concocting trippy vignettes out of the boxwoods in her garden. Pruned scenes include a child fighting with a duck, a child riding a mythical sea monster known as a hippocampus, and a series of mysterious, crescent-shaped hedges.**

A BUSH TOO FAR
Brayton's Elephant

THE GOOD LIFE AQUATIC

A Pool Shape Primer

FOR THOSE STILL CLINGING TO THE NOTION THAT A SWIMMING POOL SHOULD RESEMBLE A turquoise bean, here's a splash of cold water. The flamboyant '80s kidney was replaced long ago by the following styles, none of which scream "Cannonball."

THE POND
A naturalistic in-ground pool/garden with separate freshwater ponds for koi, a hot tub set into a boulder, jagged rock formations, and, in some cases, a waterslide. May also feature rustic waterfalls, stepping stones, slippery moss, and bridges. **SINK OR SWIM:** If executed poorly, this rock-garden homage can feel more like a set from *The Bachelor* or the Skull Mountain ride at your local Six Flags.

THE EMPEROR'S BATH
A half-moon-shaped pool surrounded by classical statuary (with mythical figures dancing across the bottom of the pool) can recall Lake Como villas or Slim Aarons's famous portraits of the jet set's aquatic playgrounds. **SINK OR SWIM:** The modern-day interpretation can scream Celine Dion at Caesar's Palace.

THE INFINITY
It's become *the* thing not to know where your pool ends, particularly if it sits on a Malibu bluff or windswept cliff in Honolulu. **SINK OR SWIM:** Once the bleeding edge in pool design, now every three-bedroom on a Tucson cul-de-sac has one.

THE "GRAY" LAP POOL
Simply serene and almost Zen-like, its long and rectangular shape is more aesthetic than useful. The gunite gives the water a deep, grayish, quasimeditative tint. While dark red brick or slate is often used to frame these pools, grass always makes a better statement. **SINK OR SWIM:** Forget about finding that sapphire ring you lost while skinny-dipping. Or noticing how shallow it is when you dive in drunk. *Thwack!*

THE ETERNAL TACKINESS OF FOUNTAINS

Fountains may have been fitting for the Medici princes, but today, water features tend to suggest "SkyMall catalog" more pointedly than "Italian nobility." Even if you were picturing something a bit grander than a faux-rock babbling brook from Sharper Image, there's a chance you might be pegged as a Bellagio swinger if you indulge on this front. Before you take the plunge, please consider two of the country's foremost fountain fanatics: Candy Spelling and Donald Trump, whose shared love of gurgling, gargoyle-rimmed birdbaths is as revealing about their personalities as their perma-smiles.

"NO TOPS, NO BOTTOMS"

Why the Rich Swim Nude

LIKE THEIR SPIRITUAL KIN AT THE bottom of the ladder, upper-class men are refreshingly unshackled from middle-class emotions like shame. This may help explain why their bathing suits actually shrink in proportion to their bank accounts. And considering the disturbing popularity of male bikinis on the world's better beaches, it's no surprise that they adore dropping trou completely in their own backyards—no matter who's watching. The most famous American exemplar is probably President John F. Kennedy, who brought a naturalist's love of nude bathing to the White House pool after decades of high-end free-balling in Palm Beach and Hyannisport (First Lady Jackie was also a lifelong devotee). No East Coast libertine, Lyndon Johnson similarly indulged when he assumed the reins, frolicking naked on at least one occasion with televangelist Billy Graham.

Though no one can say for sure, flamboyant Broadway producer Evan Frankel (known around town as the "Squire of East Hampton") was probably the first American plutocrat to put the unspoken into print, banning swimsuits altogether at his estate, Brigadoon, with a large sign reading "No Tops, No Bottoms." As he ingeniously reasoned, "A pool is not a Laundromat." Famous guests who followed the rule included Marilyn Monroe, Jackson Pollack, and Winston Churchill's daughter, Sarah.

SWIMMING WITH SHARKS
Fiat Don Gianni Agnelli

Some have even taken this pubis-bearing penchant public. In addition to bankrolling PBS, one of billionaire philanthropist John D. MacArthur's lesser-known contributions to society is the nudist playground he built on Singer Island just off Palm Beach. In town searching for a site to build his Magic Kingdom, MacArthur's squeaky clean buddy Walt Disney could even be convinced to disrobe al fresco. And while it's probably less surprising, Edward Craven Walker, inventor of the lava lamp, used the windfall from his psychedelic gizmo to develop a seaside nudist resort in England. Echt-WASP Roger Nash Baldwin, patrician founder of the ACLU, also swam starkers while summering on Martha's Vineyard, home to the unfortunately named Gay Head nudist colony, conveniently located near Jackie O's beachfront compound.

In short, be prepared to lose the suit.

DIRECTORY

STARCHITECTS

TADAO ANDO
Japanese minimalist who channels Louis Kahn.
Clients: Tom Ford; Giorgio Armani
Tadao Ando Architect & Associates
5-23 Toyosaki
2-Chome Kita-ku
Osaka 531-0072, Japan
Tel.: 81 6 6375 1148

NORMAN FOSTER
Eco-savvy structural expressionist famous for his skyscrapers.
Clients: The German government (he rehabbed the Reichstag); Hearst
Foster + Partners
Riverside
22 Hester Road
London SW11 4AN, UK
Tel.: 44 020 7738 0455
FosterAndPartners.com

FRANK GEHRY
Universally adored, stunningly impractical.
Clients: Michael Eisner; Dennis Hopper; the Guggenheim
Gehry Partners
12541 Beatrice Street
Los Angeles, CA 90066
Tel.: 310-482-3000
Foga.com

CHARLES GWATHMEY
Palatial pads for Hollywood hitters.
Clients: Steven Spielberg; David Geffen; Universal chief Ron Meyer; Jeffrey Katzenberg; Jerry Seinfeld
Gwathmey, Siegel & Associates
475 10th Avenue
New York, NY 10018
Tel.: 212-947-1240
Gwathmey-Siegel.com

ZAHA HADID
Fluid concrete forms. Diva.
Clients: Eli Broad; BMW
Zaha Hadid Architects
Studio 9
10 Bowling Lane Green
London EC1R OBQ, UK
Tel.: 44 20 7253 5147
Zaha-Hadid.com

MICHAEL HAVERLAND
Low-key modernism—with heart!
Clients: Calvin Klein; Robert Marc; artist David Salle
Michael Haverland Design
26 East 10th Street
New York, NY 10003
Tel.: 212-780-9188
MichaelHaverland.com

REM KOOLHAAS
The mad Dutchman.
Clients: Prada; the Guggenheim
Office for Metropolitan Architecture
Heer Bokelweg 149
3032 AD Rotterdam
The Netherlands
Tel.: 31 10 243 82 00
Oma.eu
and
180 Varick Street, Suite 1328
New York, NY 10014
Tel.: 212-337-0770

RICHARD MEIER
Terrariums for tycoons.
Clients: Art hustler Larry Gagosian; The Getty Foundation
Richard Meier & Partners
475 Tenth Avenue, 6th floor
New York, NY 10018
Tel.: 212-967-6060
RichardMeier.com
and
1001 Gayley Avenue
Los Angeles, CA 90024
Tel.: 310-208-6464

JEAN NOUVEL
Whimsical—with gravitas!
Clients: Brad Pitt; über innkeeper André Balazs
10 Cité d'Angoulême
Paris 75011, France
Tel.: 33 1 49 23 83 83
JeanNouvel.com

JEFFERY W. SMITH
The pasha of Palm Beach.
Clients: The Lauders; the Kochs; the Mercks; Terry Allen Kramer, et al.
206 Phipps Plaza
Palm Beach, FL 33480
Tel.: 561-832-0202
SmithArchitecturalGroup.com

INTERIOR DESIGNERS

MURIEL BRANDOLINI
Studied eclectic.
Clients: Prince and Princess Pavlos of Greece; Christopher and Pia Getty
Muriel Brandolini Inc.
525 East 72nd Street
New York, NY 10021
Tel.: 212-249-4920
MurielBrandolini.com

THIERRY DESPONT
French twist.
Clients: Calvin Klein; Bill Gates; Conrad Black
10 Harrison Street
New York, NY 10013
Tel.: 212-334-9444
Despont.com

JAMIE DRAKE
(Slightly) edgy elegance.
Clients: NYC mayor Mike Bloomberg (both Gracie Mansion and his private townhouse); Madonna (who is said to have paid in the $500,000 range—per room).
Drake Design Associates Inc.
315 East 62nd Street
New York, NY 10065
Tel.: 212-754-3099
DrakeDesignAssociates.com

STEVEN GAMBREL
Neo-classical American glam.
Clients: Liz Lange; gay Wall Streeters
S. R. Gambrel Inc.
270 Lafayette Street, Suite 805
New York, NY 10012
Tel.: 212-925-3380
SRGambrel.com

ALBERT HADLEY
Partner of Sister Parish.
Clients: Al Gore; Diane Sawyer;

various Astors, Gettys
Albert Hadley Inc.
24 East 64th Street, 4th floor
New York, NY 10065
Tel.: 212-223-8447

TONY INGRAO
Tasteful decadence.
Clients: Kim Cattrall; Howard Stern
Ingrao Inc.
17 East 64th Street
New York, NY 10065
Tel.: 212-472-5400
Ingrao.com

CHRISTIAN LIAIGRE
Jet-set journeyman.
Clients: The Mercer Hotel; Rupert Murdoch
122 rue de Grenelle
75007 Paris, France
Tel: 33 1455 61642
Christian-Liaigre.fr

DAVID NETTO
Bauhaus cribs not included.
Clients: Gwyneth Paltrow; Rachel Weisz
David Netto Design
270 Lafayette Street, 1204
New York, NY 10021
Tel: 212-343-7415
DavidNettoDesign.com

CAMPION PLATT
Comfy contemporary.
Clients: Al Pacino; Russell Simmons; Meg Ryan; Conan O'Brien
152 Madison Avenue, Suite 900
New York, NY 10016
Tel.: 212-779-3855
CampionPlatt.com

WILLIAM SOFIELD
Retro remixed.
Clients: Gucci; P. Diddy; Martha Stewart
Studio Sofield, Inc.
380 Lafayette Street, 4th floor
New York, NY 10003
Tel.: 212-473-1300

SILLS HUNIFORD ASSOCIATES
Urban legend.
Clients: Vera Wang; Anna Wintour; the Newhouse family; Tina Turner; Lauren and Richard Dupont; several Rockefellers
30 East 67th Street
New York, NY 10065
Tel.: 212-988-1636
SillsHuniford.com

MICHAEL S. SMITH
Extreme makeover: mogul edition.
Clients: Rupert Murdoch; Steven Spielberg
Michael S. Smith Inc.
1646 19th Street
Santa Monica, CA 90404
Tel.: 310-315-3018
MichaelSmithInc.com

ROSE TARLOW
Master of mix-and-match.
Clients: Barbara Walters; David Geffen; Eli Broad
Melrose House
8454 Melrose Place
Los Angeles, CA 90069
Tel.: 323-651-2202
RoseTarlow.com

VICTORIA HAGAN
The last word in muted luxe.
Clients: Jack Welch; sundry Bronfmans
Victoria Hagan Interiors
654 Madison Avenue
New York, NY 10021
Tel.: 212-888-1178
VictoriaHagan.com

THE KEYS TO QUALITY

At home, your goal is the attainment of perfection, and nothing less. According to interior designer and architect Campion Platt, every niche market has its own club of exceptionally talented craftspeople. Here are the ones you should know about:

EXOTIC STONE

PUCCIO
The premier onyx supplier in the U.S.
661 Driggs Avenue
Brooklyn, NY 11211
Tel.: 718-387-9778
Puccio.info

PYROLAVE
Bespoke lava surfaces.
11 rue Beaugrenelle
Paris 75015, France
Tel.: 33 145 71 08 30
Pyrolave.fr

RHODES ARCHITECTURAL STONE
Rocks from the Yangtze River.
2011 East Olive Street
Seattle, WA 98122
Tel.: 206-709-3000
Rhodes.org

COUTURE UPHOLSTERY

RONALD JONAS INTERIORS
44 West 18th Street
New York, NY 10011
Tel.: 212-685-5610

CARPETS

VEEDON FLEECE LTD.
Tibetan wool and pashmina silks for soft furnishings.
42 Nightingale Road
Guilford, Surrey GU1 1EP, UK
Tel.: 44 0 1483 575758
VeedonFleece.com

LEATHER

TEDDY & ARTHUR EDELMAN LIMITED
Best hides for leather walls.
80 Pickett District Road
New Milford, CT 06776
Tel.: 860-350-9600 or 800-886-TEDY
EdelmanLeather.com

M. P. L. THAILAND CO., LTD.
Custom dyed and treated sharkskins.
120/525 Moobaan Maneeya, Soi 101/1
Sukhumvit Road, Bang-na
Bangkok, Thailand 10260
Tel.: 662 361-1626-8
MPLThailand.com

LIGHTING

NULUX
Museum-quality luminations.
1717 Troutman Avenue
Ridgewood, NY 11385
Tel.: 718-383-1112
Nulux.com

RSA LIGHTING
Custom fixtures.
9660 Topanca Canyon Blvd.
Chatsworth, CA 91311
Tel.: 800-356-3030

MATTRESSES

BOND BEDDING
Handmade mattresses.
P.O. Box 17089

Hudson City Station
Jersey City, NJ 07307
Tel.: 212-943-4898
BondBedding.com

PLASTER MOLDINGS

HYDE PARK FINE ART OF MOULDINGS INC.
29-16 40th Avenue
Long Island City, NY 11101
Tel.: 718-706-0504
Hyde-Park.com

WINE CELLARS

KEDCO STORAGE SYSTEMS
For the true connoisseur.
564 Smith Street
Farmingdale, NY 11735
Tel.: 516-454-7800

HOME SECURITY

ELECTRONIC SYSTEMS ASSOCIATES
Tracking systems for fine art.
11 West 42nd Street
New York, NY 10036
Tel.: 212-843-3600

EMPIRE SAFE COMPANY
Custom vaults for family jewels.
6 East 39th Street
New York, NY 10016
Tel.: 212-226-2255, ext. 218
EmpireSafe.com

WOODWORKS

MONTEATH MOULDING
Specialty wood cuts.
P.O. Box 757
South Amboy, NJ 08879
Tel.: 800-922-1029
Monteath.com

SHUTTERS

BACK BAY SHUTTER CO.
16-A Garfield Circle
Burlington, MA 01803
Tel.: 781-221-0100
BackBayShutter.com

WINDOWS

HOPE'S WINDOWS
84 Hopkins Avenue
P.O. Box 580
Jamestown, NY 14702
Tel.: 716-665-5124
HopesWindows.com

ZELUCK
The supermodel of custom windows.
5300 Kings Highway
Brooklyn, NY 11234
Tel.: 718-251-8060
Zeluck.com

BATHROOMS

3-D LABORATORY
Bespoke radiators and towel warmers.
268 Water Street
New York, NY 10038
Tel.: 212-791-7070
3-Dcon.com

KOHLER COMPANY
New G-3 toilet has a remote control.
444 Highland Drive
Kohler, WI 53044
Tel.: 414-457-4441
Kohler.com

TOTO USA
Luxury bath products from Japan.
25 Mercer Street
New York, NY 10013
Tel.: 888-295-8134
TotoUsa.com

WATERWORKS
Fine fixtures.
60 Backus Avenue
Danbury, CT 06810
Tel.: 800-899-6757
Waterworks.com

BED LINENS

FRETTE
Foro Buonaparte, 51
Milan 20121, Italy
Tel.: 39 039 6046 360
and
799 Madison Avenue
New York, NY 10021
Tel.: 212-988-5221
Frette.com

LEONTINE LINENS
Bergdorf Goodman
754 Fifth Avenue
New York, NY 10022
Tel.: 212-872-8787
LeontineLinens.com

OLATZ
43 Clarkson Street
New York, NY 10014
Tel.: 212-255-8627
Olatz.com

PRATESI
829 Madison Avenue
New York, NY 10021
Tel. 212-288-2315
Pratesi.com
Other locations:
Beverly Hills: 310-274-7661
Boston: 617-262-5998
Chicago: 312-943-8422
San Francisco: 415-291-9480
Palm Beach: 561-655-4414

HOME SPA DESIGN

CLODAGH DESIGN
670 Broadway, 4th floor
New York, NY 10012
Tel.: 212-780-5300
Clodagh.com

HOME THEATER DESIGN

THEO KALOMIRAKIS THEATERS
247 West 35th Street
6th floor
New York, NY 10001
Tel.: 212-244-2404
TKTheaters.com

LANDSCAPE ARCHITECTURE

ROBERT TRUSKOWSKI
1110 North Coast Highway
Laguna Beach, CA 92651
Tel.: 949-494-6650
Truskowski.com

CHAPTER THREE / THE ART OF STAFFING UP

IT TAKES A VILLAGE

"Why should I walk when I can hire someone to do it for me?"
—WOOLWORTH HEIRESS BARBARA HUTTON

SERVICE WITH A SMILE

BEING FILTHY RICH IS A full-time job filled with complexities and concerns unimaginable to the average plebe. Maintaining one estate is hard enough. How on earth do you manage nine? Thankfully, America's uneasy legacy of domestic servitude is alive and thriving. So put on your boss face, because it's time to staff up!

It's not that you're lazy or spoiled. (Unless you are.) You didn't become mind-bogglingly loaded by sitting on your ass. (Unless you did.) It's just that maintaining a lifestyle that the vast majority of the earth's population can't even begin to fathom demands constant vigilance and commitment. Obviously, hours spent truffling with the Spielbergs on the Rothschild estate will mean less time for ironing and parenting. Better to dispense with the workaday chores and leave the details to the pros.

Regrettably, this isn't as simple as posting an ad on craigslist. Without the proper knowledge and contacts, recruiting a qualified staff can be excruciating. And once you've got everyone on board, the fun really starts. Like all plutocrats, you are now a corporation in miniature, and how you treat your employees will mean the difference between long-term success and public flameout.

For instance, harshly scolding your servants (or, God forbid, belting them upside their heads with cell phones, Naomi Campbell–style) will only land you in the columns. Unless you enjoy being mocked, do not do this. Other potential pitfalls are less obvious. Is requiring your butler to wear tails and address you as "Sir" the ultimate in refined taste—or the mark of a hopeless striver? As you'll soon find out, it depends on your locale.

Regardless of whether you believe in such things, staffing up could turn out to be the most karmically rewarding experience of your filthy rich life. Rarely do humans have the opportunity to live and work so closely with complete strangers. Tread carefully, hire wisely, conduct yourself with integrity, and your staff will bring nothing but joy into your home. Do otherwise and, well—we'll get to that.

THE PECKING ORDER

A Guide to the Household Hierarchy

MAJORDOMO

COMMONLY CALLED AN ESTATE MANAGER, the sexier, more pretentious European term is preferable. From the Medieval Latin *major domūs* (literally, "head of house"), the majordomo is responsible for the care and maintenance of all your domiciles, including the hiring, firing, and overseeing of staff. He (it's never a she) manages the household accounts, opens and closes seasonal properties, relays your directives to the appropriate minions, and owns several waxed Barbour jackets. He's your eyes and ears among the folks "downstairs" and, when needed, your cold-blooded hatchet man. **SALARY RANGE:** $85,000 to $225,000* **SPENDS DAY OFF:** Getting tanked at the local T.G.I. Friday's; bow hunting

PERSONAL ASSISTANT

NATIVE TO HOLLYWOOD, THIS POLITICALLY correct update on the "personal secretary" of yore is now an indispensable part of any filthy rich retinue. He or she is responsible for doing things that are beneath you, including (but in no way limited to) scheduling, canceling, and rescheduling lunches with your frenemies; finding a behavioral psychologist for your suicidal dachshund; scoring a prom date for your socially retarded nephew; hacking into your cheating spouse's Gmail account; apologizing for your rude and thoughtless behavior; complimenting you on your wit; and procuring marijuana. Of all your staff relationships, this one is the most vital and complicated. She knows your secrets and could ruin you, but never would, because she'd sooner slit her own throat. Or write a thinly veiled roman à clef. (See "Clip-'n-Save NDA!", p.69) **SALARY RANGE:** $35,000 to $300,000 **SPENDS DAY OFF:** Crying on the phone to her mother in Duluth; blogging about you

BUTLER

FORMALLY TRAINED AND HIGHLY EXPERIENCED, he supervises and coordinates the activities of the household and its employees on a daily basis. He answers the phone, serves meals and drinks, runs basic errands, and eavesdrops on your guests. In some cases, he is referred to by an inscrutable title, like butler administrator, but to you, he's Giles or Tibbets or Clifton. If he doesn't have a suitable name, you're well within your rights to call him something else. The word "butler" derives from the Old French *bouteillier* (meaning "cupbearer"), from *bouteille* ("bottle"), and a properly trained butler will know his wines cold. These days, he wears a business suit or business casual, never tails. Unless you're in your nineties, live in Newport, and he taught you how to drive in a Model T. **SALARY RANGE:** $45,000 to $100,000 **SPENDS DAY OFF:** Attending musical theater

* *Salary ranges are approximate and include room and board.*

HOUSEKEEPER

RELATIVELY COMMON EVEN IN UPPER-middle-class homes, a housekeeper performs domestic chores: cleaning, shopping, light babysitting, and dog walking. She will not speak fluent English, and will hate your cook even more than you do. **SALARY RANGE:** $26,000 to $32,000 **SPENDS DAY OFF:** In church; burning through prepaid phone cards to Guatemala since you won't let her call long distance

THE NANNY

STANDARD PROTOCOL CALLS FOR A 2:1 nanny-to-kid ratio. With good reason. Your nanny (or "manny," in some oddball cases) is so *in loco parentis* her duties can include everything from filling out preschool applications and planning bat mitzvahs to tutoring darling Peyton in Pashtun. Coveted nannies are Australian and English. **SALARY RANGE:** $20,000 to $90,000 **SPENDS DAY OFF:** Hungover in bed

CHAUFFEUR

DUTIES INCLUDE FERRYING YOU AND your immediate family around, maintaining all vehicles, pretending he isn't listening to your cell phone conversations, and idling in bad neighborhoods while your teenage son scores crack. The best ones hail from the former Eastern Bloc, where they did "bad tings" they'd rather not discuss. Particularly when working for celebrities, Vlad often doubles as a bodyguard, trained in martial arts, menacing stares, and evasive driving techniques. **SALARY RANGE:** $50,000 to $90,000 **SPENDS DAY OFF:** Practicing English at the local OTB; selling passports

VALET

WHEN YOU HAVE MORE CLOTHES THAN the third floor at Barneys, common sense says you need someone to manage it all. Your valet's primary responsibility is the care and mainte-

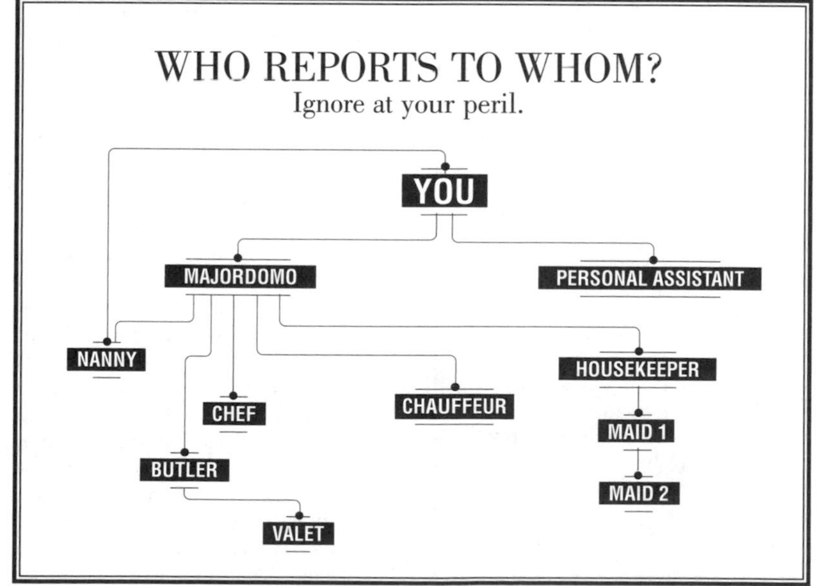

THE SERVANT BLOTTER

EDMOND SAFRA

- In 1999, ailing Lebanese banking tycoon **Edmond Safra** and his nurse, Vivien Torrente, burned to death inside Safra's sprawling flat in Monaco. Weakened by Parkinson's, the billionaire was attended by a phalanx of orderlies, one of whom, Ted Maher, served eight years in prison for homicide. Maher claimed he lit the blaze with the intention of rescuing Safra in a bit of staged heroism. His plan failed.

- First Lady **Nancy Reagan**'s personal valet, Anita Sanabria Castelo, was indicted in 1986 for conspiring to smuggle illegal arms to Paraguay. In addition to organizing Reagan's extensive wardrobe, Castelo, with the help of two others, had planned to buy hundreds of thousands of .22-caliber rifle rounds for shipment to the South American backwater, reportedly for use by nascent narco-traffickers. What a relief: There was no guerrilla movement in Paraguay at that time.

- In addition to laundry and light dusting, Polish housekeeper-to-the-stars Lucyna Turyk-Wawrynowicz cleaned out actor **Robert De Niro** to the tune of $95,000. Another client's credit card was hammered 18 times during a three-day bender at Barneys. Asked after her arrest in 2005 why she hadn't pilfered anything from actress **Isabella Rossellini**, the maid said, "She treated me well."

nance of your personal wardrobe, and daily assistance with dressing, clothing storage, alterations, shoe care, and the packing and unpacking of clothes with tissue paper when traveling. A certain level of passionate gayness is required, so prepare your spouse accordingly. **SALARY RANGE:** $50,000 to $70,000 **SPENDS DAY OFF:** Wearing your clothes and dropping your name in the next town over

MAIDS

DIRECTED BY THE housekeeper, two maids work around the clock to keep your home immaculate and do the things the aforementioned housekeeper won't deign to do. Duties include all heavy housework; washing, ironing, and stain removal; bonding with your Pomeranian; cleaning up after your children; and sleeping with your chauffeur. **SALARY RANGE:** $10,000 to $20,000 **SPENDS DAY OFF:** Working for your neighbor

CHEF

IN EVERY STEREOTYPE, THERE'S A KERNEL of truth. In the case of chefs, there's a cob: they're the prickliest, vainest, most difficult members of any staff—because they can be. Eating well is at least 50 percent of living well, so competition for culinary talent is fierce. Along with dishing out attitude, a poach-worthy chef will be proficient in organizing, maintaining, and supplying a kitchen, menu planning, meal presentation, florid cursing, and the latest fad diet. **SALARY RANGE:** $75,000 to $500,000 **SPENDS DAY OFF:** Writing business plan for eponymous restaurant

I PAY YOU FOR THAT?

Nonessential jobs you never knew existed.

CULTURAL ATTACHÉ

Megaproducer Brian Grazer famously has one on permanent retainer, charged with keeping the *American Gangster* producer abreast of who's cool and interesting in culture so that he doesn't have to. In a typical month, Grazer's attaché arranges one-hour meetings with up to ten "emerging influencers" all over the world, from heads of state to magazine editors to artists to athletes. Grazer's a very busy guy, and doesn't have time to network in the traditional sense. Instead, he employs someone else to keep him connected and in the loop. No wonder he knows everybody.
APPROXIMATE WAGE RANGE: $100,000 to $200,000 per year

MODEL WRANGLER

Wondering who that short, swarthy man tapping away on his Sidekick is sitting next to Joe Billionaire at Mr. Chow? More likely than you'd think, he's a model wrangler. Extremely rich men on the make have always had what used to be called procurers—charismatic young bucks who traffic in companionship—but only recently has the role become big business. Typically club promoters, this growing cadre of entrepreneurial hustlers put the charms they employ to lure pretty young things to nightclubs like Hyde in service of their benefactor's libido. They're not pimps, per se. We prefer the term "sexual attachés."
APPROXIMATE WAGE RANGE: $1,000 a week retainer

"JEWELRY HANDLER"

In the higher echelons of hip-hop, many rappers employ what's referred to as a "jewelry handler." Considering their well-known penchant for rock-encrusted watches and chains costing hundreds of thousands of dollars, those outside the know are forgiven for assuming this is for insurance purposes. Common code for bagman, the "handler" carries on his person whatever illicit substances his employer might enjoy—typically, an ounce or more of high-grade marijuana. Under increasing police scrutiny, many artists (and the men who write their checks) don't want to risk arrest for possession and instead hire an old friend or flunky to take the risk for them. Of course, the job has its dangers: Rapper Busta Rhymes's longtime "jewelry handler" Israel Ramirez was gunned down at a video shoot in New York in 2006 when an assailant tried to snatch his bag.
APPROXIMATE WAGE RANGE: $30,000 to $50,000 per year

WEALTH COUNSELOR

Once the twins know they're worth a cool billion, it may be hard to rein in their spending, particularly in light of the example you've been setting. That's when it's time to call in the big guns. A counselor will meet with you as a family to discuss financial trusts, potential foundations, investing, and philanthropy. Generally a young, ambitious bow-tied type with a background in private banking, he will ensure that no lemonade stand occurs without a spreadsheet analyzing the profit potential. Before long, your little ones will be pulling their weight.
APPROXIMATE WAGE RANGE: $625 an hour

HOMEWRECKER HALL OF FAME

Live-Ins Who Worked Overtime

BASIA "BARBARA" PIASECKA

THERE WASN'T A BAND-AID in the world big enough to cover the wound J. Seward Johnson Sr. inflicted when he married his third wife, Polish sexpot Basia Piasecka, his longtime chambermaid, cook, and mistress, in 1971. When he died 12 years later, his will left nearly his entire share of the Johnson & Johnson pharmaceutical fortune to his former servant. Innumerable headlines later, "Barbara" was awarded half a billion dollars and a top slot on the Forbes 400. Soon after, she converted the family estate in Princeton, New Jersey—which she'd dubbed Jasna Polana ("Bright Meadow")—into a country club and moved to Monte Carlo.

DAISY WRIGHT

IN THE SUMMER OF 2005, *Talented Mr. Ripley* actor Jude Law's former nanny, 26-year-old Briton Daisy Wright, sold a London tabloid the story of her month-long affair with the onetime "Sexiest Man Alive," who was then engaged to underemployed ingénue Sienna Miller. Wright, who cared for the children Law shares with ex-wife Sadie Frost, told tales of suggested three-ways and spectacular sex on a pool table. By week's end, Law's engagement to Miller was kaput. Wright reportedly went public after being sacked by Frost, who learned of her live-in's romps with her ex-husband by reading her diary. Take a lesson.

HILLEVI SVENSSON

IN 2005, METRO NETWORKS billionaire David Saperstein, owner of the largest house ever built in Los Angeles, ditched his 45-year-old wife, Suzanne, for a younger model: the 32-year-old Hillevi Svensson, nanny to their three kids. But things are looking up: The world's foremost consumer of haute couture and 18th-century furniture, Suzanne stands to win the largest divorce settlement in history, dwarfing even the $890 million that arms dealer Adnan Khashoggi paid his jilted ex back in '82.

SPENCER WAGNER

MARLA MAPLES, THE FORmer Georgia beauty queen who told the *New York Post,* "Donald Trump Is The Best Sex I Ever Had!" lost her grip on the real estate mogul in 1996 when she was caught *in flagrante delicto* on a beach with her bodyguard, Spencer Wagner. The aspiring actress, who began her own affair with Trump while he was still married to long-time wife Ivana, was unable to explain herself. Shortly after, Trump filed for divorce. He would later crow that the wreckage was limited: They had an air-tight prenup, which granted Maples a measly $5 million of his estimated $2.7 billion fortune (if you believe *Forbes*).

CLIP-'N-SAVE NDA!

AS BALZAC OBSERVED, BEHIND EVERY GREAT FORTUNE THERE'S A CRIME. BUT THAT doesn't mean everyone has to know about it! All filthy rich families have secrets. Protect yours with this handy nondisclosure agreement.

POCKET

NONDISCLOSURE AGREEMENT

Between Mr./Ms. ____________________ **(Employee Name)**
and Mr./Ms. ________________________ **(Your Name)**

I, __________________ **(Employee Name)**, agree that any and all information disclosed to me during the term of my employment by __________________ **(Your Name)** will be considered proprietary and confidential, including, but in no way limited to, the brand names and dosage levels of any prescription medications found in the Employer's medicine cabinet, where his/her spouse actually sleeps, the real reason everyone hates Grandfather, how much money is left in the trust, or that some members of the household prefer drag.

I understand that my Employer will seek all legal remedies available, both civil and criminal, should I disclose information to Page Six of the New York Post, the Daily Mail, or the IRS without their prior consent, and that evidence of any and all disclosures is grounds for immediate termination, loss of severance, and a stream of ugly (if empty) threats of ruination.

Confidential information shall not include information previously known to Dominick Dunne or me.

I agree that for a period of __________________, I will hold all confidential and proprietary information in confidence and will not use such information except as authorized by my Employer and will prevent its unauthorized dissemination, unless I am specifically asked to leak it. I acknowledge that unauthorized disclosure could cause irreparable harm and significant injury to my Employer, particularly if any resulting novel fails to make The New York Times bestseller list or be optioned for film.

ACCEPTED AND AGREED TO BY:

Employer Signature ______________________________
Printed Name ______________________________
Date ______________________________

Employee Signature ______________________________
Printed Name ______________________________
Date ______________________________

DIRECTORY

STAFFING AGENCIES

GREYCOAT INTERNATIONAL
Grosvenor Gardens House
35-37 Grosvenor Gardens
London SW1W 0BS, UK
Tel.: 44 20 7233 9950
GreycoatPlacements.co.uk

HAMPTONS DOMESTICS
P.O. Box 40
Sag Harbor, NY 11963
Tel.: 800-853-9006
HamptonDomestics.com
Other locations:
The Hamptons: 631-725-1527
New York: 212-838-5900
Palm Beach: 561-848-4777
Miami: 305-674-1960

INTERNATIONAL GUILD OF PROFESSIONAL BUTLERS
134 West 82nd Street, Suite 3B
New York, NY 10024
Tel.: 646-290-6527
ButlersGuild.com

MASSEY'S AGENCY
50 Fitzroy Street
London W1T 5BT, UK
Tel.: 44 20 3033 0000
MasseysAgency.co.uk

PAVILLION AGENCY
15 East 40th Street
Suite 400
New York, NY 10016
Tel.: 212-889-6609
PavillionAgency.com

PROFESSIONAL SERVICES AND DOMESTIC INSTITUTE
2000 Carriage Road
Powell, OH 43065
Tel.: 740-881-3358
HouseStaff.net

REIMER EMPLOYMENT AGENCY
249 Peruvian Avenue
Palm Beach, FL 33480
Tel.: 561-655-4171
ReimerAgency.com

ROBERT HANSELMAN DOMESTIC AGENCY
P.O. Box 1312
Madison, GA 30650
Tel.: 888-838-4404
PlanetDomestics.com

STARKEY INTERNATIONAL INSTITUTE FOR HOUSEHOLD MANAGEMENT
1350 Logan Street
Denver, CO 80203
Tel.: 800-888-4904
StarkeyIntl.com

COOKS

PRIVATE CHEFS, INC.
204 S. Beverly Drive, Suite 105
Beverly Hills, CA 90211
Tel.: 310-278-4707
PrivateChefsInc.com
Other locations:
Palm Beach: 561-582-6810
Dallas: 214-513-CHEF
London: 44 208 980 4472
New York: 800-921-CHEF
Las Vegas: 702-641-2433
San Francisco: 800-491-CHEF
Washington, DC: 800-825-CHEF

BODYGUARDS

BLACKWATER
When you're really screwed.
P.O. Box 1029
Moyock, NC 27958
Tel.: 252-435-2488
BlackwaterUSA.com

GAVIN DE BECKER & ASSOCIATES
Security expert to the stars.
11684 Ventura Boulevard
Suite 440
Studio City, CA 91604
and
11 Penn Plaza, 5th floor
New York, NY 10001
GavinDeBecker.com

BACKGROUND CHECKS

KROLL
Blue-chip snoops with sixty offices worldwide.
900 Third Avenue, 8th floor
New York, NY 10022
Tel.: 888-209-9526

UNIFORMS FOR SERVANTS

BEST BUY UNIFORMS
Pinafores and more.
500 East 8th Avenue
Homestead PA, 15120
Tel.: 800-345-1924
BestBuyUniforms.com

KITCHEN AIDS

Tools to keep your cook happy

STOVE

BONNET
BonnetCidelcem.com

AGA
AgaCookShop.co.uk

VENTILATION HOOD

CHENG DESIGN
ChengDesign.com

ESPRESSO MACHINE

LA CIMBALI
Cimbali.com

DISHWASHERS

FISHER AND PAYKEL
FisherPaykel.com

REFRIGERATORS

PERLICK
BringPerlickHome.com

TRAULSEN
Traulsen.com

CHAPTER FOUR / LOOKING THE PART

BUYING A BETTER YOU

"Whoever said money can't buy happiness simply didn't know where to go shopping."
—BO DEREK

PROJECTING THE RIGHT image is important for two reasons. First, it identifies you to your fellow tribe members, who actually know what a decent eye lift costs. And second, it indicates to service people that you deserve special treatment, like a corner banquette at the hot spot du jour, or the last life jacket on a rapidly sinking yacht.

If you're a filthy rich woman, the stakes are even higher. Squeezing into a sample-size gown four nights a week takes monastic dedication. Stack on a few stress pounds and the society snappers might shun you. Retain just a bit of that baby weight and the bimbos smell blood.

But there is some consolation: Once you've trained yourself to survive on thin slivers of Parmesan, Moët fumes, and Adderall, it's time to go shopping!

HAUTE STUFF

Now there's something you can really sink your porcelain veneers into—every day if you like, and never gain an ounce. (A cup size, maybe, but more on that shortly.)

To transform yourself tastefully into a walking argument for socialism, you'll need very deep (preferably Pucci silk-lined) pockets, an open mind, and at least a modicum of personal style. Barring that, you'll need the humility to hire someone who does.

With unlimited funds at your disposal, you have an opportunity to remake yourself from head to toe into the person you have always thought you were. That, or a surgically mangled fashion victim whose face frightens small children.

Which is to say: Know your limits. In the wrong hands, a Black Card can be a very dangerous thing.

BILLIONAIRE

SOCIAL SYLPH

Famished and fabulous

THE LOOK: Protruding clavicles, rib-cagey décolletage, furry arms
HOW TO GET IT: Cut out saturated fats, unsaturated fats, carbs, and calories, and commit to a single food group, like lettuce or Swedish Fish. Supplement daily with 18 Diet Cokes and 25 Parliament Lights.

PEAR-SHAPED PRINCESS

Loads of dough—tons of fun

THE LOOK: "Zaftig"
HOW TO GET IT: For most of America, it's a cinch. For you, it requires crackling wit, a warm demeanor, and a who-gives-a-shit air peculiar to a certain type of heiress. Someone has to buy all those size 12 Badgley Mischkas!

YUMMY MUMMY

Jonesing for Gyrotonics

THE LOOK: Silky hair, tennis arms, perky everything
HOW TO GET IT: After finally convincing Richard to leave his wife, undergo fertility treatments, and give birth to twins; channel self-loathing into obsessive daily workouts.

BODY TYPES *A Six-Figure Guide*

FAT BASTARD

Appetite for destruction

THE LOOK: Barrel-shaped gut, beefy paws, awkward limp

HOW TO GET IT: Devour anything and anyone who crosses your sight line—from your hopelessly incompetent assistants to the beef cheeks at Babbo. Thank God for portable defibrillators ("Clear!").

MANOREXIC

Extreme makeover: mogul edition

THE LOOK: 60-year-old face, 30-year-old body

HOW TO GET IT: The minute you hit your mid-40s, start obsessing about your looks. Hire the hottest celebrity trainer you can find, take whatever "vitamins" he sells you, and get pumping.

LITTLE BIG MAN

Huge ego, small package

THE LOOK: 5-foot-7 and under (unless standing on his wallet)

HOW TO GET IT: Among the most common filthy rich physiques, it's only available at birth—followed by decades of cruel taunting that eventually metastasizes into a full-blown complex and *raison d'être.*

LUST FOR LIFE

The Health Nut Hall of Fame

"The door to the cabinet is to be opened using a minimum of fifteen Kleenexes."

—HOWARD HUGHES, IN A "PROCEDURES MANUAL" FOR HOUSEHOLD STAFF

KING KHALID OF SAUDI ARABIA

(1912–1982)

CURSED WITH A WEAK TICKER, HIS Highness underwent open-heart surgery at the renowned Cleveland Clinic in the late 1970s. Lest further Midwestern adventures disrupt his reign, he promptly outfitted his 747 with a cardiac intensive care unit staffed by a team of top-drawer docs. Though probably just a nasty rumor, it's said he also kept a "heart donor" on permanent retainer, just in case.

DR. JOHN HARVEY KELLOGG

(1852–1943)

THE BOWEL-OBSESSED inventor of the cornflake was a *greeeeeat!* believer in the moral superiority of the vegetarian lifestyle. In the early 20th century, tycoons from all over flocked to his Battle Creek Sanitarium in Michigan for yogurt enemas, calisthenics, and lectures on the importance of fiber. Oddly, masturbation fell just after meat on his list of societal evils.

HOWARD HUGHES

(1905–1976)

ALTHOUGH A CRIPPLING codeine addiction and all-steak diet would seem to disqualify history's richest loon from induction, his extreme germaphobia induced staggering displays of health-nuttiness. Decades before Purell and the Ionic Breeze, Hughes installed industrial-strength air filters in all his homes and cars, and wore tissue boxes on his feet to avoid touching the ground.

DAVID MURDOCK

(b. 1924)

THE OCTOGENARIAN OWNER OF Dole Foods puts his money where his mouth is, offering staffers up to $100,000 to lose their guts. He recently spent $1 billion developing the California WellBeing Institute, a "medi-hotel" where guests can get full-body physicals, DNA testing, hypnotherapy, acupuncture, and a "Life Quality Profile" assessing their physical, emotional, social, and spiritual state.

EXTRA-LARGE AND IN CHARGE

Filthy Rich Fatties Waddle On

MR. BIG Taft

GOOD NEWS, GENTS: Manorexia may be all the rage, but the fat cat of yore is still alive and wheezing in the upper echelons of American wealth. For most of human history, of course, being grotesquely overweight was the height of fashion. Consider Socrates, dropping knowledge on the shiftless rich kids of ancient Athens (and hummus on his tunic), or President William Howard Taft *(left)*, the only 340-pound sphere to ever rule a republic.

Although most modern tycoons are more familiar with the yoga studio than the vomitorium—and are certainly outnumbered by their salade-niçoise-nibbling peers—supersized titans can still be spotted strapping on the feed bag at power-lunch *boîtes* across the country and around the world. Behold, the Goliath-sized gourmands who blazed their extra-wide trail!

HENRY VIII
Rotund royal
Lardass lady-killer proved disgusting corpulence needn't be a barrier to bedding sexy babes. (Note: If you're loaded.)

MARVIN DAVIS
Hollywood heavyweight
A custom-moon-shaped desk ensured this studio sultan always had room for thirds. Thanks to an embarrassing incident at Spago, he even traveled with his own steel-reinforced chair. These days, his grandson, Jason, carries the family fork.

CARLOS SLIM HELÚ
Fleshy financier
Mexico's filthy richest resident gorges on Latin America's telecom sector like it's an all-you-can-eat fajita bar. (Slim, by the way, is his father's name, not some cruel playground taunt.)

HARVEY WEINSTEIN
Portly producer
After decades of yo-yo dieting, Hollywood's most infamous angry fat guy seems to have finally settled into his own distended skin, as happy—and husky—as he's ever been. He's even bagged a super-skinny bride.

TITANS ON THE TREADMILL

How the Upper Class Sweats

LIKE ALL MORTALS, THE SERIOUSLY MINTED CAN'T JUST SLATHER ON THE TRUFFLE BUTTER and expect to see ninety. To keep their waistlines in check, they've got to work it, just like everyone else. Sort of.

TRENDING DOWNWARD

THE FADDIST

THE FIRST TIME SHE SAW JANE FONDA on Betamax, the Faddist ordered two dozen pairs of magenta leg warmers and flew her down to Jupiter Island for a one-on-one. Years later—bored of capoeira—she summoned Billy Blanks to Aspen to teach her Tae Bo. She was there for stepping, for Israeli Krav Maga, and for the BOSU ball. She had a stripper pole installed in her exercise pavilion, naturally, and was the first wife at the Maidstone with her own Pilates Reformer.

Whatever it is they're flogging at the Reebok Sports Club these days, you can bet her perfect ass she's been doing it forever.

THE IRON MAN

STAYING IN SHAPE ISN'T JUST ABOUT aesthetics. It's about *winning*. An increasingly common super-species of filthy rich male, the Iron Man fancies himself an *übermensch*. He might have rowed crew at Princeton, which taught him the rewards of obsessive self-discipline. In all areas of his life, he is a perfectionist. He is anal. He loves telling you his "times." On weekends in places like Darien and Palo Alto, Iron Men can be spotted in T-shirts and baseball caps touting their latest athletic achievements. Whether in Boston for the marathon or the Italian Alps for the Winter Triathlon World Cup, they know that winning hurts, and have the heel spurs to prove it.

GUNS AND MONEY

THE YOGI

WITH ALL THEIR TALK OF CHAKRAS, all their downward dogging and namastes, it's tempting to imagine that loaded yoga-heads like Donna Karan, Russell Simmons, ex–Time Warner boss Gerald Levin, and Sting have ascended to a higher spiritual plane. Don't kid yourself. Yoga is the favored exercise activity of the exceptionally well-to-do because it helps them commune with their favorite higher power—themselves. Give them a swank studio in Sag Harbor and tell them they'll look like buffer-than-thou yogis-to-the-stars Rodney Yee or Colleen Saidman, and even the most hard-bitten mogul will be om-ing in no time. As they close their eyes, exhale, and feel the positive vibes of being so very VIP, they'll know they've earned it.

TOTAL POSER

THE VOYEUR

THIS OUT-OF-SHAPE SUPERFAN NEVER deigns to lift a barbell. And why should he? He's already underwritten at least one sports team at his kid's prep school, if not its entire I. M. Pei–designed athletic center. He owns a piece of his local NBA franchise, where he's a court-side regular, and if he hasn't taken the plunge already, is considering an America's Cup gambit. Like Caesar surveying his gladiators, the vested Voyeur doesn't have to break a sweat. He pays other people to do it for him.

CAVEAT EMPTOR

THE AMBITIOUS TRAINER

Everything was going swimmingly with Sven. The daily kettlebell circuits and visualization techniques he'd developed for Anastasia were actually working. She had shed eight pounds and what felt like a decade. She was so relaxed she even slept with him (leading her to drop yet another two pounds). Thanks to her recommendations, he was soon training half her circle–which is when things got messy. First, he asked to use her name to get a Thursday night table for eight at The Waverly Inn. She let it slide. Not so a week later, when she read his quote in *Vogue* ("Sven and Now: Secrets of an A-list Trainer") about how "scarily out of shape" she was at their first session. When he finally returned her call, he was apologetic. His quotes were taken out of context, he said. He was about to embark on a six-week national tour in support of his new motivational book and DVD series, *The Power of Sven*, but would make it up to her when he returned. Oh, and did she happen to know anyone at Oprah's book club? It occurs to her only now that he wasn't in it for the $250 an hour or the treadmill liaisons, and that, come to think of it, Sven is an unusual name for a Greek guy from Las Vegas.

"DADDY, I HATE MY NOSE!"

Prime Cuts: A Cradle-to-Grave Guide

IN THE COURSE OF HER LIFETIME, A FILTHY RICH WOMAN WILL BRAVE THE KNIFE so often she can spot a botched nose job at 100 yards and recall her surgeon's birthday faster than her firstborn's. (August, was it?)

FACE LIFT

NOTHING TURNS 50 INTO 40 FASTER THAN a good old-fashioned face lift. Unfortunately, once you've launched your preemptive war against gravity, you'll need to lift up the hood every few years to make sure everything stays in place. **COVER STORY:** "Sweetie, did I tell you we were going to be in Palm Beach this weekend? We're stuck in Aspen and I'm bundled up with the flu. It's *highly* contagious." **COST:** $5,000–$15,000

RHINOPLASTY

CHANCES ARE DARLING DYLAN WILL be begging for this universal rite of passage before her pre-bat mitzvah sitting with Annie Leibovitz—particularly if she's cursed with "daddy's bump." Over 10 percent of all rhinoplasties are performed on patients under the age of 19, and for good reason. It's *so* much easier to return from "summer camp" with a new beak and two black eyes. Kids are terribly naive. **COVER STORY:** "I had a *horrible* deviated septum/sinus infection/off-piste skiing debacle/car accident and the doctor said surgery was my only option." "Puberty" also works. **COST:** $4,000–$12,000

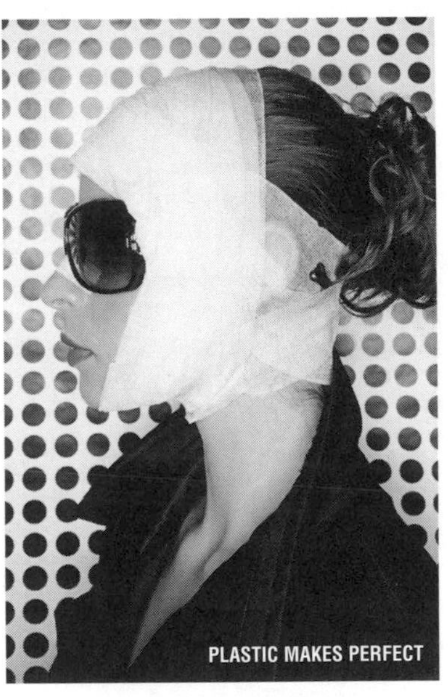
PLASTIC MAKES PERFECT

LIPOSUCTION

YOU'VE SNAGGED A HUSBAND AND sired some heirs, but even annual stints in a Balinese boot camp aren't doing the trick. To get back to your finishing school weight, have the fat melted and sucked out of you via tiny tubes. **COVER STORY:** "It's so true what they say. Breast-feeding *torches* the calories." **COST:** $2,000–$11,000

BREAST AUGMENTATION

OH, HOW MUCH BETTER LIFE WOULD BE if you had the perfect pair! Tired of dreaming, you decide to take action. The cup size to aim for is a medium C, less so if you're skinny (unnaturally round globes scream "stripper"). Just make sure he goes in through your armpits or say good-bye to topless tanning. **COVER STORY:** "Weird, right? I'm on this new pill and my hormones have just gone *insane*." **COST:** $3,000–$8,000

TOE TUCK

FEW THINGS RUIN THE LINES OF A Louboutin like a chubby pinky toe. Once considered exotic (or "insane"), the removal of excess fat from an unsightly phalange is an increasingly popular procedure on the benefit circuit. For an additional $250, regular shots of collagen to the foot soles provide extra support while social climbing. **COVER STORY:** "I tripped." **COST:** $1,250 per toe

UMBILICOPLASTY AND VAGIOPLASTY

YOUR SEX LIFE SUCKS AND YOU KNOW it's because you are hideous. The former gives your belly button a more youthful appearance post-pregnancy, while the latter tightens and tones what its name implies. You never did like your vulva. **COVER STORY:** "On strictest orders from my doctor, I'm repairing to St. Barts to treat my seasonal affective disorder." **COST:** $9,700

SCAR SEARCH

A Beginner's Guide to Surgery Spotting

In some cities, determining who's had work is practically a blood sport. Except at the following places, where the answer is "everyone":

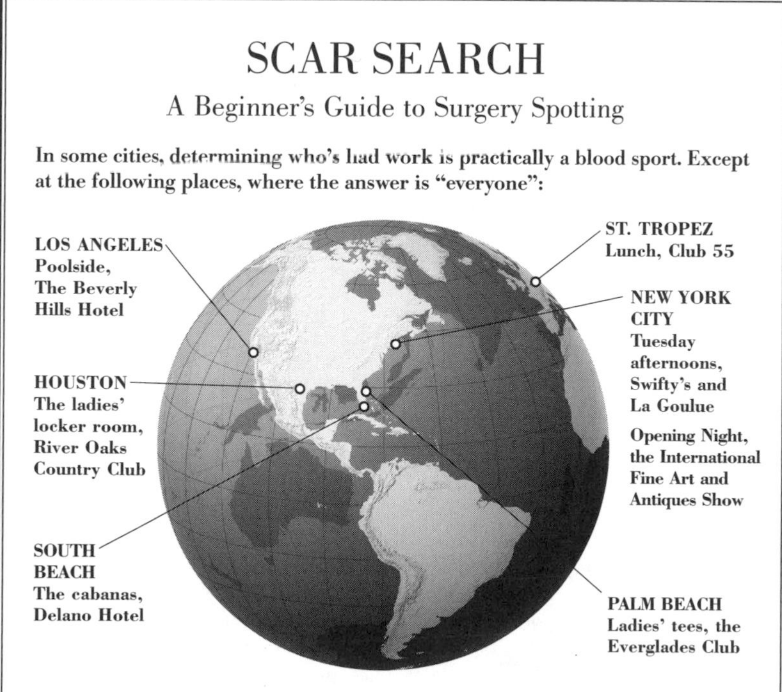

PUNISHMENT FOR GLUTTONS

Where the Top Tier Tunes Up

BEFORE THE ONSET OF NEW AGE FASCISM, "spa" was a code word for "fat farm." At now-defunct facilities like the Bircher-Benner clinic in Zurich and Elizabeth Arden's Maine Chance Spa in Arizona, society matrons deposited their pearls (and dignity) in the lobby safe for a week of zero-calorie meals, soggy seaweed wraps, and brutal calisthenics. Afterward, they were beaten with birch twigs. This was all in the name of keeping their husbands.

Although their founding mission is often concealed behind a smoke screen of lemon-ginger incense and Oprah-babble, filthy rich women still adore old-fashioned spas. The rules are calming. No caffeine or alcohol. Vigorous daily beach walks at dawn in unflattering jumpsuits. For those who were born into money, it's like a return to boarding school. For others, it's a "safe space" to unload creeping addictions to Peter Luger steaks, Vicodin, or Ladurée macaroons. A week at a proper one will cost you upwards of $10,000, but think of it as preventive medicine. Keep up that nightly bottle of Oban and a month at Promises Malibu will run you $40,000.

Feeling bloated? Why not head to the world-renowned Ashram in Calabasas, California, where they'll run you ragged 'til you drop a pants size? On your path toward unbearable lightness you'll enjoy a week of roommates who overshare about their bowels, 5 A.M. wakeup calls from aggressively chipper "counselors," and the choice of an apple or glass of orange juice for breakfast. After a day of ass-numbing yoga and uphill hikes in 100-degree heat, you can wind down with an evening of handwriting analysis. (Or, if you're lucky, some contraband Ambien.)

DINNER IS SERVED

If the stateside options lack that masochistic *je ne sais quoi,* there's always the Mayr Health Spa in Austria's Carinthian mountains, where the jumbo jet set is fed stale spelt bread to teach it to chew slower. Mandatory lights out: 9:30 P.M. (See p. 93 for full contact info on the Ashram, Mayr Health Spa, and other suitable retreats.)

PLUTOCRATS ON THE COUCH

Inside the Filthy Rich Mind

To see what was really going on upstairs, we gave an empty head to the following three tycoons and asked them to fill in the blank.

DAMIEN HIRST
Art Superstar

PATRICIA HEARST
Heiress/Ex-Hostage

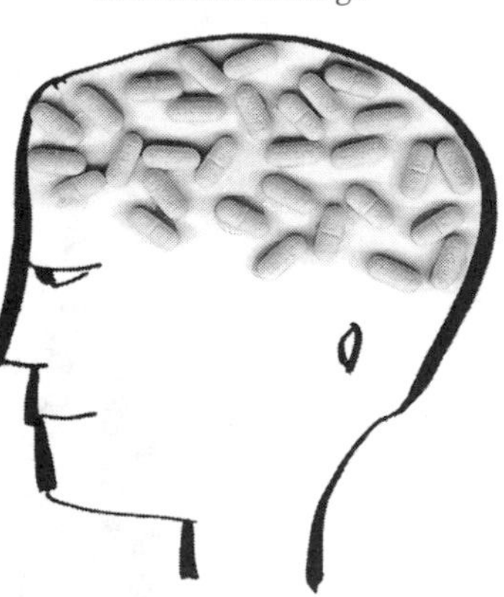

CLAUS VON BÜLOW
Bon Vivant

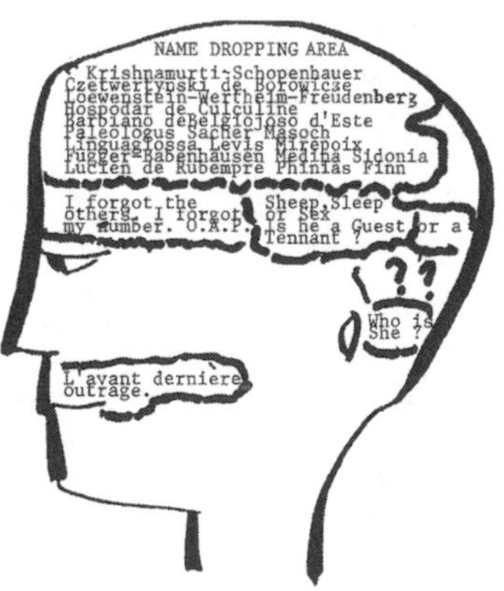

RETAIL THERAPY

Hire Up to Keep Your Head in Check

GURU

Sometimes all the money in the world can't fix your problems. If reading *The Secret* or Debbie Ford doesn't do it for you, there are legions of yogis, astrologers, Kabbalah teachers, and "investment advisors" from various cults who would love to help you find yourself. **APPROXIMATE COST:** A $1,000,000 donation demonstrates commitment, but surely you could do better. Think of what's at stake!

THERAPIST

The only person who knows you're a high school dropout with abandonment issues, your therapist doubles as the nurturing parent you never had. "Talking it out" will help with your control issues and low self-esteem, but you'll also need a top-drawer psychopharmacologist to tone down the nasty temper that keeps landing you on Page Six. **APPROXIMATE COST:** $500 and beyond an hour

LIFE COACH

When the going gets tough, it's time to phone your therapist's unlicensed alter ego. Instead of bringing up your childhood emotional traumas, a life coach will offer empowering pick-me-ups (with hefty doses of exclamation points): "Attitude is a little thing that makes a big difference!!!" **APPROXIMATE COST:** $10,000 monthly retainer

WHAT PRICE VANITY?

The High-Maintenance Medicine Cabinet

- **Vicodin bottle with the label peeled off**
For that "heli-skiing injury" back in '04. *$2,000, purchased from your trainer*

- **Elemis Deep Drainage detoxifying capsules with black radish, parsley, and plantain seed**
Taken nightly with a dirty martini.
$42/60 capsules

- **UltraClear Plus Metabolic Detoxification for Imbalanced Detoxifiers by Metagenics**
If those crackpot black radish pills don't do the trick, it's time to call in the big guns.
$75.15/32.6 oz

- **Crème "High Maintenance" by Dr. Sebagh**
Combats the strains of high altitude on delicate skin. A must after Aspen, Bhutan.
$400/100ml

- **Plus-sized Crème de la Mer**
Invented by an astronaut to treat third-degree burns. Imagine what it does for bags.
$1,350/16.5 oz

- **Ambien**
Take it regularly, and you can forget almost anything.
$20 copay/30 pills

- **Bulgari mini-shampoos and conditioners**
Unused bottles are the perfect servant stocking stuffer.
$0, not counting the $1,300 daily room rate at the Four Seasons Chiang Mai, where you swiped them.

- **Cartier bespoke fragrance**
Smells like Megève in March, Mustique in April, and Punta del Este in May. But only because you were there.
$70,000 and up for "development." The resulting scent is extra.

- **South African hoodia extract**
Shaky hands make snacking difficult.
$39.95/90 capsules

- **Xanax hidden in an Altoids container**
Mogul's little helper.
$20 copay/30 pills

LOGO A-GO-GO

Dressing Up in the Age of "Mass Class"

THE DEMOCRATIZATION OF LUXURY HAS MADE IT POSSIBLE for everyone to afford Polo, but there are still a few remaining bastions of exclusivity. For the time being, at least, the following labels are Filthy-Rich approved:

Alexander McQueen
Asprey
Balenciaga
Bottega Veneta
Carolina Herrera
Chanel
Charvet
Fendi
Givenchy
Gucci
Hermès
Hogan
Kiton
Lanvin
John Lobb
Martin Margiela
Michael Kors
Oscar de la Renta
Prada
Pucci
Tod's
Turnbull & Asser
Valentino
Versace
Yohji Yamamoto
Yves St. Laurent

CARING FOR YOUR CLOTHING

"They were careless people, Tom and Daisy—they smashed up things and creatures and then…let other people clean up the mess."

—F. SCOTT FITZGERALD, *THE GREAT GATSBY*

EXTREME NEGLIGENCE is a prized habit of the well-to-do, copied from flaky WASPs; treating one's wardrobe with casual disdain is a way of telling the world you could always buy another one. Fret too much over that scuff mark on your custom brogues and you'll start to look a bit desperate.

The Filthy Rich frequently leave their uncapped Montblanc pens in their white Fendi bags (where they jostle for space with broken pairs of $1,300 Alain Mikli sunglasses), wear their $10,000 suede driving jackets in the rain, and use their Dennis Basso mink stoles to make their dachshund puppies feel "safe" in their air-travel containers.

Generally, the most appropriate place for new clothes is on the floor of your dressing room, where you can walk on them. Someone else will pick them up eventually.

BLESS THIS MESS

CAVEAT EMPTOR

AND THE BRAND PLAYED ON

These once-beloved labels have been copied, co-opted, or otherwise sapped of any lasting elitist appeal.

BURBERRY
They still make a nice Macintosh, but slavish devotion to its signature check by footballers' wives like Victoria Beckham has stripped this English staple of its snotty allure.

TIFFANY & CO.
The bean necklace is darling on your 14-year-old daughter, but the "Little Blue Box" at your local mall doesn't deliver like it used to.

MANOLO BLAHNIK
Ever since *Sex and the City* introduced millions of desperate *hausfraus* to these status shoes, going on about your Manolos just sounds sad.

DOLCE & GABBANA
This oversexed Italian design duo is the clothier of choice for today's hottest tabloid starlets. All you need to know.

LOOKING

FOR HER

A FILTHY RICH WOMAN must first decide if her aim is to grace the International Best-Dressed List or simply fit in with the ladies at the club. If it's the former, important vintage pieces from Doyle's couture auction house and avant-garde tunics from Yohji Yamamoto should do the trick. If it's the latter, a month's worth of neutral Chanel suits, beige four-

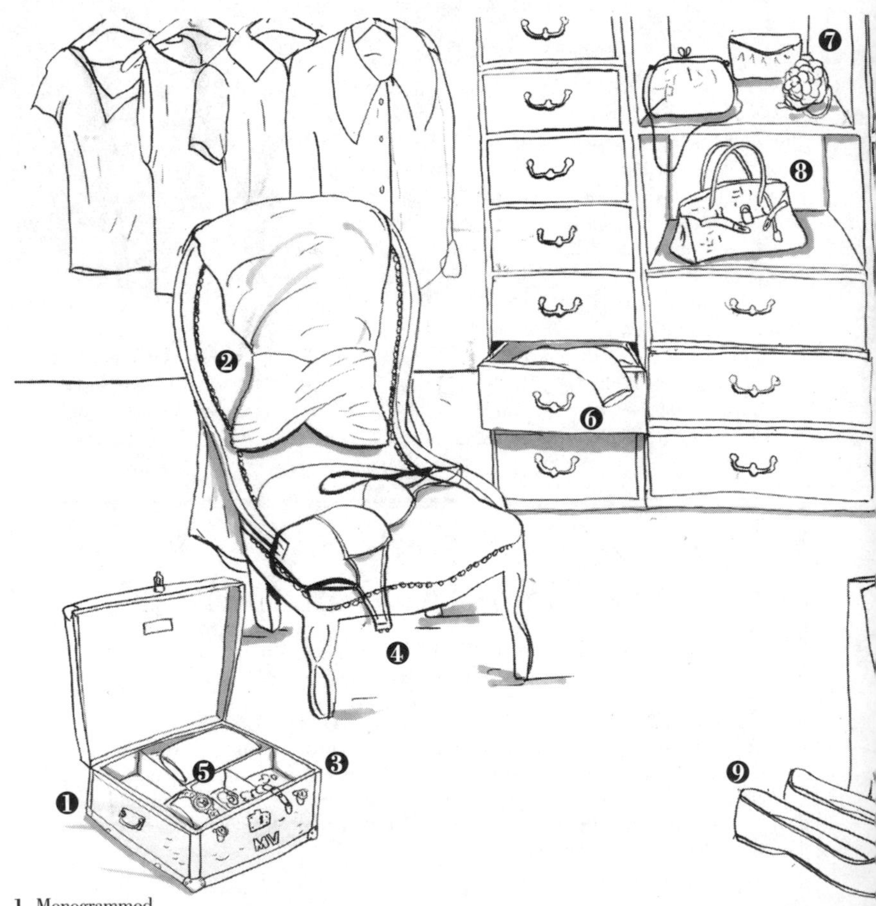

1. Monogrammed **Goyard Palace trunk** ($5,200)
2. **J. Mendel gown** for the Food Allergy Ball ($20,000)
3. **Diane von Furstenberg** sutra bracelet for H. Stern ($200,000)
4. **La Perla** bra and panties ($375 a set)
5. **Chopard H** watch ($26,000)
6. **Linen pj's.** A gift from Olatz Schnabel, of course
7. **Judith Leiber** sparkly evening clutch shaped like an insect ($4,375)

THE PART

ply cashmere sweaters, and Mikimoto pearls always works. As usual, regional rules apply: In Dallas, wearing a crisp white shirt with your black Balenciaga jodhpurs will get you mistaken for the help. Still, there are certain "pieces" that always convey an understanding of the sartorial pecking order. In general, the longer the waiting list, the better. Bonus points if the designer saved one just for you.

8. Hermès Porosus Lisse Birkin bag in croc (6-year waiting list; $148,000)

9. Delman Traveler flats in gold ($294)

10. Psychedelic **Pucci sheath** for sailing off Cartagena with the Santo Domingos ($294)

MY STYLIST, MY SOUL MATE

At your bedside each morning for your 7 A.M. blowout, Franz sees you at your most vulnerable. You may have all your girl-friends fooled, but he knows exactly what you look like without your war paint and which blind items in the *Post* left you red-eyed. No wonder his opinion holds such sway. Suddenly, you're explaining to your decorator that Franz thinks azure won't work for the pool-house drapes, and inviting him to Aspen with his Argentinean boyfriend. You even read his stupid Kabbalah book. But it's all worth it so long as that shade of butter blonde stays yours and yours alone.

FOR HIM

THOUGH LESS SUSCEPTIBLE to fashion's whimsy, the plutocrat *homme* is equally concerned with his wardrobe. His tailor's digits—cadged over single malt whiskeys on a fly-fishing trip in the Scottish Highlands—are his most closely guarded secret (after that "embezzling thing" in the late '80s and his starter marriage). Once he settles on a look, whatever it may be, he is often a creature of habit. On his shopping list you'll find a new suit that

1. **"K-50" custom suits from Kiton** in Naples (50 hours of labor by 45 tailors; $50,000 and up)
2. Monogrammed **Charvet dress shirt** (five weeks' delivery time, but very Gianni Agnelli; $425)
3. **Ghurka Steward III** suitcase ($1,400) and **Cavalier III** weekend bag ($1,500)
4. Four-ply cashmere **Lucien Pellat-Finet** "skull" sweater ($3,500)
5. **Loro Piana** trench coat ($1,400)
6. **Stubbs & Wootton** black velvet evening slippers, a somewhat fey gift from your third wife, Binky ($310)

looks identical to the other 48 in his closet and several pairs of caramel-colored driving shoes, varying only in the stitching patterns holding them together. That said, should he need to fill some gaps in his walk-in wardrobe, he can safely swipe some plastic on the following tycoon-approved classics (or delegate the task to his winsome valet).

6

LOBB

LOBB

7

7. Custom stingray lace-ups from **John Lobb** ($4,500 and up)

8. Cashmere night-shirt and socks from **The Private House** ($800)

9. **Creed's Angélique Encens cologne,** commissioned by Marlene Dietrich in 1933 ($590/500ml)

10. Unworn **promotional polo shirts** from various banks and charities ($0)

MEN IN UNIFORM

A Certain Type of Mogul Finds a Look and Sticks with It

STEVE JOBS, 2006

STEVE JOBS, 2007

STEVE JOBS, 2001

FRENCH FOR EXPENSIVE

When Off-the-Rack Won't Do

WHILE ANY OLD "UPPER" can waltz into Chanel in SoHo and pick up a gilet and a pair of Double C skis, it takes sophisticated social maneuvering to gain entrée to the atelier of a Parisian *haute couture* designer.

Twice a year, the jet set converges on Paris for the spectacles mounted by Christian Lacroix, John Galliano, Armani, Valentino, and others. After dark, the designers lavish attention on their loyal couture clients, who number fewer than 2,000 in the world. Of those, only 200 are regular buyers, dropping bank on multiple custom-made pieces each season. It's a small world. Tread lightly.

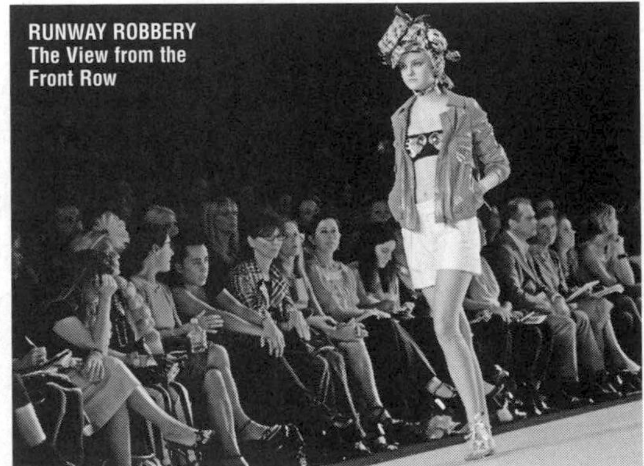

RUNWAY ROBBERY
The View from the Front Row

J.A.R. YOU SERIOUS?

Tucked away off the Place Vendôme in Paris, there's an unassuming shop designated only by the initials etched in glass above the door: J.A.R. Inside, an obsessively private, Bronx-bred jeweler named Joel Arthur Rosenthal creates 70 or so custom pieces each year for clients like Elizabeth Taylor, Diane von Furstenberg, Ann Getty, and Princess Firyal of Jordan. If he agrees to meet with you, and there's a good chance he won't, be prepared to wait up to two years to own a piece so utterly fabulous it looks completely fake. Cost? $30,000 and up into the very high six figures.

PICTURE PERFECT

The Idiot's Guide to Iconic Style

MAKING THE PAGES OF *VOGUE* OR *W* ISN'T AS SIMPLE AS SWADDLING YOURSELF IN head-to-toe Margiela and buying up Birkins in every color. Herewith, four field-tested shortcuts to fashion immortality:

BE SPONTANEOUS. San Francisco doyenne **Dodie Rosencrans** drew gasps at a Paris dinner party in the '80s when she doubled up her ruby and emerald Indian Moghul necklace and fastened it around her neck with the ribbon from a box of Fauchon chocolates. Striking couture collector Tatiana Sorokko has been known to wear her coats inside out (very Little Edie Bouvier).

HAVE A "THING." Inimitable British stylist **Isabella Blow**'s astounding collection of Edwardian-influenced couture hats by milliner-to-the-royals Philip Treacy catapulted her into the upper reaches of the fashion stratosphere. Perhaps you could bring back the bustle?

HATS OFF Headwear Legend Isabella Blow

PLAY DRESS UP. Standard Oil heiress **Millicent Rogers** captivated Jazz Age New York by dressing like a starving artist. Sure, her whimsical ensembles of Tyrolean aprons, dirndls, and embroidered vests were cribbed from the city's boho underclass, but she wore them better.

GO SLUMMING. New York society princess **Heather Mnuchin** mixes $35 white tees from Le Petit Bateau (the French Banana Republic) with ball skirts from Oscar de la Renta.

IN VOGUE Socialite Scribbler Plum Sykes

Socialite author **Plum Sykes** pairs jeans from Comptoir des Cotonniers (the French Gap) with her Balenciaga bomber. I know, right?

DRESSIN' TEXAN

Where Cowgirls Learned to Spend

FASHION INSIDERS AGREE ON VERY LITtle, but they agree on this: Texans shop harder, faster, bigger, and louder than just about anyone else. Since opening its plus-sized Dallas flagship in 1914, Neiman Marcus has been where they do it.

Desperate to prove that Dallas was not just another behind-the-times boomtown, Gilded Age belles flooded the fashionable shop in its early years. Ranching heiress Electra Waggoner Wharton supposedly dropped $1,000,000 in a single day. Then, in 1952, Stanley Marcus added a live Black Angus bull and sterling silver barbecue cart ($1,925) to the store's Christmas catalog as a publicity stunt, and a Lone Star legend was born. Subsequent catalogs have included a bag of uncut diamonds ($250,000), a Noah's Ark filled with endangered species ($588,247), a Maserati Quattroporte ($125,000), and countless variations on the "His 'n Hers" theme: His 'n Hers ancient Egyptian tombs, His 'n Hers hot-air balloons, and His 'n Hers jets, to name just a few.

Of course, the rich aren't the only ones tempted by Neiman's wares. In 1985, a shopgirl named Angie King jacked over $531,000 worth of merchandise, which she resold to area matrons at a discount. When word got out, she landed in the clink. After her release, the charismatic ex-con landed herself a millionaire and was soon back at her old stomping ground, holding court at Neiman's famed trunk shows. Clearly, the store has a tolerance for colorful characters. Like the man who used his one phone call from jail to ring the store and ask for bail money. He was, after all, a very loyal customer.

SPURS NOT INCLUDED
His 'n Hers hot-air balloons from the Neiman Marcus catalog

DIRECTORY

RETREATS & SPAS

THE ASHRAM
P.O. Box 8009
Calabasas, CA 91372
Tel.: 818-222-6900
TheAshram.com

CAL-A-VIE
29402 Spa Havens Way
Vista, CA 92804
Tel.: 760-945-2055
Cal-a-Vie.com

CANYON RANCH
165 Kemble Street
Lenox, MA 01240
Tel.: 800-742-9000
CanyonRanch.com

THE GOLDEN DOOR
P.O. Box 463077
Escondido, CA 92046
Tel.: 760-744-5777
GoldenDoor.com

GREEN VALLEY SPA
1871 West Canyon View Drive
St. George, UT 84770
Tel.: 435-628-8060
GreenValleySpa.com

THE GREENHOUSE
P.O. Box 1144
Arlington, TX 76004
Tel.: 817-640-4000
TheGreenhouseSpa.net

MAYFLOWER INN AND SPA
118 Woodbury Road
Washington, CT 06793
Tel.: 860-868-9466
MayflowerInn.com

MAYR HEALTH SPA
Gesundheitszentrum
Golfhotel am Wörthersee
Golfstraße 2
A-9082 Maria Wörth-Dellach
Kärnten, Austria
Tel.: 43 4273 2511 0
MayrAndMore.at

MIRAVAL
5000 East Via Estancia
Miraval
Catalina, AZ 85739
Tel.: 800-825-4000
MiravalResort.com

MAINTENANCE

DR. FREDERIC BRANDT
Cosmetic dermatologist.
8798 NW 15th Street
Miami, FL 33172
Tel.: 800-234-1066
DrBrandtSkinCare.com

DR. RICHARD ELLENBOGEN
Plastic surgeon.
Beverly Hills Body
9201 Sunset Blvd., Suite 202
Los Angeles, CA 90069
Tel.: 310-276-3183
BeverlyHillsBody.com

OZ GARCIA
Nutritionist to the stars.
10 West 74th Street
New York, NY 10023
Tel.: 212-362-5569
OzGarcia.com

DR. JANA KLAUER
Weight-loss specialist.
780 Park Avenue
New York, NY 10021
Tel.: 212-288-9595
JanaKlauerMd.com

ELIZA PETRESCU
Eyebrow sorceress.
Exhale Mind Body Spa
980 Madison Avenue
New York, NY 10021
Tel.: 212-564-1722
ElizasEyes.com

HOSPITALS

Along with smarty-pants doctors, the country's top-ranked hospitals offer just enough five-star services to keep you in your comfort zone. A sampling of accommodations (treatments not included) . . .

JOHNS HOPKINS
Baltimore, MD
Patients in the Marburg Pavilion ($2,000 a day) are waited on by tuxedo-clad staffers (using the same hospitality model as the Ritz-Carlton). And, yes, those are Oriental throw rugs on the hardwood floors. Jhintl.net

CEDARS-SINAI
Los Angeles, CA
At A-list Hollywood's go-to infirmary, Picasso-lined suites with gourmet kitchens run $1,600 a day. Expectant trophy wives and sitcom stars jockey for the four O.B. suites, which come with a doula and billion-thread-count linens. Cedars-Sinai.edu

THE CLEVELAND CLINIC
Cleveland, OH
Opt for one of the elegant Founders Suites where, for a blood pressure-elevating $2,000 a night, you can convalesce in luxurious peace alongside Fortune 500 CEOs and foreign dignitaries. ClevelandClinic.org

MOUNT SINAI
New York, NY
Frette robes, views of Central Park, and a menu of manicures await patients recovering in the Eleven West unit of the Guggenheim Pavilion. A standard suite goes for $1,900 a night; rooms with panoramic views, up to $2,900. It's Manhattan, after all. MountSinai.org

THE MAYO CLINIC
Rochester, MN; Jacksonville, FL; and Scottsdale, AZ
Where kings and presidents go for tune-ups. Top-tier suites hover in the $2,000 range. If they can't fix you here, you probably can't be fixed. MayoClinic.org

SPIRITUALITY

THE CHURCH OF SCIENTOLOGY
Celebrity Centre International
5930 Franklin Avenue

Hollywood, CA 90028
Tel.: 323-960-3100
Scientology.cc

THE KABBALAH CENTRE
1062 S. Robertson Blvd.
Los Angeles, CA 90035
Tel.: 310-657-5404
KabbalahCentres.com

ST. BART'S EPISCOPAL CHURCH
109 East 50th Street
New York, NY 10022
Tel.: 212-378-0222
StBarts.org

ST. PATRICK'S CATHEDRAL
400 Madison Avenue
New York, NY 10017
Tel.: 212-753-2261
SaintPatricksCathedral.org

TEMPLE EMANU-EL
1 East 65th Street
New York, NY 10065
Tel.: 212-744-1400
EmanuelNYC.org

URBANE OUTFITTERS

CHARVET
Handmade dress shirts.
28 Place Vendôme
Paris 75001, France
Tel.: 33 1 4260 3070

CHRISTIAN LOUBOUTIN
Jimmy who?
941 Madison Avenue
New York, NY 10021
Tel.: 212-396-1884
ChristianLouboutin.fr

KITON
Italian suits for your inner Agnelli.
4 East 54th Street
New York, NY 10022
Tel.: 212-486-5250
Kiton.it

JOHN LOBB
Treat your feet for an arm and a leg.
88 Jermyn Street
London SW1Y 6JD, UK
Tel.: 44 20 7930 8089
JohnLobb.com

LUCIEN PELLAT-FINET
Groovy cashmere with cachet.
1 rue de Montalembert
Paris 75007, France
Tel.: 33 1 4222 2277
LucienPellat-Finet.com

STUBBS & WOOTTON
Who says velvet slippers aren't appropriate male evening attire?
4 Via Parigi
Palm Beach, FL 33480
Tel.: 561-655-6857
StubbsAndWootton.com

ROGER VIVIER
Sophisticated stilettos.
750 Madison Avenue
New York, NY 10065
Tel.: 212-861-5371
RogerVivier.com

EMILIO PUCCI
Psychedelic resort-wear is always a "do."
24 East 64th Street
New York, NY 10065
Tel.: 212-752-4777
EmilioPucci.com

GHURKA
Colonial nostalgia you can carry.
683 Madison Avenue
New York, NY 10065
Tel.: 212-826-8300
Ghurka.com

MAISON GOYARD
Hand-painted leather goods so ugly they're beautiful.
233 rue St. Honoré
Paris 75001, France
Tel.: 33 01 42 60 57 04
Goyard.com

VALEXTRA
Chicly impractical white leather luggage.
Via A. Manzoni, 3
Milan 20121, Italy
Tel.: 39 02 99 78 60 60
Valextra.it

FRED SEGAL
Your one-stop shop for celebrity sightings, $3,000 bikinis.
420 & 500 Broadway
Santa Monica, CA 90401
Tel.: 310-394-9814 (Ask for the general manager.)
FredSegal.com

MONOGRAMMING

CAROLINE BRACKENRIDGE
225 East 73rd Street
New York, NY 10021
Tel.: 212-288-8864
MonogramInc.com

PERSONAL SHOPPERS

BERGDORF GOODMAN
Where sultans and socialites brave the racks.
754 Fifth Avenue
New York, NY 10022
Tel.: (women) 212-872-8700; (men) 212-339-3045
BergdorfGoodman.com

JEFFREY
3500 Peachtree Road, Suite A-3
Atlanta, GA 30326
Tel.: 404-237-9000

NEIMAN MARCUS
Request either a couture or designer specialist.
9700 Wilshire Boulevard
Beverly Hills, CA 90212
Tel.: 877-634-6263
NeimanMarcus.com

VINTAGE COUTURE

DOYLE NEW YORK
175 East 87th Street
New York, NY 10128
Tel.: 212-427-4141 ext. 208
DoyleNewYork.com

L'HÔTEL DROUOT AUCTION HOUSE
9, rue Drouot
Paris 75009, France
Tel.: 33 01 48 00 20 20
Drouot.com

COUTURE CLEANING

MADAME PAULETTE
1255 Second Avenue
New York, NY 10021
Tel.: 212-838-6827
MadamePaulette.com

BOUTIQUE CLOTHING STORAGE

Garde Robe
137 Duane Street
New York, NY 10013
Tel.: 212-227-7554
GardeRobeOnline.com

CHAPTER FIVE / OUT & ABOUT

THE SOCIAL WHIRL

"Money can't buy friends. But you can afford a better class of enemy."
—LORD MANCROFT

YOU MAY NOT KNOW IT YET, BUT YOU'RE being watched. Not only by the IRS, but by your new peers, who've been conducting their own detailed audit, accounting solely for taste. Every invite you decline, name you mispronounce, and pariah you pose with factors into a silent equation that will determine your true social worth.

For the Filthy Rich, socializing isn't just about having drinks with old friends at the local Italian. It's about having the *right* drinks with the *right* Italians on the *right* yacht off Capri. And there's almost always a subtext. Corporate marriages are formed between sips of Screaming Eagle. Prices are fixed over toast points.

It's an unforgiving world you now find yourself in, and the urge to withdraw is tempting. But don't. Save that for later when you're bitter and alcoholic after decades of nonstop party hopping. Like a bored socialite contemplating Everest, you must verse yourself in the latest high-end climbing techniques to ensure a smooth ascent. You may not reach the summit, but as your guru always tells you, it's about the *journey*. Just remember: There's only one way down.

WORK HARD, PLAY HARD

SCHMOOZE OR LOSE

Secrets of the Chattering Class

CONTRARY TO POPULAR MYTHOLOGY, the Filthy Rich are incredible bores. Not all of them, mind you, but most. They don't start out that way, but spending the better part of one's life in the spirit-sapping capitalist trenches or the Ambien embrace of inherited wealth has a way of dulling the mind. Which is fabulous news for you! To paraphrase hard-partying dark prince Henry Kissinger, now, when you bore people, they'll actually think it's *their* fault. The following list of go-to conversation topics should put you well on your way. *Clink!*

- Who's in AA (unless it's you)
- Who's under investigation (unless it's you)
- Who's had their face done (unless it's you)
- Who's cheating on his wife (unless it's you)
- Who's secretly gay (unless it's you)
- Articles from that month's *Vanity Fair*
- Items from that day's Page Six
- How ridiculously screwed all these hedge guys are
- How expensive everything is
- The size of [insert name]'s new gigayacht/compound/jet/divorce settlement/tits

"WHEN ANDY AND I . . ."

People Everyone Claims They Were Friends With

PRINCESS DI
Jet-set saint

ANDY WARHOL
Oddball artist

SIR JIMMY GOLDSMITH
British übermogul

BROOKE ASTOR
Society legend

NAN KEMPNER
Uptown clothes horse

EDIE SEDGWICK
'60s "It" mess

C. Z. GUEST
WASP style icon

DIANA VREELAND
Original Voguette

"ANTHONY WHO?"

People No One Admits They Were Friends With

CARLOS MENEM
Argentinian kleptocrat

IVAN BOESKY
'80s villain

IMELDA MARCOS
Shoe fetishist

ANTHONY PELLICANO
Tinseltown wiretapper

JACK ABRAMOFF
Indian tribe bilker

SAM WAKSAL
Pharmaceutical fast talker

JEFFREY EPSTEIN
Billionaire teen lover

DANA GIACCHETTO
Celebrity cheat

"A VOICE FILLED WITH MONEY"

Memorize the following and keep the eye rolls to a minimum.

	AS IN...	IT'S...	NOT...
CANNES	The French resort; film festival	Can	Khan (as in Aga)
CAPRI	The Italian playground	Kah-PREE	KAY-pree
CARIBBEAN	The sea	KAH-ruh-BEE-in	KA-RIB-ee-uhn
CRUDITÉS	The vegetable appetizer	KREW-dih-tay	KRUD-ites
DIANE	The designer, von Furstenberg	DEE-on	DYE-ann
GSTAAD	The Swiss mecca	GUSH-tahd	GUS-tad
HERMÈS	The French luxury label	AIR-mez	HER-meez
HOBE	The Florida Sound	Hohb (as in "strobe")	Ho-BEE
KLUGE	The zillionaire, John	Klewg-EE	KLOOG
KOCH	The zillionaire, Charles	Coke (as in "joke")	Koch (as in Mayor Ed)
LA GRENOUILLE	The New York restaurant	Lah Gren-OOH-ye	Lah GREN-ool
LAUREN	The WASPloitationist, Ralph	LAW-ren	Law-REN
MOËT	The bubbly	MO-wet	MO-way
PROENZA SCHOULER	The upstart fashion label	pro-EN-za SKOOL-er	pro-EN-za SHOO-ler
RUSCHA	The painter	REW-shay	REW-skuh/ RUSS-kuh
TAKI	The raconteur, Theodoracopulos	TAH-kee	TAY-kee

TALK THIS WAY
The Lingua Franca

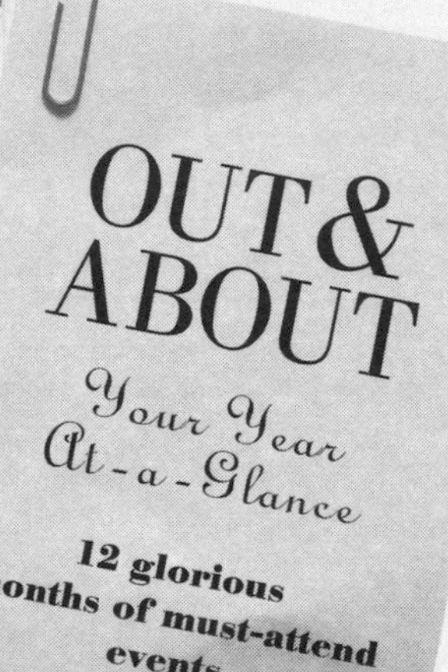

JANUARY

HAUTE COUTURE SHOWS (Paris)
Whisper conspiratorially with your neighbors while pretending to take notes on your favorite "pieces." Chain-smoke and repeat.

SUNDANCE FILM FESTIVAL (Park City, Utah)
Hollywood infidels colonize Mormon country for a week of slopeside deal-making and debauchery. Pack your Bogner, Advil.

OPERA GUILD'S LA BELLA NOTTE GALA (Nashville, Tennessee)
Feeling Republican? Brush off your tux and cowboy boots for a Southern society high-art hoedown.

CARTIER POLO WORLD CUP ON SNOW (St. Moritz, Switzerland)
The Romans had their gladiators; the Filthy Rich have their polo players. Keep an eye on your daughters.

FEBRUARY

ARMORY ART SHOW (New York)
As a category of things others can't afford, you find contemporary art fascinating. Hustle an invite to the VIP preview or don't bother. By opening night, the better booths have been picked clean.

LEUKEMIA BALL (Washington, D.C.)
For one night only, Dems can wear red without plummeting in the approval ratings as the Washington Convention Center hosts the capital's largest "nonpolitical" fund-raiser.

***VANITY FAIR* OSCAR PARTY (Los Angeles)**
Kiss editor Graydon Carter's bespoked bottom when you see him at his New York clubhouse, The Waverly Inn, for a chance to watch Steve Jobs chat up an Olsen.

WESTMINSTER KENNEL CLUB DOG SHOW (New York)
Queen Victoria and her Scottish deerhounds. J.P. Morgan and his collies. Since 1877, Westminster has attracted the world's poshest pups and their barking-mad owners, desperate to hear those three life-affirming words: "Best in Show." It's the Super Bowl for grande dames.

WORLD ECONOMIC FORUM (Davos, Switzerland)
Share whatever bits of worldly wisdom you've accumulated at this annual meeting of international eggheads. Try not to laugh during Angelina Jolie's PowerPoint presentation.

23RD: PALM BEACH SOCIAL SEASON ENDS
Bid adiós to your favorite sugar barons, the Fanjuls.

A RICH BITCH AT WESTMINSTER

MARCH

PRINCESS GRACE FOUNDATION'S ROSE BALL (Monte Carlo)
Waltz with Monegasque royals, Saudi sheiks, and Filthy Rich scene queen Elton John in the Salle des Etoiles. Hard-living hostess Princess Caroline of Hanover personally picks the theme (2006: "reggae"), so keep your titters to a minimum.

"WEIRD AL" OF MONACO
Gets Freaky

FRICK COLLECTION'S YOUNG FELLOWS BALL (New York)
If someone bombed the fabled Frick museum on this particular evening, there'd be no one left to lunch.

TEFAF MAASTRICHT ART FAIR (Maastricht, The Netherlands)
Over 300 collector-packed private jets invade the land of hash and windmills for a serious weeklong art binge. Not for dabblers.

APRIL

15TH: THE TAXMAN COMETH
Call Mr. Tibbetts in Grand Cayman to confirm that last bank transfer. (Can't be too careful.)

ANTIGUA RACING WEEK (Falmouth Harbor, Antigua)
The largest regatta in the Caribbean (remember, that's KAH-ruh-BEE-in), where hypercompetitive captains of industry take to the waves and mast size matters.

OLD WORLD SYMPHONY BALL (Houston)
Actors in period clothes and powdered wigs work the room at this *tout* le Texas black-tie blowout filled with oil tycoons and their helmet-haired spouses. (Shoulder pads optional, but recommended.)

BOOT AND RALLY

GUMBALL RALLY (London)
For a £28,000 entry fee, the world's most fortunate sons race (sorry, "rally") their Bugattis, Ferraris, and Porsches 3,000 miles across Europe in eight days at top speeds while ingesting ungodly amounts of mind-bending substances. It doesn't get filthy richer.

KENNEDY CENTER SPRING GALA (Washington, D.C.)
Billionaire campaign donors and the power brokers who love them raise millions for the performing arts.

MAY

SHAREHOLDER MEETING SEASON (various)
Wall Street shaman Warren Buffett recounts his vision to Berkshire Hathaway's 20,000 shareholders at the "Woodstock of Capitalism" in Omaha.

AMERICAN BALLET THEATER'S SPRING GALA (New York)
Pretend to like ballet.

SLOAN-KETTERING CANCER CENTER'S AWARDS FOR EXCELLENCE (New York)
The city's old guard turns out to support their long-beloved charity. Pour out a little Dom for the late Nan Kempner, who raised $75 million for the center.

KENTUCKY DERBY (Lexington, Kentucky)
Oh, how the rich love horses! And gambling! And hats! Mix in a pinch of mint and a jigger of Maker's Mark, and you're off to the races.

THE ROBIN HOOD FOUNDATION GALA (New York)
The biggest, baddest fund-raiser in America attracts 4,000 plutocrats for an evening of A-list entertainment and million-dollar bidding. The 2007 take: $72 million.

MET COSTUME INSTITUTE BALL (New York)
Vogue empress Anna Wintour summons the world's taste-makers to her annual dress-up party. Win points by making nice with daughter, Bee.

LIFE BALL (Vienna)
The continent's flashiest AIDS fund-raiser: catwalk, costume party, Sir Elton John.

MEMORIAL HERMANN FOUNDATION'S CIRCLE OF LIFE GALA (Houston)
Mosey on down to the health-care charity's black-tie benefit and throw a little sumthin' on the $3-million pile.

JUNE

ROYAL ASCOT (Ascot Racecourse, England)
A classic, if crusty, weeklong horseracing event where gents wear morning suits and ladies, silly hats. Snag a coveted spot in the No. 1 car park to watch titled aristos tailgate like Packers fans before inevitably losing their loafers in ankle-deep muck.

BUCKAROO BALL (Santa Fe, New Mexico)
It's furs and spurs at New Mexico's biggest fund-raiser for at-risk children. Also, the Charlie Daniels Band, or someone like them.

ART BASEL (Basel, Switzerland)
The art world goes on a European bender. Wake up Monday morning wondering why the hell you paid $2.2 million for a papier-mâché sculpture of a unicorn fellating itself.

BRUCE MUSEUM'S RENAISSANCE BALL (Greenwich, Connecticut)
Local hedge fund zillionaires cover the museum's annual budget in a single night.

CANNES FILM FESTIVAL (Cannes, France)
Movies are depressing. Why not spend the week getting wasted with everyone else aboard Paul Allen's *Octopus*? Not like he'll notice.

LOVE HEALS (Sagaponack, New York)
Another day, another AIDS fund-raiser. Roll off your chaise and into something linen for this auction/dinner/dance at the Luna Farm estate.

SWAN BALL (Nashville, Tennessee)
The must-attend event of the Southern season supports the Cheekwood Botanical Garden and Museum of Art, with performances by boomer favorites like Earth, Wind & Fire.

JULY

NEWPORT REGATTA (Newport, Rhode Island)
Two hundred and fifty of the world's better sailboats do battle in Narragansett Bay. Which is nothing compared to the combat onshore.

WIMBLEDON (Wimbledon, England)
Each year, tennis tourney guests guzzle 150,000 Pimm's Cups; 62,000 pounds of strawberries; and 1,850 gallons of cream. Game, set, match.

SLICE OF THE GOOD LIFE

FESTIVAL OF SPEED (West Sussex, England)
Pull on your Wellies for the Earl of March's annual "hill climb," where cars race through his steep and narrow Goodwood Estate.

AUGUST

ROLEX MONTEREY HISTORIC AUTOMOBILE RACES (Monterey, California)
The cars are a little older and a tad slower, but they still cost more than your first house. Spoiler alert: vintage autophile Jay Leno wins every year.

MONTEREY POP

THE MASTERS, U.S. PGA CHAMPIONSHIP (varies)
The top-of-the-tour heap. Quiet on the green.

COACHING WEEKEND (Newport, Rhode Island)
Every three years, Newport's unembalmed gather for a day of horse-and-buggying and a night of black-tie shimmying at The Breakers to benefit the local preservation society. He may not know where he is, but Archibald can still samba.

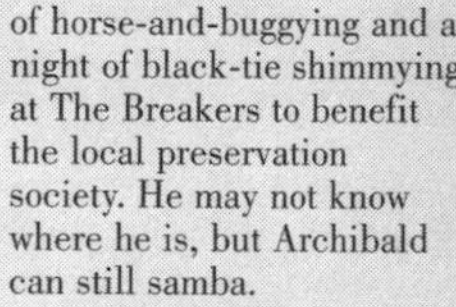

THE HAMPTON CLASSIC HORSE SHOW (Bridgehampton, New York)
The high-WASP social event of the summer with over 50,000 spectators and $500,000 in prize money. Host a lunch in the VIP tent on Grand Prix Sunday and pretend to watch the horses.

SEPTEMBER

24TH: F. SCOTT FITZGERALD'S BIRTHDAY
Get extravagantly plastered.

MAXI YACHT ROLEX CUP
(Porto Cervo, Italy)
Gigayachts ahoy for the highlight of the sailing season, the Aga Khan's weeklong regatta in Sardinia. Hair of the dog at Berlusconi's place!

GREEN TIE BALL
(Chicago)
Where the Windy City's big-shouldered billionaires write Oprah-sized checks for the beautification of Chicagoland.

THE NATURAL RESOURCES DEFENSE COUNCIL'S LADIES' LUNCHEON
(Los Angeles)
Hollywood enviro-queens Elizabeth Wiatt (wife of William Morris überagent Jim) and Laurie David (ex-wife of *Seinfeld* creator Larry) sell the benefits of "going green" over salade frisée.

NEW YORK FASHION WEEK (SPRING/SUMMER COLLECTIONS)
When garment bags filled with new "looks" start arriving on your doorstep, remember: It's time to give back to those who've loaned you so much. Slip into your favorite designer's latest for a front-row photo op.

UNDER THE BIG TOP

OCTOBER

28TH: BILL GATES'S BIRTHDAY
Back up your hard drive.

FRIEZE ART FAIR
(London)
Browse 150 galleries in Regent's Park while collecting anecdotes that'll last all year. ("I was talking to Damien—*yes,* Hirst, darling, who else?—and you'll never *believe* what he wants to do to Mitzi.")

LES VOILES DE SAINT-TROPEZ
(Saint-Tropez, France)
Armadas of old-fashioned nautical nuts cruise in for the world's premier classic wooden yacht race. Try not to stare at the Moldavian gangsters holding court at Club 55 (*"Cinquante-Cinq,"* to you).

A HOPEFUL USHER

CAROUSEL OF HOPE
(Los Angeles)
Billionaire widow Barbara Davis's biennial gala raises over $4 million for her diabetes foundation and draws 1,100 glitterati to the Beverly Hilton. Take home a celeb-decorated Mercedes-Benz pedal car, or ceramic plate for the maid.

WHITNEY MUSEUM'S FALL GALA
(New York)
Renowned for its elaborate décor and name-heavy guest list, it's a no-brainer.

RINGSIDE FOR MERCY'S SAKE
(Chicago)
Traders from the Chicago Mercantile Exchange beat each other up in seven live three-round boxing matches for the Mercy Home for Boys & Girls. Seriously.

NOVEMBER

LA BAL CRILLON DES DEBUTANTES (Paris)
At the brass ring of deb balls, international maidens "come out" in their favorite Paris couture gown and Mikimoto pearls. Past debs include: Lauren and Ashley Bush, Lydia Hearst-Shaw, Amanda Hearst, and Louise de Rothschild. Next year: your darling Daphne!

THE GAME (Cambridge, Massachusetts, or New Haven, Connecticut)
Harvard and Yale compete in the only football matchup that matters.

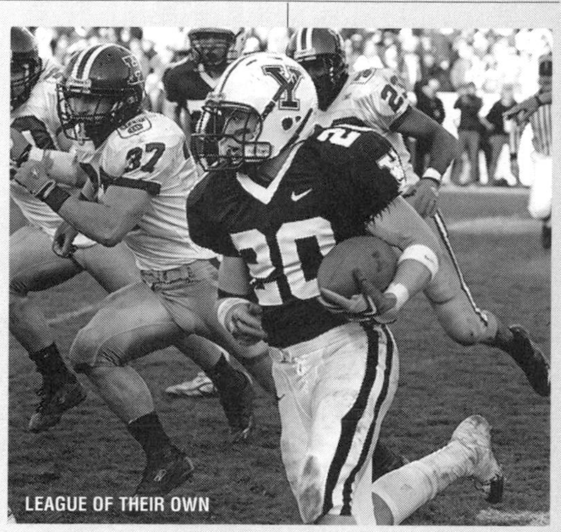
LEAGUE OF THEIR OWN

DECEMBER

ART BASEL (Miami Beach, Florida)
A bedazzled offshoot of the Swiss original, it's utterly trashtastic, but in a "fun" way.

BUT IS IT ART?

NEUE GALERIE GALA (New York)
Old and new money mingle beneath Gustav Klimt's *Adele Bloch-Bauer I* at cosmetics mogul Ron Lauder's bash for Austrian art's sake. Stop by to see what $135 million buys you.

NEW YORK BOTANICAL GARDENS WINTER WONDERLAND BALL (Bronx, New York)
For one night a year in the Boogie Down Bronx, the White Man's Overbite rules the dance floor.

HUTCH HOLIDAY GALA (Seattle, Washington)
The Pacific Northwest's *nerdoissie* raise $5 million in Microsoft money for the Fred Hutchinson Cancer Research Center.

THE GUGGENHEIM MUSEUM'S YOUNG COLLECTORS COUNCIL ARTIST'S BALL (New York)
Debu-tards and B-list reality stars frolic to raise funds for works by "emerging artists."

RON PERELMAN'S NEW YEAR'S EVE BIRTHDAY BASH (St. Barts)
Soak up the fabulosity aboard the Revlon chieftain's newly christened *Ultima VI* in Belgravia harbor. Sing happy birthday as you ring in the New Year. Wonder where the time went.

DOMESTIC AFFAIRS

If You're Indicted, You're Invited . . .

ON THE LIST

HAVING OD'D ON SALTED ENDIVE AND been pressured to dress in theme, it's your turn to host. For obvious reasons, cocktails are easier to pull off. Ply your guests with enough booze and the entertainment takes care of itself. What's more, you can invite everyone you want to see as well as those you don't, thus deferring dozens of insufferable lunches and awkward Wednesday night dinners with a series of air kisses in the foyer. If you're single, they're also quite useful for getting laid.

Dinner parties are vastly more taxing (for your staff), but there are plenty of reasons to host those, too. For instance, to give your friends the impression you care enough to feed them; to honor a visiting dignitary or celebrity more famous than yourself; to pry the details of a recent sexcapade straight from the scandalized's mouth; or to pump your corporate lawyer friends for news of unannounced mergers. Whatever the occasion, the most important factor is "the mix."

As a rule of thumb, every guest list should include at least two of the following types:

- Elected politicians
- Titled Brits
- Bestselling authors
- Supermodels
- Wizened old coots
- Winners (Nobel, Pulitzer, Oscar, what have you)
- Friendly gossip columnists
- Fortune 500 CEOs
- "Name" artists
- Witty queens

In addition to the above, there are those you'll want, but only in moderation. In general, two of the following is always too many:

- Celebrity hairdressers
- High-end prostitutes
- Famous drunks
- Coke dealers
- Coke addicts
- Comedians
- Lawyers
- Vegans
- Recovering alcoholics
- Post-op transsexuals

MEGARICH MIXOLOGY

A Cocktail Party Primer

HAVE GODFREY SHAKE UP THE FOLLOWING RECIPES FOR a no-fail bar menu:

Perfect Manhattan

In 1874, Jennie Jerome hosted a party at New York's Manhattan Club to celebrate the election of Governor Samuel J. Tilden. She asked the bartender to mix up something special, and a drink was born. When toasting a celebrated New York editor's thinly veiled roman à clef ("Oh, come on! I set it in 1870. How could that *possibly* be you?"), there's no better elixir.

GLASS ENVY
A Manhattan

2 oz. Jameson
½ oz. sweet vermouth
½ oz. dry vermouth
1 dash Angostura bitters
Maraschino cherry, or lemon twist

Stir Jameson, vermouth, and bitters in a tall cocktail shaker with ice. Strain into a chilled cocktail glass that's been rinsed with dry vermouth. Garnish with cherry or twist.

Hot Toddy

Invented in India ("toddy" is bastardized Sanskrit for "sugar cane extract"), it's an après-ski staple. If, after drinking one, you want another, the bartender made a mistake.

1 jigger (or more, really) Rémy Martin
1 tablespoon honey
¼ teaspoon lemon juice
1 cup tea

Place honey, lemon, and cognac in a tumbler. Top off with tea.

G&T

Back in the good old days, British colonialists drank tonic water spiked with quinine to stave off malaria. Being British, they added gin.

1 part Tanqueray No. 10
3 parts tonic water
Lime slice

Stir gin and tonic in a highball glass with solid cubes of ice. (Shaved ice is for snow cones, juleps.) Garnish with lime.

Old-Fashioned

Born in rural Kentucky, this classic rose to prominence in the bar at the Waldorf-Astoria. (Perhaps you can relate.)

1 sugar cube, or ½ teaspoon sugar
2 dashes bitters
1 splash soda water
1½ ounces bourbon
Orange slice

Combine sugar, bitters, and soda in an old-fashioned glass. Muddle to combine. Fill the tumbler with ice cubes, add liquor. Stir. Garnish with an orange slice, or twist.

Champagne Cocktail

As old as champagne itself, the recipe was first published in 1862 in *The Bartender's Guide*, the premier mixed-drink compendium used by those in the know.

1 sugar cube
2–3 splashes Angostura bitters
Veuve Clicquot

Place a sugar cube in the bottom of a champagne glass and saturate it with bitters. Fill the glass with Cristal, or like-minded bubbly, and serve. When ordering outside the home, make sure you see the bottle.

Pimm's Cup

British fishmonger James Pimm concocted this gin sling for his London oyster house in 1823. Unfortunately, you'll need a gallon to get drunk.

1 part Pimm's No. 1
3 parts "lemonade"
Chunks of cucumber, orange, strawberry, mint, apple, lemon

Pour Pimm's into an ice-filled highball glass. Top with "lemonade" (Brit-speak for Sprite). Put in a vegetable and several pieces of fruit. Talk about "ruggah."

FOOD FOR THOUGHT

As host, your primary duty is to maximize sexual tension, so keep the drinks hard and the conversation soft. Serve enough hors d'oeuvres to satisfy, but not enough to sober. In high-WASP circles that's not too hard to do—just order up some cold cuts and serve them on the family silver, along with Triscuits, Philadelphia cream cheese, and a smattering of grapes. Or just take a cue from legendary uptown feeding ground Swifty's. In the late '80s, when Glenn Birnbaum, owner of the Upper East Side society clubhouse Mortimer's, moved on to make seating charts in heaven, his chef and maître d' secured backing from the day's reigning doyenne, Nan Kempner, and a host of other hoity-toits to keep the party going. In a nod to their old employer, they named their new spot after his beloved pug—who, in turn, had been named after super-agent and famed party-thrower Irving "Swifty" Lazar. See how this works?

Swifty's "Billionaire's Bacon"*

The late chef and food consultant Gene Hovis gave the recipe for this decadent bacon to Mortimer's. It was subsequently adopted by Swifty's and is served at cocktail parties both on- and off-site.

Serves 8–10

1 pound bacon

1½ cups light brown sugar

1. Preheat oven to 425 degrees.
2. Separate strips of bacon and blot dry with paper towels.
3. Put sugar into a wide dish. Coat both sides of bacon in sugar, firmly pressing sugar into each strip. Lay the coated bacon out on sheet pans (some sugar will fall off).
4. Cook bacon in oven, turning once, until browned and lacquered, about 15 minutes. Transfer to lightly oiled sheet pan and let cool. Break slices into thirds.

**Decidedly not kosher*

NOTA BENE

The Importance of Saying Thanks

EVEN IF THE AFTER-DINNER ENTERTAINMENT involved a kilo of Bolivia's finest and four circus donkeys, the moment you emerge from your blackout, it's time to put pen to paper. And we're not talking Crane's. A proper thank-you note is floridly written, filled with exclamation points, and written on 50-pound card stock from either Smythson or Mrs. John L. Strong ("Ginny Strong" to you). Your full name or initials should be engraved at the top in Copperplate Light. Thankfully, to avoid the pain of drafting an entire 5" x 7" worth of false sentiment, some particularly overscheduled genius invented the "one-word wonder." It's amazing how an oversized "Wow!" "Cheers!" "Charmed!" or "Merci!" can convey so very little, while appearing to say so much. Don't forget to run a haphazard dash through your name or initials. No one is exactly sure why this is done, it just is.*

ERH

Amanda, darling!
Your dinner last night was beyond beyond. You
outdid yourself—as you will outdo yourself in
the very near future, if that's humanly possible.
Much like the company, the truffle gelato was
divine. You must, must messenger the recipe
over to Stefano immediately. I'll fax you the
Bergdorf bills when I blow up like a giant →

***That's not true. It's to assure the recipient that you wrote the note yourself. The rich are very suspicious.**

A BIG TO-DO

A Party Planning Checklist

❑ Determine what type of party you'll be hosting: A cozy dinner for 12 to toast your guru's arrival from Tibet? A sprawling post-divorce soirée?

❑ Draft a guest list (see p. 104).

❑ Check with cronies to make sure miniaturized comfort food isn't "over."

❑ Select invitations from Mrs. John L. Strong ($100 for 12).

❑ Call your sommelier in Napa. A case, or three, of 1990 Louis Roederer Cristal ($300) should do it.

❑ Call the calligrapher and ask her to address the invitations in a "handwritten" style, like you did them yourself. Your perfect self.

❑ Count the Haviland, and replace any casualties: $350/five-piece setting.

❑ Count the Alain Saint-Joanis flatware while cursing Minnie's kleptomania. Order more: $660 setting.

❑ Ship the Borzois to that puppy camp in Connecticut they adore.

❑ Call Ladurée for your favorite macaroons: $31 for 18.

❑ Embark on a draconian juice fast.

❑ Secure the Belon oysters: roughly $300 for 100 oysters.

❑ Order Indonesian Kopi Luwak coffee (beans plucked from the drippings of wild civets): $600 a pound.

❑ Have the fromager stock the cheese cave.

❑ Order the gardener to resod the lawn.

❑ Draft a seating chart. The basic rules, of course, are boy-girl-boy-girl and always split up couples. In the case of gays, seat them talker-listener-talker-listener, or try pretty-ugly-pretty-ugly. *Note: At parties of ten or fewer, seating is traditionally done on the fly—a ritual whereby you (the host) get to point to people and say, "You sit here, you sit there." Never explain your decisions.*

❑ Get full-body scrub and microdermabrasion.

❑ Pop a Xanax.

❑ Smile. They're here!

PARTY FOULS

- Parsley
- Name tags
- Wine charms
- Cosmos
- Pictionary
- Heroin
- Swing dancing
- A cappella
- Magicians
- Live butterfly releases

THE BEST OF TIMES

Famous Fêtes

Trimalchio's Banquet, *The Satyricon* of Petronius

(A.D. 61)

IN HIS THINLY VEILED ROMAN À CLEF, Nero's personal party planner, Petronius, lampooned a feast suspiciously like the ones he's said to have thrown for his fiddling boss. "Fictional" highlights included slaves showering guests with snow water and then having sex with the host. The menu: a roast boar, which—when carved—released live birds; sweetmeats molded to resemble piglets; 12 dishes representing every sign in the zodiac; fish spouting pepper sauce; and rabbits fitted with wings.

Alva Vanderbilt's Housewarming

(1883)

TO GET NEW YORK TALKING, MRS. Vanderbilt had Richard Morris Hunt design a white limestone mansion the likes of which the town had never seen. Painfully aware that the reigning social gatekeeper, Caroline Astor (who famously hated new money), had yet to welcome her, she set a trap. After inviting *tout le monde's* sons and daughters to perform quadrilles in her Versailles-inspired ballroom—but just before showtime—she sent word that the younger Caroline Astor wasn't welcome since her mother had failed to "call." Astor promptly sent over her calling card. And with that, Vanderbilt snubbed her way into New York society.

Don Carlos de Beistegui's Costume Party

(September 3, 1951)

DON CARLOS DE BEISTEGUI, THE HEIR to a Mexican mining fortune, invited 1,500 guests to appear in 18th-century costumes at his $50,000 ball set in the Palazzo Labia. Gawkers paid up to 80,000 lira just to watch the party from neighboring buildings; black-market invitations fetched $500. Invitees arrived from Paris, New York, and London in costumes created by Dior and Pierre Cardin. "I don't think that we will ever see anything like this again," the Aga Khan remarked, a bit hastily.

PUT ON A HAPPY FACE

REIGNING QUEENS Katharine Graham and Truman Capote

The Black-and-White Ball

(November 28, 1966)

In the wake of *In Cold Blood*'s explosive success, Truman Capote held a black-and-white masquerade ball in the Plaza Hotel, ostensivly to honor *Washington Post* publisher Katharine Graham. The crème de la crème jockeyed for invitations, but only 500 made the cut. The most talked about party in Filthy Rich history, it can't possibly have been as much fun as everyone says it was.

Saul Steinberg's 50th Birthday Party

(August 5, 1989)

"Honey, if this moment were a stock, I'd short it," ill-starred '80s raider Saul toasted his wife, Gayfryd, at his 17th-century-themed birthday feast. Steinberg was well known for his collection of Old Masters, so the party tent was set up to resemble a Flemish eating house. Live models reenacted ten of his favorite paintings, including Rembrandt's nude *Danae,* while twins posed as mermaids by the beach.

Malcolm Forbes's 70th Birthday Party

(September 1989)

Publishing tycoon and Fabergé egg–addict Malcolm Forbes threw himself an over-the-top 70th birthday party in Tangier, a $2 million affair that featured 200 Berber horsemen and hundreds of belly dancers. He kindly chartered three planes (a Concorde, DC-8, and 747) to bring his 800 guests to the Palace Mendoub.

Dennis Kozlowski's Sardinian Bash

(June 10–16, 2001)

Tyco CEO Dennis Kozlowski flew 75 friends to Sardinia for his second wife Karen's week-long Roman-themed birthday bash, which later landed Kozlowski in hot water when it was discovered his company footed half the $2 million bill. Toga-clad models hand-fed guests and Jimmy Buffett flew in. Most memorably, an ice sculpture of Michelangelo's *David* peed vodka.

Oprah Winfrey's 50th Birthday Party

(February 2004)

Because an elaborate on-air celebration—complete with a serenade by Tina Turner and a 400-pound cake delivered by Jay Leno—and a ladies' luncheon for fifty famous friends just weren't enough, Oprah marked her 50th year with a black-tie gala in Santa Barbara. Fifty violinists lined the staircase to serenade arriving guests, and images of Versailles were projected onto a tent adorned with 800 yards of Italian chiffon, chandeliers imported from Italy, and 200,000 orchids, hydrangeas, and magnolias. Each guest was assigned a personal waiter and the four-course meal was served in unison. For dessert, Stevie Wonder performed. The following year Oprah invited 25 "influential women of color" to her 51st birthday party and gave them each a pair of $200,000 Cartier diamond studs.

Amit Bhatia and Vanisha Mittal's Wedding

(February 20, 2004)

Nothing but the best would do for the only daughter of Indian steel tycoon Lakshmi Mittal, who sent out 20-page invitations summoning 1,000 guests to Paris for a five-day affair that included a party at Versailles, a Kylie Minogue concert at a temporary wooden castle erected in Parc de Saint Cloud, and a wedding ceremony at Château de Vaux le Vicomte. The guests drank over $1.5 million of wine, including 5,000 bottles of Mouton Rothschild. Total tab: $60 million.

Elizabeth Brooks's Bat Mitzvah

(November 26, 2005)

To usher his daughter Elizabeth into womanhood, Long Island defense contractor David H. Brooks rented two floors of New York's Rainbow Room. Kenny G warmed up the cocktail hour—and the 18-foot JumboTron—before Tom Petty, Stevie Nicks, Don Henley, Aerosmith, Ciara, and 50 Cent took to the stage, the latter changing the lyrics of his hit, "In Da Club" to "Yo, Elizabeth, it's your bat mitzvah, we gonna party like it's your bat mitzvah." (Yes, really.) At the end of the evening, Aerosmith's Steven Tyler said he'd play an encore only if Brooks handed over his gold watch. Surprisingly, he refused. Brooks was later charged with paying for the $10 million blowout with funds looted from his employees' pension fund.

GIVE GOOD GIFT

What do you get for the person who has everything? More.

- British retail billionaire **Sir Philip Green**'s wife, **Christina**, gave him a solid gold Monopoly set featuring his own properties.
- **Tom Cruise** gave his wife **Katie Holmes** a $20 million jet, so she could fly home when his Gulfstream was in use.
- Formula One racing king **Flavio Briatore** gave model **Naomi Campbell** his 170-foot yacht, *Lady in Blue*, for her 33rd.
- **Jay-Z** gave his girlfriend **Beyoncé** a 1959 Rolls-Royce convertible worth more than $1 million for her 25th.
- As an engagement gift, Tyco boss **Dennis Kozlowski** gave a loyal analyst a $20,000 private investigator to check out his bride-to-be.
- Heiress **Athina Onassis Roussel** gave her husband, Olympic medalist **Alvaro Alfonso de Miranda Neto**, a prize cow valued at $320,000.
- Wall Street investment banker **Stan Lai**'s wife gave him the naming rights of a newly discovered toad species.

STARS FOR SALE

The Best Acts Money Can Buy

THE FILTHY RICH LOVE NOTHING MORE THAN HAVING THEIR FAVORITE ACTS CROON just for them. With the exception of Bruce Springsteen and U2, who consistently refuse, you can buy almost any rock band's affection for a 15- to 60-minute set. (Mingling not included.)

JIMMY BUFFETT

GOING RATE: $250,000 **SUGGESTED ENCORE:** "Cheeseburger in Paradise" **PREVIOUS ENGAGEMENT:** Dennis Kozlowski's wife Karen's infamous Sardinian birthday bash **LINER NOTES:** A recording of Buffett covering "Brown-Eyed Girl" was submitted as evidence in Kozlowski's fraud trial.

ROD STEWART

GOING RATE: $1 million **SUGGESTED ENCORE:** "Some Guys Have All the Luck" **PREVIOUS ENGAGEMENT:** Blackstone CEO Steve Schwarzman's 60th birthday **LINER NOTES:** Apparently, Schwarzman can't get enough of his favorite pop-act-for-hire. Months after his own party, he attended a costume party for New York Jets owner Woody Johnson dressed as Rod the Mod.

ROBBIE WILLIAMS

GOING RATE: $1.8 million, donated to charity **SUGGESTED ENCORE:** "Ego a Go Go" **PREVIOUS ENGAGEMENT:** London broker Michael Spencer's 50th at Châteauneuf de Grasse in the south of France **LINER NOTES:** Williams sang 15 songs over the course of an hour. Later, lesser-priced '70s sensation Sister Sledge performed.

SNOOP DOGG

GOING RATE: $300,000

SUGGESTED ENCORE: "Hoes, Money & Clout" **PREVIOUS ENGAGEMENT:** The bar mitzvah of Mark Chaplin, son of Wayne Chaplin, president and COO of Southern Wine & Spirits of America **LINER NOTES:** The theme of the event was the Super Bowl, and Snoop was the halftime show. Miami Dolphins defensive end Jason Taylor and linebacker Zach Thomas graciously signed autographs.

DOGG'S RULE Want Snoop? Make Sure There's a PlayStation

CHRISTINA AGUILERA

GOING RATE: $3.7 million, for three songs **SUGGESTED ENCORE:** "What a Girl Wants" **PREVIOUS ENGAGEMENT:** Russian oligarch Andrei Melnichenko's wedding to Serbian model Alexandra

Kokotovic **LINER NOTES:** Aguilera's rendition of "Beautiful" reportedly brought the audience to tears—and they did not even know it cost $5,034 per second!

JENNIFER LOPEZ

GOING RATE: $1.2 million, for 40 minutes ($2.5 million less than Melnichenko paid for fifteen minutes of Aguilera's time) **SUGGESTED ENCORE:** "Love Don't Cost a Thing" **PREVIOUS ENGAGEMENT:** Andrei Melnichenko's 35th birthday **LINER NOTES:** Reportedly, it cost him $800,000 just to fly Lopez and her entourage to London, put them up in the Mandarin Oriental, and chopper them out to Surrey for the party.

GEORGE MICHAEL

GOING RATE: $3.5 million, for one hour **SUGGESTED ENCORE:** "Freedom '90" **PREVIOUS ENGAGEMENT:** Moscow billionaire Vladimir Potanin's New Year's Eve party **LINER NOTES:** Bizarrely, much of Michael's equipment was destroyed after he finished his set when a member of the crew, experimenting with some unused pyrotechnics, inadvertently torched the stage.

THE ROLLING STONES

GOING RATE: Undisclosed, but a recent party they played cost over $10 million **SUGGESTED ENCORE:** "You Can't Always Get What You Want" **PREVIOUS ENGAGEMENT:** Texas billionaire David Bonderman's birthday bacchanal **LINER NOTES:** Rubber-faced funnyman Robin Williams emceed a roast and John Mellencamp opened. Guests were treated to a brunch the next morning in a room decorated with stacks of colorful socks, a Bonderman signature.

YOU HAVE AN ANNOUNCEMENT

When PDA Is Okay

If your marriage isn't announced in *The New York Times* or frothed over in *Vogue*, it's almost as if it didn't happen. It's simply a requirement, like the blood test and the $200,000 Olivier Theyskens gown.

Because you're filthy rich, which counts for quite a lot at the *Times*, it won't be too difficult to secure a coveted slot the weekend of your wedding, but to get additional inches, you'll need to make your case.

Your parents were boarding school roommates back at Choate? How ironic! You both Peace Corped in Mali? Amazing! You met, broke up, and reunited two divorces later? Cute! Ivy League degrees count, as does graduate education, particularly if it occurred in England. Any connection to the New York media world or an old-money family like the Mellons or Du Ponts should certainly be highlighted. And if anyone in the family ever invented anything (Marshmallow Fluff? Velcro?), do mention it. Word to the wise, however: The *Times* employs fact-checkers to sniff out elaborate lies. So, tell the truth. Just stick to the highlight reel and leave out the rehab.

If you are selected for a longer "Vows" profile make sure to demand photo approval. Pass on the interactive video, however. It's terribly middle class.

MEMBERS ONLY

Country Club Confidential

THE FIRST AMERICAN CLUBS, LIKE THEIR BRITISH COUNTERPARTS, WERE MEN-ONLY affairs, like the Somerset in Boston, the Union League in Philadelphia, the Knickerbocker in New York, and the Bohemian Club in San Francisco. As the country became more industrialized, urban moguls soon found themselves longing for a pastoral haven removed from the troubles of trade and the longing gazes of the less fortunate. In this spirit, they invented the country club.

OLD MONEY CLUBS

IT'S A PERVERSE BUT INALIENABLE TRUTH that the older the money, the shabbier the clubhouse. The price of entry is similarly "understated." The catch is, unless your blood runs blue, you'll never have the opportunity to write that insignificant check. Your best chance for entrée is to marry a member.

Which is to say, despite how society has changed, that the most renowned old-money clubs are not for everybody. While a few celebrated tokens squeak through, these clubs are obstinately retro, and quietly proud of it. You must be nominated by a member in good standing, seconded by another, and supported in writing by as large and prominent a selection of the "in" crowd as possible. (All recommendations are not created equal.) But even if you make the waiting list, don't start scheduling tee times. If a club's "ethnic" quota has been filled, for example, you could be kept on a wait list for decades. And unless you're the "right sort," throwing money at the problem won't help. Tennis anyone?

KEY

OLDER CROWD

EXCESSIVELY SPORTY

BLUE BLOODS ONLY

INTERMINABLE WAIT LIST

COME ONE, COME ALL

THE COUNTRY CLUB

Brookline, Massachusetts

(FOUNDED 1882)

DIGS: When his friends tired of leaning on J. Murray Forbes's hospitality, they suggested that everyone pitch in for parties at a barn just outside Boston, and unwittingly started a craze. With its iconic yellow clubhouse, passion for croquet and curling, and an impenetrable wait list, it's still the model for the American private club. **MEMBERS:** 1,300 of Boston's Brahminest.

AUGUSTA NATIONAL GOLF CLUB

Augusta, Georgia

(FOUNDED 1933)

DIGS: The public gets a peek inside during the Masters Tournament. The rest of the year, corporate titans fly in from around the country to don green jackets at the club that Bobby Jones built. In reply to a 2002 letter from the National Organization for Women challenging its exclusion of ladyfolk, then chairman Hootie Johnson wrote, "There may well come a day when women will be invited to join our membership, but that timetable will be ours, and not at the point of a bayonet." **MEMBERS:** You don't apply, you get tapped. Membership is limited to 300 and so is the wait list. When a member dies, an announcement is mailed out and chairman Billy Payne brings a lucky newbie into the fold, which includes Berkshire Hathaway CEO Warren Buffett; Coors Brewing chairman Pete Coors; American Express chairman Kenneth Chenault; IBM chairman Lou Gerstner; ex-Citigroup CEO Sandy Weill; Motorola's Chris Galvin; JPMorgan Chase's William Harrison.

ROLLING ROCK CLUB

Ligonier, Pennsylvania

(FOUNDED 1917)

DIGS: Founded by philanthropist Richard Beatty Mellon on 12,000 acres of inherited land, what was once a casually organized retreat for friends escaping the city is now a premier private hunting, shooting, fishing, and golf club. **MEMBERS:** The hush-hush members generally keep out of the limelight, but that was not the case in 2003 when Dallas investment banker Dan Cook took his pal Dick Cheney shooting. Their "canned hunt," in which 500 pheasants were released and 417 met their end, drew heavy fire from animal rights groups—and he hadn't even shot anyone yet. Not that it's kept Dick away; he's been spotted hunting with former U.S. senator Rick Santorum and NRA bigwig Wayne LaPierre.

CHEROKEE TOWN & COUNTRY CLUB

Atlanta, Georgia

(FOUNDED 1956)

DIGS: Reigning supreme over the Southern social scene from day one, it has two locations: the country club, where the golfers play, and the town club in Buckhead, with a 90,000-square-foot clubhouse and 16 tennis courts. **MEMBERS:** Consistently ranked the best and most exclusive in the nation, it's where Georgians gather to discuss the etiquette of monogramming and their Coca-Cola stock. The wait list is five years long.

BATH AND TENNIS CLUB

Palm Beach, Florida

(FOUNDED 1927)

DIGS: Built by architect Addison Mizner, this deeply snooty outpost on Ocean Boulevard stole the winter colony away from The Breakers. **MEMBERS:** Although they're slowly coming to

---

CLUB SODA
The Southside

Invented in Chicago to cover up the taste of bootleg booze, this cocktail is now a house favorite at clubs across the country. The Devon Yacht Club, in Amagansett, New York, is purported to serve the best. There are infinite variations, but the classic recipe is as follows:

½ lemon, squeezed

1 teaspoon sugar*
2 sprigs spearmint

1½ oz. Mount Gay rum, or Tanqueray gin

Muddle the lemon juice, sugar, and mint in a shaker.

Combine with liquor and ice. Shake and strain into a highball glass filled with crushed ice.

**Lazy bartenders often replace the sugar and lemon solution with Collins mix. Accept no substitutes.*

accept Trump's purchase of Mar-a-Lago, the Palm Beach grande dames remain loyal to their home base.

MAIDSTONE CLUB

East Hampton, New York

(FOUNDED 1891)

DIGS: Bearing the original name for East Hampton, this exceedingly proper club follows the strictest standards, right down to the golf course. Completed in 1899, it is one of only a handful of courses in America that meets the Scottish definition of a links (between the ocean and farmland, no irrigation, etc.). **MEMBERS:** Although other Hamptons clubs like the National and Shinnecock accept corporate power brokers, Maidstone invites only the true blue-blood Northeasterners to play. Former President Bill Clinton was denied a tee time during the Monica Lewinsky sex scandal and writer George Plimpton was blackballed.

LOS ANGELES COUNTRY CLUB

Los Angeles, California

(FOUNDED 1898)

DIGS: Famous for being the only club to ever decline an invitation to host the U.S. Open, it also refused Hugh Hefner's request for direct access to the course from his mansion so that his bunnies could drive out on their golf carts. **MEMBERS:** Perhaps in a bit of thinly veiled anti-Semitism, the club originally excluded actors. Ronald Reagan was the famous exception to the no-thespian rule.

BOHEMIAN CLUB

San Francisco, California

(FOUNDED 1872)

DIGS: "Weaving spiders come not here" is the motto of this hangout for high-profile politicians and businessmen best known for its annual summer retreat in Bohemian Grove, complete with skits and a mock human sacrifice. Conspiracy theorists say its fireside activities have included the planning of the Manhattan Project and the tapping of Dick Cheney for VP. Recalling his time at the Grove, former president Richard Nixon called it "the most faggy goddamn thing you would ever imagine." **MEMBERS:** Every Republican president since Calvin Coolidge; economist Alan Greenspan; Walter Cronkite; former Speaker of the House Newt Gingrich; Henry Kissinger; Colin Powell; late *National Review* founder William F. Buckley; former CIA director William Casey.

OLYMPIC CLUB

San Francisco, California

(FOUNDED 1860)

DIGS: Founded in a downtown firehouse by Germans, Italians, and various Catholics who couldn't get into Nob Hill's posh Pacific Union, the club (which has a ten-year waiting list) hosts old-fashioned Ocean Beach swims, Lake Merced relay races, and crab feeds. **MEMBERS:** More than 5,000 active members work out wearing the club's winged "O."

RIVER OAKS COUNTRY CLUB

Houston, Texas

(FOUNDED 1923)

DIGS: Look for an oak-lined drive complete with mood-setting Spanish moss and a clubhouse that channels the White House. **MEMBERS:** Snootier "Establishment" types like George Bush Sr. prefer the more understated Houston Country Club, but River Oaks is the social epicenter for modern-day oil barons and their pastel-suited wives.

NEW MONEY CLUBS

TODAY, THE CLUB CONCEPT HAS BLURRED SIGNIFICANTLY AS EVERY MARKETING marksman has his arrow poised at the new leisure class. While older-money clubs spoke to the entrenched elite with flat tonic water, casual racism, and decrepit locker rooms, the new-money clubs seek to please with pet concierges, towel butlers, and helicopter pads. Rather than smothering their members with stern rules, they take their cues from the world's better five-star resorts, offering amenities like functioning exercise equipment and 40-page wine menus. Although just as exclusive as their old-money competitors, here the only color that matters is green.

THE ATLANTIC GOLF CLUB

Bridgehampton, New York

(FOUNDED 1992)

DIGS: Known for extreme difficulty, its Rees Jones–designed course brings Manhattan power brokers to blows over slow play. Unlike the Hamptons triumvirate (Maidstone, National, Shinnecock), it has a strong Jewish contingent. **PRICE TAG:** $275,000 membership fee, plus annual dues. **MEMBERS** (limited to 160): Jets owner Woody Johnson; Warner Music CEO Edgar Bronfman Jr.; NYC mayor Mike Bloomberg; New Jersey governor Jon Corzine and senator Frank Lautenberg; Blackstone biggie Steve Schwarzman; Loews Hotels honcho Jonathan Tisch. ☺

THE BRIDGE

Bridgehampton, New York

(FOUNDED 2002)

DIGS: Art "installations" and a Pilates studio complete the TriBeCa-at-the-beach vibe at this 18-holer built by ex-Treasury chief Bob Rubin amidst the retro ruins of the Bridgehampton Motor Racing Circuit. Self-made men are most welcome, provided they can pony up the cash. **PRICE TAG:** $600,000 membership fee, plus annual dues. **MEMBERS:** Related Companies founder Steve Ross; Bear Stearns CEO Alan C. Greenberg; Cantor Fitzgerald CEO Howard Lutnick; Warner Music macher Lyor Cohen; posh painter Richard Prince. ☺

HOW TO MEET YOUR FOOD MINIMUM

When visiting an old-money club, you will never be disappointed by the booze and will always be aghast at the food. This is the way it is and there is no point in complaining about it. The WASP keepers of the American country club system grew up in households where Cracker Barrel on Triscuits was considered an acceptable hors d'oeuvre, and they make the rules. In order to see your friends—and meet your food minimum—you will find yourself choking down limp club sandwiches, overdressed salads sprinkled with canned seafood, gelatinous mac 'n' cheese, chewy steaks, and dry turkey soaked with lukewarm gravy. Don't worry: You'll get used to it. You might be better off ordering a grilled cheese from the kids' menu, but then you'd miss the deviled eggs.

CLUB GRUB
Play It Safe

BIGHORN GOLF CLUB

Palm Desert, California

(FOUNDED 1991)

DIGS: Two 18-hole courses, a 40,000-square-foot clubhouse, and a 13,000-square-foot spa and salon at the foothills of the Santa Rosa Mountains. Each year on "Snow Day" 150 tons of snow are carted into the desert for a party. **PRICE TAG:** $350,000 membership fee, plus annual dues. **MEMBERS:** Producer Jerry Weintraub; golf champ Annika Sorenstam.

MAR-A-LAGO CLUB

Palm Beach, Florida

(FOUNDED 1995)

DIGS: A ballroom modeled on Versailles, three bomb shelters, and an onsite "futurologist" complete Donald Trump's vision of moneyed excess. **PRICE TAG:** $150,000 membership fee, plus annual dues. **MEMBERS:** The Donald; Telecom tycoon Peter Loftin; fad-diet heiress Veronica Atkins.

NANTUCKET GOLF CLUB

Siasconset, Massachusetts

(FOUNDED 1998)

DIGS: A perfect facsimile of the quintessential northeastern golf club, it looks just as old as neighboring Sankaty Head. So there. **PRICE TAG:** $400,000 membership fee, plus annual dues. **MEMBERS:** Senator John Kerry; former Cendant chairman Walter Forbes; ex-General Electric CEO Jack Welch.

SEBONACK GOLF CLUB

Southampton, New York

(FOUNDED 2006)

DIGS: Thumbing its nose at its uptight neighbors, this is a decidedly rugged course designed by Jack Nicklaus and Tom Doak on 300 acres of waterfront property. Check out panoramic views of Great Peconic Bay and Cold Spring Pond, but chuck your BlackBerry—they're banned. **PRICE TAG:** $650,000 membership fee, plus annual dues. **MEMBERS** (capped at 200): Reichmont chairman Johann Rupert; former Soros Fund chief Stan Druckenmiller; NetJets CEO Richard Santulli.

SHERWOOD COUNTRY CLUB

Thousand Oaks, California

(FOUNDED 1989)

DIGS: Billionaire Dole chairman David Murdock developed this club in Hidden Valley, 35 miles west of Beverly Hills. Spread over 1,900 acres, it has two Jack Nicklaus–designed golf courses, more than a dozen tennis courts, and two tournament croquet greens. **PRICE TAG:** $200,000 membership fee, plus annual dues. **MEMBERS:** There are presently 475, but for the first six months there was only one—Murdock. Sean Connery once sued Sherwood for using his image to promote itself.

YELLOWSTONE CLUB WORLD INTERNATIONAL

(FOUNDED 2006)

DIGS: Timber billionaire Tim Blixseth's extreme time-share transports members via private yacht or jet to a portfolio of high-end properties, including a private Scottish golf club, a sprawling 14th-century French château, a $40 million beachfront villa in the Mexican rain forest, a fly-fishing camp in Wyoming, and a Turks and Caicos compound. **PRICE TAG:** $3.5 million (increasing to $10 million over time) membership fee, plus annual dues. **MEMBERS** (capped at 150, by invitation only): Microsofty Bill Gates; former vice president Dan Quayle; Cablevision CEO Jim Dolan; News Corp president Peter Chernin; Comcast president Steve Burke; Brad Pitt.

DIRECTORY

STATIONERY

MRS. JOHN L. STRONG
Blue-blood paperie.
699 Madison Avenue, 5th floor
New York, NY 10021
Tel.: 212-838-3775
MrsStrong.com
Other locations:
Atlanta: 404-231-3004
Dallas: 214-528-8118
Los Angeles: 310-276-4400
Palm Beach: 561-805-9335

SMYTHSON OF BOND STREET
Embossed everything.
40 New Bond Street
London W1S 2DE, UK
Tel.: 44 020 7629 8558
Smythson.com

CALLIGRAPHY

BERNARD MAISNER CALLIGRAPHY & FINE STATIONERY
Martha Stewart calls it "The most beautiful calligraphy I've ever seen."
165 West 66th Street, 5L
New York, NY 10023
Tel.: 212-477-6776
BernardMaisner.com

PARTY PLANNING

DAVID E. MONN, LLC
The "Architect of Style" supervised the Costume Institute Gala, Henry Grunwald's funeral.
807 Sixth Avenue
New York, NY 10001
Tel.: 212-242-2009
DavidMonn.com

DAVID TUTERA
Mick Jagger hired him. Then again, so did Star Jones.
470 Seventh Avenue
11th floor
New York, NY 10036
Tel.: 212-229-9280
DavidTutera.com

NADINE JOHNSON INC.
Belgian dynamo sets the jet-set agenda.
312 West 19th Street
New York, NY 10011
Tel.: 212-228-5555
NadineJohnson.com

PARTY PHOTOGRAPHY

IZOLA WEDDINGS
331 West 21st Street
Suite FW
New York, NY 10011
Tel.: 866-683-0007
IzolaWeddings.com

PATRICK McMULLAN
Hire a legend.
321 West 14th Street, B
New York, NY 10014
Tel.: 646-638-2000
Booking Fax: 646-638-2223
(ask for Billy)
PatrickMcMullan.com

LUCIEN CAPEHART
PB's resident chronicler.
4111 S. Country Road #201
Palm Beach, FL 33480
Tel.: 516-8333-7507
LucienCapehart.com

PUBLICITY & DAMAGE CONTROL

MIKE SITRICK
Enabler of the moment.
Sitrik & Co.
1840 Century Park East
Suite 800
Los Angeles, CA 90067
Tel.: 310-788-2850

DAN KLORES
Celebrity spinmeister.
Dan Klores Communications
386 Park Avenue South
10th floor
New York, NY 10016
Tel.: 212-685-4300

HOWARD RUBENSTEIN
Shilled for all the greats.
Rubenstein Communications
1345 Avenue of the Americas
New York, NY 10105
Tel.: 212-843-8000
Rubenstein.com

SPECIALTY FOODS

CAVIAR HOUSE
Almas caviar, from a 100-year-old beluga sturgeon, sells for $25,000 per tin.
161 Piccadilly
St. James Street
London, England
Tel.: 44 020 7409 0445
CaviarHouse.com

LADURÉE
Haute macaroons.
75 Avenue des
Champs Elysées
Paris 75008, France
Tel.: 33 1 45 63 45 78
Laduree.fr

LA MAISON DU CHOCOLAT
Top-tier truffles.
1018 Madison Avenue
New York, NY 10021
Tel.: 212-744-7117
LaMaisonDuChocolat.com

HOSTESS GIFTS

BERNARDAUD
French flatware, expensive breakables.
900 North Michigan Avenue
Chicago, IL 60611
Tel.: 312-751-1700
and
489 Park Avenue
New York, NY 10022
Tel.: 212-758-8444
Bernardaud.fr

THE CONRAN SHOP
For the thoroughly modern bride.
Michelin House
81 Fulham Road
London, England
Tel.: 44 020 7589 7401
Conran.com

HERMÈS
$1,075 cashmere throws.
691 Madison Avenue
New York, NY 10021
Tel.: 212-751-8143
Hermes.com

MOSS
Chairs not meant for sitting.
150 Greene Street
New York, NY 10012
Tel.: 212-204-7100
MossOnline.com

TAKASHIMAYA
Exotic Japanese imports.
693 Fifth Avenue
New York, NY 10022
Tel.: 212-350-0100

ENTERTAINMENT

CREATIVE ARTISTS AGENCY
Does Clooney do birthdays? Ask Bryan.
2000 Avenue of the Stars
Los Angeles, CA 90067
Tel.: 424-288-2000
Caa.com

ENDEAVOR
And what's Chris Rock been up to lately . . .
9601 Wilshire Blvd., 3rd floor
Beverly Hills, CA 90210
Tel.: 310-248-2000

HANK LANE MUSIC AND PRODUCTIONS
Book the legendary bandleader who played P. Diddy's 35th.
65 West 55th Street, Suite 302
New York, NY 10019
Tel.: 212-767-0600
HankLane.com

PLATINUM RYE ENTERTAINMENT
For the right price, founder Ryan Schinman could get Beyoncé to headline a bris.
22 West 21st Street, 8th floor
New York, NY 10010
PlatinumRye.com

WILLIAM MORRIS AGENCY, MUSIC & PERSONAL APPEARANCE DEPARTMENT
The Eagles are always up for a party.
1325 Sixth Avenue
New York, NY 10019
Tel.: 212-586-5100
Wma.com

ACCENT REDUCTION

JENNIFER PAWLITSCHEK
The rain in Spain falls mainly on the plain.
Tel.: 212-518-3553
PowerfulSpeaking.net

FEEDING GROUNDS

Filth Rich tested, publicist approved.

ASPEN, COLORADO

CARIBOU CLUB
Lunch/dinner; main dining room is the place to be seen; snag the Hunt Room, Pow Wow Room, or Wine Room for privacy.
411 East Hopkins Avenue
Aspen, CO 81611
Tel.: 970-925-2929

ATLANTA

BONE'S
Lunch/dinner; old-fashioned man food.
3130 Piedmont Road NE
Atlanta, GA 30305
Tel.: 404-237-2663

CHOPS LOBSTER BAR
Dinner; invite-only private club in the basement.
70 West Paces Ferry Road
Atlanta, GA 30305
Tel.: 404-262-2675

BOSTON

ABE & LOUIE'S
Lunch/dinner; ask for a table near the front windows.
793 Boylston Street
Boston, MA 02116
Tel.: 617-536-6300

CHARLESTON, SOUTH CAROLINA

HOMINY GRILL
Breakfast/lunch/dinner; champagne and grits.
207 Rutledge Avenue
Charleston, SC 29403
Tel.: 843-937-0930

CHARLOTTE, NORTH CAROLINA

THE CAPITAL GRILLE
Lunch/dinner; where Bank of America execs grab a porterhouse.
201 North Tryon Street
Charlotte, NC 28202
Tel.: 704-348-1400

CHICAGO

BLACKBIRD
Lunch/dinner; moneyed scenesters.
619 West Randolph Street
Chicago, IL 60661
Tel.: 312-715-0708

GIBSON'S
Lunch/dinner; enormous porterhouse; kiss up to frontman John Colletti.
1028 North Rush Street
Chicago, IL 60611
Tel.: 312-266-8999

ITALIAN VILLAGE
Lunch/dinner; landmark mob scene.
71 Monroe Street
Chicago, IL 60603
Tel.: 312-332-7005

MORTON'S
Lunch/dinner; lawyers galore.
65 East Wacker Place
Chicago, IL 60601
Tel.: 312-201-0410

NOMI
Dinner; best views in town.
800 North Michigan Avenue
Chicago, IL 60611
Tel.: 312-239-4030

CORAL GABLES, FLORIDA

CHRISTY'S
Lunch/dinner; grab a table against the back wall.
3101 Ponce de Leon Boulevard
Coral Gables, FL 33134
Tel.: 305-446-1400

DALLAS

THE MANSION ON TURTLE CREEK
Lunch/dinner; sit near the fireplace . . . or at Manolo Blahnik's table on the veranda.
2821 Turtle Creek Boulevard
Dallas, TX 75219
Tel.: 214-559-2100

DETROIT

TRIBUTE
Lunch; where auto industry execs collude.
31425 West Twelve Mile Road
Farmington Hills, MI 48334
Tel.: 248-848-9393

HOUSTON

CAFÉ ANNIE
Lunch/dinner; oil tycoons and their yammering wives; deep-fried quail, upon request.
1728 Post Oak Boulevard
Houston, TX 77056
Tel.: 713-840-1111

LOS ANGELES

AGO
Lunch/dinner; outdoor terrace; co-owned by Bob De Niro.
8478 Melrose Avenue
West Hollywood, CA 90069
Tel.: 323-655-6333

DAN TANA'S
Dinner only; low-key industry hangout since 1964.
9071 Santa Monica Boulevard
West Hollywood, CA 90069
Tel.: 310-275-9444

GIORGIO
Lunch/dinner; wait outside for one of 12 tables, no matter who you are.
114 West Channel Road
Santa Monica, CA 90402
Tel.: 310-573-1660

THE GRILL ON THE ALLEY
Lunch; table requests not accepted.
9560 Dayton Way
Beverly Hills, CA 90210
Tel.: 310-276-0615

THE IVY
Lunch; wave to the paps!
113 North Robertson Blvd.
West Hollywood, CA 90048
Tel.: 310-274-8303

KATE MANTILINI
Lunch/dinner; deluxe fast food.
9101 Wilshire Boulevard
Beverly Hills, CA 90210
Tel.: 310-278-3699

MATSUHISA
Lunch/dinner; cramped, celeb-packed sushi heaven.
129 North La Cienega Boulevard
Beverly Hills, CA 90211
Tel.: 310-659-9639

MR. CHOW
Dinner; Michael Chow's West Coast outpost.
344 North Camden Drive
Beverly Hills, CA 90210
Tel.: 310-278-9911

NATE-N-AL'S
Lunch; saucy waitresses sling deli classics; sit at the counter.
414 North Beverly Drive
Beverly Hills, CA 90210
Tel.: 310-274-0101

THE POLO LOUNGE
Lunch/dinner; cut a deal over Neal McCarthy salads.
The Beverly Hills Hotel
9641 Sunset Boulevard
Beverly Hills, CA 90210
Tel.: 310-276-2251

SPAGO
Lunch/dinner; industry standby; sit in the garden.
176 North Canyon Drive
Beverly Hills, CA 90210
Tel.: 310-385-0880

TOSCANA
Dinner; almost unmarked, across from Hamburger Hamlet.
11633 San Vincente Boulevard
Los Angeles, CA 90049
Tel.: 310-820-2448

MIAMI

CASA TUA
Dinner; spectacular old-fashioned Italian (for Florida); know someone or be prepared to wait . . . and wait.
1700 James Avenue
Miami Beach, FL 33139

JOE'S STONE CRAB
Lunch/dinner; an FR staple since 1913; reservations are not accepted.
11 Washington Avenue
Miami Beach, FL 33139
Tel.: 305-673-0365

MINNEAPOLIS

D'AMICO CUCINA
Lunch/dinner; Twin City VIPs; lobster gnocchi.
100 N. Sixth Street
Minneapolis, MN 55403
Tel.: 612-338-2401

NASHVILLE

MIDTOWN CAFÉ
Lunch/dinner; where music execs schmooze.
102 19th Avenue South
Nashville, TN 37203
Tel.: 615-320-7176

NEW YORK

BALTHAZAR
Breakfast; weekdays only; order the brioche French toast.
80 Spring Street
New York, NY 10012
Tel.: 212-965-1414

CIPRIANI DOWNTOWN
Dinner/drinks; tables in back; everyone's named Paulo, Lapo.
376 West Broadway
New York, NY 10012
Tel.: 212-343-0999

DA SILVANO
Lunch/dinner; six tables near the entrance; make nice with local pope, Silvano Marchetto.
260 Sixth Avenue
New York, NY 10014
Tel.: 212-982-2343

ELAINE'S
Dinner; tables in front; pay respects to literary den mom Elaine Kaufman (or else).
1703 Second Avenue
New York, NY 10128
Tel.: 212-534-8103

THE FOUR SEASONS
Lunch; Grill Room only; power host Julian Niccolini choreographs daily.
99 East 52nd Street
New York, NY 10022
Tel.: 212-754-9494

GINO
Dinner; no-frills red sauce joint; old-school classic.
780 Lexington Avenue
New York, NY 10021
Tel.: 212-758-4466

LA GRENOUILLE
Lunch; grande dames convene most Tuesdays.
3 East 52nd Street
New York, NY 10022
Tel.: 212-752-1495

PETER LUGER
Lunch; überflack Howard Rubenstein's cash-only boys' club.

178 Broadway
Brooklyn, NY 11211
Tel.: 718-387-7400

MICHAEL'S
Lunch; symphony of media/business insiders; manager Joe Armstrong conducts; front room only.
24 West 55th Street
New York, NY 10019
Tel.: 212-767-0555

MR. CHOW
Dinner; traditional Chinese in haute Parisian-style setting; celeb central; try not to stare.
324 East 57th Street
New York, NY 10020
Tel.: 212-751-9030

NELLO'S
Lunch/dinner; whatever you do, don't mess with Nello; just sit back, relax, and watch next week's gossip column items unfold in real time!
696 Madison Avenue
New York, NY 10021
Tel.: 212-980-9099

RAO'S
Dinner; traditional Italian in a faux mob setting.
455 East 114th Street
New York, NY 10029
Tel.: 212-722-6709

SETTE MEZZO
Dinner; billionaire playpen; cash or house charge only.
969 Lexington Avenue
New York, NY 10021
Tel.: 212-472-0400

SWIFTY'S
Lunch; beloved WASP's nest.
1007 Lexington Avenue
New York, NY 10021
Tel.: 212-535-6000

VIA QUADRONNO
Breakfast; cappuccino perfecto.
25 East 73rd Street
New York, NY 10021
Tel.: 212-650-9880

THE WAVERLY INN
Dinner; front room only; smoking allowed for a privileged few.
16 Bank Street
New York, NY 10014
Tel.: 212-243-7900

'21'
Lunch/dinner; jacket required; so FR, tables have plaques; store your vino downstairs.
21 West 52nd Street
New York, NY 10019
Tel.: 800-721-CLUB

OMAHA, NEBRASKA

GORAT'S STEAK HOUSE
Lunch/dinner; no-nonsense favorite of Buffett and Gates.
4927 Center Street
Omaha, NE 68106
Tel.: 402-551-3733

PALM BEACH, FLORIDA

TA-BOO
Lunch; lots of tiki; best seats are fireside.
221 Worth Avenue
Palm Beach, FL 33480
Tel.: 561-835-3500

PALO ALTO, CALIFORNIA

IL FORNAIO
Lunch/dinner; backroom boys' club.
520 Cowper Street
Palo Alto, CA 94301
Tel.: 650-853-3888

PHILADELPHIA

LE BEC-FIN
Lunch/dinner; best tables are near the fireplace.
1523 Walnut Street
Philadelphia, PA 19102
Tel.: 215-561-1000

PHOENIX

THE CAPITAL GRILLE
Lunch/dinner; order a Stoli Doli and the steak au poivre; sit in the center booths.
2052 East Camelback Road
Phoenix, AZ 85016
Tel.: 602-952-8900

SANTA BARBARA, CALIFORNIA

THE HITCHING POST
Dinner; house-bottled pinot noir at the bar.
3325 Point Sal Road
Casmalia, CA 93429
Tel.: 805-937-2216

SAN FRANCISCO

A16
Dinner; Meatball Mondays; perfect wine list.
2355 Chestnut Street
San Francisco, CA 94123
Tel.: 415-771-2216

CHEZ PANISSE
Dinner downstairs, lunch upstairs; book ahead.
1517 Shattuck Avenue
Berkeley, CA 94709
Tel.: 510-548-5525

SLANTED DOOR
Lunch/dinner; Charles Phan's mod Vietnamese; refreshingly divey.
1 Ferry Building, Number 3
San Francisco, CA 94111
Tel.: 415-563-4755

ZUNI CAFÉ
Lunch/dinner; inside tables only.
1658 Market Street
San Francisco, CA 94102
Tel.: 415-552-2522

SEATTLE

CANLIS
Dinner; east room on the lower level; the Caché for privacy.
2576 Aurora Avenue N
Seattle, WA 98109
Tel.: 206-283-3313

WASHINGTON, D.C.

MORTON'S
Lunch/dinner; three-year wait for wine lockers; NOT the other five D.C. locations.
1050 Connecticut Avenue NW
Washington, DC 20036
Tel.: 202-955-5997

THE OVAL ROOM
Lunch; nonpartisan favorite of Bubba, Karl, and Condi.
800 Connecticut Avenue NW
Washington, DC 20006
Tel.: 202-463-8700

CHAPTER SIX / SUMMER IS A VERB

TRAVEL & LEISURE

"Travel only with thy equals or thy betters; if there are none, travel alone."
—BUDDHA

LIKE A PARTICULARLY PICKY FLOCK OF water fowl, countless times each year the Filthy Rich take to the air armed with Evian misters and eight-ply cashmere blankets, only to reconvene en masse elsewhere and air kiss the same hundred people they air kiss back home.

Contrary to popular mythology, these seasonally determined summits are not just for pleasure. They're where the plutocrats find relief.

Away from the gazes and judgmental glares of the have-nots, they can wear eight-carat diamonds to the drugstore, swap Ferrari stories above a whisper, and gripe about the cost of Gulfstream maintenance without fear of being punched. Ensconced among their equals—whether in Palm Beach, Aspen, Lyford Cay, or Careyes—they can dispense with the "stealth wealth" pretensions of home and hoist their freak flags high.

To join them, you'll need to plant your own tastefully weathered pennant. Doing so will require the cash purchase of an envy-inducing compound, proficiency in the local customs, frequent bows to the reigning gatekeepers, and the enthusiastic donning of native dress.

Sound exhausting? *Relax.* It will only be a few seasons before it's time to move on. Declaring a place "over" once you've had your fill is a sacred filthy rich tradition, so after you've done, say, Aspen or Southampton, it's off to Gstaad and St. Tropez. If you're particularly dedicated, your fourth or fifth home should be somewhere farther afield—a tad louche, even. Years later, when you inevitably find Tangier to be just as full of the folks who bored you off the wagon at the Everglades Club, it's time to think about buying an island.

After all that running around, you could use a real vacation.

HOP 'TIL YOU DROP

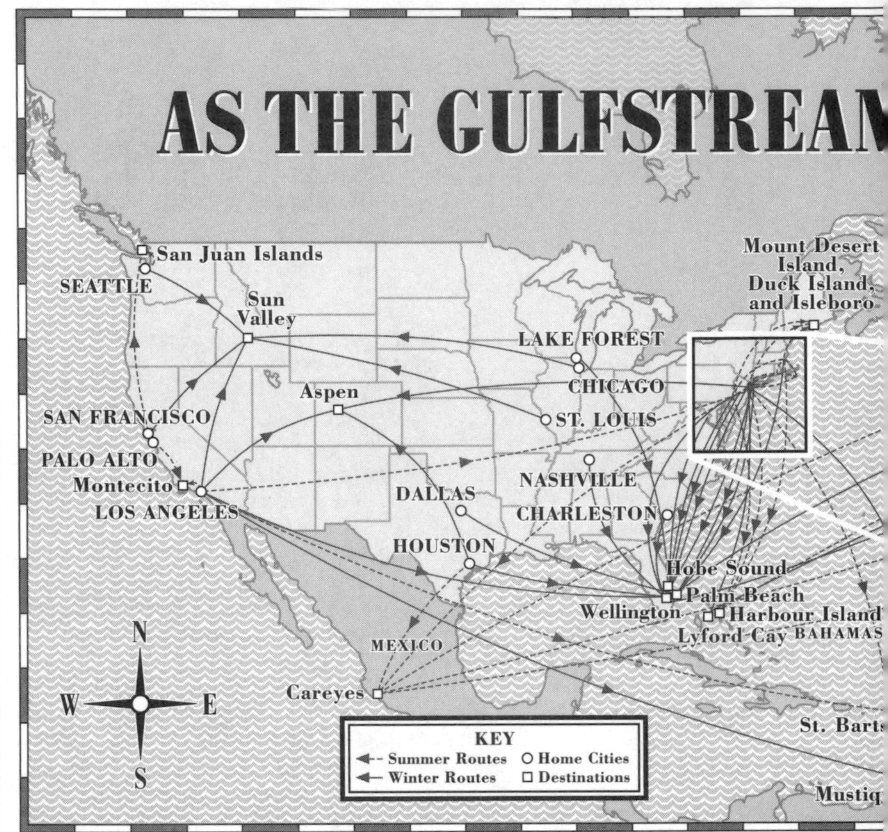

UNTIL THE MIDDLE OF THE LAST CENTURY, TYCOONS IN NEED OF A RECHARGE SIMPLY selected from a list of acceptable Eastern resorts and called it a day. As blue-blood society chronicler Cleveland Amory put it, there were just so few places "worth caring about." In order of desirability, they were Palm Beach and Hot Springs, Virginia; followed by Narragansett Pier in Newport; the Berkshires in Massachusetts; Tuxedo Park, New York; and the North Shore of Long Island. While Palm Beach basks in a renaissance, the Springs are now overrun with tchotchke shacks, Tuxedo Park is a glorified subdivision, and Newport is the world's grandest nursing home. The takeaway? Filthy Rich migration patterns shift over time. But for the moment, at least, the following pass muster:

WINTER HAVENS

ON OR AROUND DECEMBER 20, ANYTHING resembling work should be carelessly abandoned as you flit back and forth between tropical idylls and quaint mountain towns, spreading Christmas cheer with your Black Card. Just remember to return by January 7. Wouldn't want your employees to get the wrong idea.

PALM BEACH, Florida

THE DRAW: Shut out by Northeast society, Standard Oil cofounder Henry Flagler envisioned a balmy retreat where his

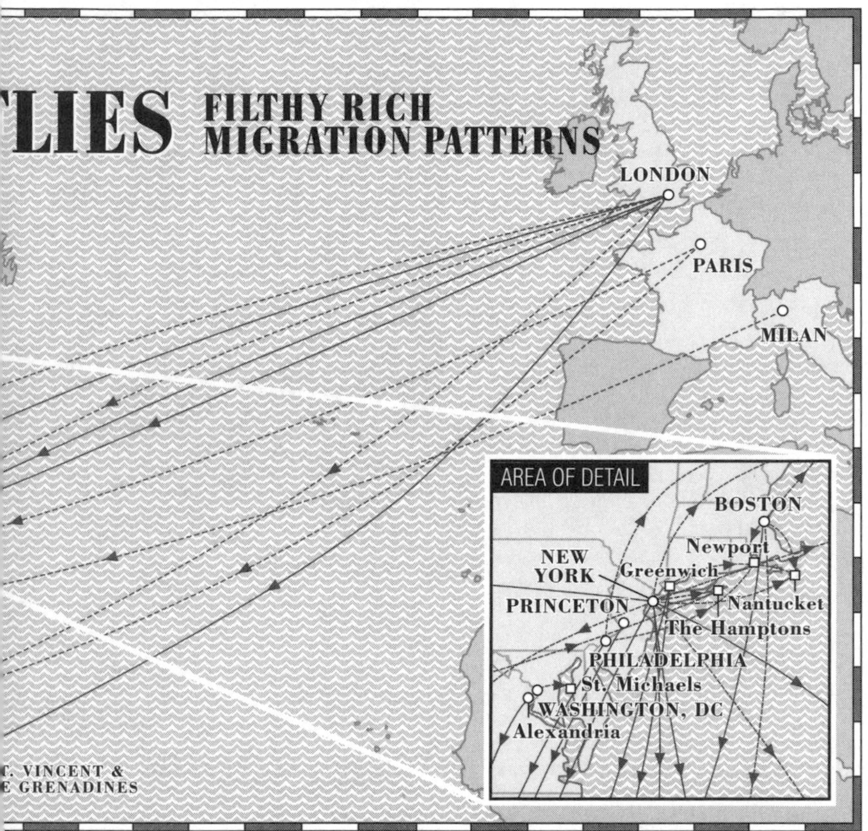

filthy rich friends could winter in peace, uninhibited by quaint Yankee notions like restraint. Today, the 3.75-square-mile island idyll he founded has more Rolls-Royces per capita than anywhere outside Monaco, a median age of 67, and a rep for exclusion untouched on these shores. Until the statute was successfully challenged in the 1980s by the ACLU, nonresidents—meaning maids, day workers, and other dusky types—were required to carry ID cards and be photographed and fingerprinted at the local sheriff's office. As you might expect, it's an irony-free oasis rendered in pastels—an insular Republican stronghold of $60 million "villas," dissolute heirs with legendary surnames, and vicious social jockeying . . . which is why dropping $100 million on one of the bougainvillea-covered monsters along Billionaires Row between the Atlantic Ocean and Lake Worth won't necessarily get you "in." ("In" being your phone number listed on Cuban sugar baron Pepe Fanjul's annual oversized Christmas card, along with 299 of the island's other major swells.) But cut enough checks, and kiss the right behinds, and you'll be accepted soon enough—two decades, max. Should you fail, don't take it too hard. The Kennedys never made it "in" either. **IN RESIDENCE:** The Khashoggis; the Trumps; the Du Ponts; the Fanjuls; the Dodges; the Fords; the Pulitzers; the Basses; the Johnsons; KKR's Henry Kravis; Blackstone biggie Steve Schwarzman; Allen & Co. heiress Terry Allen Kramer and Handmade Films helmer Nick Simunek; right-wing radio raja Rush Limbaugh; etc., etc., etc. **$125 MILLION BUYS YOU:** A 54,000-square-foot French Regency compound on North Ocean Boulevard with 475 feet of ocean front, two guest houses, and an Olympic-size pool **LOCAL COSTUME:** See "Into the WASP's Nest," p. 132.

ASPEN, Colorado

THE DRAW: Much like the Hamptons, its spiritual East Coast cousin, Aspen is hated by *everyone*. It's scene-y, it's gauche, it's full of wannabes, and the lift lines are interminable. Which is why, come January, there's no place you'd rather be. Deep beneath that heavy gloss lies an Old West mining town capable of summoning the inner cowboy in even the most dead-eyed of superagents (chaps courtesy of Ralph Lauren "vintage"). Should you care, between the Cristal-fueled bacchanals and nonstop bragging, there's also skiing. The Aspen Mountain Club, the Little Nell, and the Caribou Club are the *haute* spots to roll your eyes at how overdressed everyone is. **IN RESIDENCE:** Jack, Warren, Goldie, and the rest of the boomer A-list; sundry Saudi sheiks; Gucci guru Domenico De Sole; desktop dynamo Michael Dell; Sun Microsystems magnate Bill Joy **$9.9 MILLION BUYS YOU:** A 6,362-square-foot, ski-in-ski-out chalet with indoor pool and spa, six bedrooms, and six bathrooms **LOCAL COSTUME:** (for him) vintage RL by Ralph Lauren denim shirts; Zegna "barn" jackets; Lucchese cowboy boots; (for her) fur-trimmed Moncler ski jackets; Gorsuch shearling coats; Prada gilets

MUSTIQUE, St. Vincent and the Grenadines

THE DRAW: Jet-setters come for the Anglo hospitality and pristine Macaroni Beach, and stay for the sense of smug satisfaction that comes with own-

ing a home on one of the world's most exclusive islands. With dreams of ruling over his own aristo-bohemian colony, wildly eccentric Scottish lord Colin Tennant (alas, no relation) blew his sizable trust fund developing the 1,400-acre island in the 1960s. To help move things along, he gave ten acres to his hard-partying pal Princess Margaret, who convinced a handful of British rock stars and semi-landed gentry to join in the chic debauchery. **IN RESIDENCE:** Rock fossils Mick Jagger and David Bowie; clothes horse Tommy Hilfiger; U.K. publishing pasha Felix Dennis **$25,000 BUYS YOU:** A week in Jacaranda, a four-bedroom villa with freshwater pool on the beach in

FULL OF FLAKES
Aspen

L'Ansecoy Bay. There are only 100 properties on the island and, unless you know someone, they're certainly not for sale. **LOCAL COSTUME:** (for him) Leather "mandals" from a street market in Jaipur; Façonnable white linen shirts; starched khakis from Paul Stuart (rolled at the cuffs for that shipwrecked look); (for her) Matthew Williamson tunics; skinny white jeans; Ferragamo flats; exotic caftans of various stripes

SUN VALLEY, Idaho

THE DRAW: Since its first lift opened in 1936, Sun Valley has epitomized rugged luxury. Ernest Hemingway completed *For Whom the Bell Tolls* at the Sun Valley Lodge (room 206), and the subsequent influx of Hollywood macho men like Gary Cooper and Clark Gable cemented the slopes of Bald Mountain as *the* place to peacock in high American style. In the half-century since, Winter Olympians made it their training ground, while entertainment and media titans put off by Aspen erected superchalets in the surrounding mountains. **IN RESIDENCE:** Governator Arnold Schwarzenegger; John Kerry and his ketchup queen, Teresa Heinz; *New York Times* columnist Alex Kuczynski and her megabanking hubby, Charles Stevenson; casino bigwig Steve Wynn; *Rolling Stone*r Jann Wenner; Allen & Co. rainmaker Herb

Allen **$9.9 MILLION BUYS YOU:** An 8,649-square-foot "cabin" on five acres overlooking the Big Wood River **LOCAL COSTUME:** (for him) "tycoon casual" Merrell hiking boots; high-performance mountaineering jackets from North Face; mock turtlenecks from Prada; (for her) de Castelbajac for Rossignol ski pants; Bogner ski jackets from Theodore; Uggs

HOBE SOUND, Florida

THE DRAW: If Palm Beach strikes you as a bit obvious, look north to Hobe Sound, an unflappably discreet community of 450 estates on a barrier island scattered with sea pines. Mixed doubles and other forms of lock-jawed recreation take place at the Jupiter Island Club, renowned for blackballing Jackie Kennedy and Perry Como. **IN RESIDENCE:** Urban Outfitters overlord Richard Hayne; links sphinx Tiger Woods; publishing scion Nelson Doubleday; Martha Ingram, matriach of her family's megaconglomerate **$15.9 MILLION BUYS YOU:** A six-bedroom gated estate with wall-to-wall marble and free-form saltwater pool **LOCAL COSTUME:** See "Into the WASP's Nest," p. 132.

LYFORD CAY, Bahamas

THE DRAW: Though often derided as "Lifeless Cay," this 1,000-acre *echt*-WASP wealth preserve sees itself as a civilized sanctuary standing quietly in contrast to "flashy, trashy" Palm Beach. The candy-pink Lyford Cay Club, where chintz is still the rage, is the center of the blue-blood action (stop by for a famed Lyford Dog, a deep-fried weiner filled with cheese and wrapped in bacon strips). But despite its snooty rep, a few barbarians have shimmied through the gates: Canadian playboy Peter Nygard (a onetime paramour of Anna Nicole Smith) holds court in a 150,000-square-foot tiki-style compound, tastefully accented with multiple beach volleyball courts, a windowed party pool, and several mock Mayan sacrifice altars, which he's humbly dubbed "Nygard Cay." **IN RESIDENCE:** Avon heiress Sandra McConnell; the Bacardi family; New York socialite Jamee Gregory; grizzled Scot Sean Connery; Filthy Rich icon Babe Paley's son, Bill Jr. **$16 MILLION BUYS YOU:** A 2.1-acre canal-front estate with 650-foot dock and four guest cottages **LOCAL COSTUME:** See "Into the WASP's Nest," p. 132.

WELLINGTON, Florida

THE DRAW: From late November through mid-March, the horsey set decamps to Wellington to take in the Winter Equestrian Festival and world-class, high-goal polo. Even the Brits make a showing: The queen's second cousin Marquis George Milford Haven (442nd to the throne) ships his ponies in for the season. The Palm Beach Polo Club and the Equestrian Club are popular gilded ghettos, but a compound in Grand Prix Village—an equine fantasy located in the heart of the 179-acre show grounds—or a sprawling farm off Pierson is where you want to be. **IN RESIDENCE:** Outback Steakhouse founder Tim Gannon; Bruins' owner Jerry Jacobs; billionaire spawn Georgina Bloomberg; Calvin's ex, Kelly Klein **$14 MILLION BUYS YOU:** A 3,000-square-foot, two-bedroom, three-bathroom house on 3.4 acres in Grand Prix Village. Includes a 20-stall barn, dressage ring, jumping ring, and paddocks. While a recent dispute threatened to relocate the show grounds and force an equine exodus, the matter has been resolved, resulting in a bigger, fancier playground and even pricier real estate. **LOCAL COSTUME:** (for him and her) Tailored Sportsman breeches; custom Vogel or Der-Dau riding boots; Hermès belts; Hadfield bespoke shirts; green Devoucoux Windbreakers bequeathed by Grand Prix winners

PALM BEACH BABYLON

Local Scandals You Need to Know

It seems serene—the palm-fringed villas, the tennis whites, the limited-edition Aston Martins—but looks can be deceiving on the Intercoastal. In fact, this thin sliver of sand has a decadent history worth whispering about. A few of the lowlights:

1967

(120 El Brillo Way)

Socialite **Trink Gardiner** shoots and paralyzes her husband, William, with a .22 revolver after allegedly catching him *en flagrante* with his mistress. This may explain why he doesn't press charges.

1983

(415 N. Trail Way)

Scandal-magnet **Roxanne Pulitzer** and her hubby Herb's sensational divorce trial rips the lid off PB nightlife. In open court, Herb claims "Foxy" Roxy is an "incorrigible coke slut" who "humps anything she can get her hands on," including, in at least one instance, "a trumpet." But the couple's coke-fueled orgies with Kleenex heiress Jacquie Kimberly at the Holiday Inn in West Palm are the biggest bombshell. Surely they could have sprung for The Breakers?

1984

(301 Australian Avenue)

Fresh out of Hazelden, **Bobby Kennedy's** 28-year-old son David is banished from the family compound on North Ocean over Easter break. Holed up in room 107 of the Brazilian Court Hotel, he overdoses on a lethal injection of cocaine, Mellaril, and Grandma Rose's Demerol. A family curse is rekindled.

FOXY ROXY
Pulitzer in *Playboy*

1987

(920 S. Ocean Blvd.)

Financier **James Sullivan** puts a hit out on his estranged wife Lita, the same day a judge is to divvy up their assets. The fatal gunshot is delivered with candy and flowers in Buckhead, Atlanta, by an assassin disguised as a delivery boy. Sullivan flees PB for Thailand, where he lived on the lam until 2004.

1991

(1095 N. Ocean Blvd.)

After a raucous night at Au Bar, Camelot creep-master **William Kennedy Smith** convinces a local named Patricia Bowman to join him and Uncle Teddy for a nightcap back at the compound. Innumerable headlines later, he's acquitted of rape charges.

2003

(1495 N. Ocean Blvd.)

Anti-drug hardliner **Rush Limbaugh's** $370-a-week housekeeper tells cops of the GOP propagandist's habit of trading Cuban cigar boxes stuffed with cash for sandwich bags full of OxyContin.

2006

(358 El Brillo Way)

Pervy hedge fund honcho **Jeffrey Epstein** is indicted after a yearlong investigation into his thrice-daily massage sessions with underage teen girls from the wrong side of town. Epstein, who vowed to fight back, eventually cops to solicitation charges and is sentenced to 18 months. (Apparently, he has a very bad back.)

BASKET CASE
Nantucket

SUMMER SANCTUMS

AH, SUMMER. THOSE GLORIOUS THREE TO FOUR MONTHS WHEN THE FILTHY RICH HONE their tennis serves, have messy affairs with sailing instructors, and skip along that slippery slope toward full-blown alcoholism. (Not to worry. Silver Hill is quite lovely when the leaves turn.) Here's where they do it best:

NANTUCKET, Massachusetts

THE DRAW: Arriviste Bostonians love that it's tonier than Martha's Vineyard (a bit "day-tripper" these days), while the island's white-haired doyennes long for the '70s when *everyone* was in the Social Register. Lately, even the 27-mile journey from Hyannis isn't enough to keep the newbies at bay. At the height of the season in the first two weeks of August, G-Wagon-clotted cobblestone streets, private jet jams at the airport, and Lilly Pulitzer–swathed New Yorkers yapping away on their iPhones give Main Street a decidedly Hamptonian vibe. But for now, at least, there seem to be enough shingled compounds on this fog-draped sandpile for anyone willing to pay through the nose. **IN RESIDENCE:** Retired GE honcho Jack Welch; automotive ace Roger Penske; Wayne Huizenga; Alamo Rent A Car founder Michael S. Egan; designer Tommy Hilfiger; Daisy and Paul "brother of George" Soros; ex-IBM chief Louis Gerstner; John Kerry and Teresa Heinz; Google guy Eric Schmidt **$9.6 MILLION BUYS YOU:** A five-bedroom, eight-bathroom whaling cottage with covered porches, guest cottage, and deeded access to the harbor **LOCAL COSTUME:** See "Into the WASP's Nest," p. 132.

THE HAMPTONS, New York

THE DRAW: Despite the chopper *bruit*, publicist-packed share houses, endless lines, and sharp-elbowed hedge-funders, America's Filthy Richest keep coming back. Here, the media/fashion/Hollywood/Wall Street power nexus keeps its houses fully staffed year-round and never set foot on the beach. Amagansett, Sag Harbor, and the Springs say "hippie-luxe"; East Hampton is where the vestiges of Manhattan's wilted WASPistocracy still "summer." Nouveau Southampton is considered more flash, but the bluenosed Meadow Club and the Bathing Corporation keep it grounded. (Note: Filthy Rich GPS doesn't register Westhampton or Hampton Bays, due to the preponderance of plastic surgeons.) **IN RESIDENCE:** Box office behemoth Steven Spielberg; LBO legend Carl Icahn; actor-activist Richard Gere; *SatC*-er Sarah Jessica Parker and hubby Matthew Broderick; real estate roué Mort Zuckerman; right-wing plutocrat Rudy Giuliani; hip-hop heavyweights Russell Simmons and P. Diddy; VC dynamo Tony Forstmann **$25 MILLION BUYS YOU:** A 3,500-square-foot pile in the East Hampton estate district with Olympic-size pool, greenhouses, formal English garden, and three outbuildings for staff and guests **LOCAL COSTUME:** See "Into the WASP's Nest," p. 132.

MOUNT DESERT, ISLEBORO & OTHER PRIVATE ISLANDS, Maine

THE DRAW: Where authentic Brahmin fustiness meets serious bank and terrifying swarms of vicious black flies. In general, the more obscure the island or wooded peninsula, the better. Unlike the fast-living Bush clan in Kennebunkport, true Mainiacs make their homes in turn-of-the-century "cottages" (34-room mansions in Seal Harbor) that they try their damnedest to make look downtrodden. Beat up, wood-paneled Country Squire station wagons come standard, as do rum and tonics, backgammon tourneys, and ritualized self-abuse in the form of bracing swims in 40-degree water. As undercover rich-kid Vince Vaughn notes in *Wedding Crashers:* "Sailing is sex to these people." For a smooth ride, make sure your sloop is made of wood; tinted windows and working motors are other red flags that you're "new." **IN RESIDENCE:** Martha Stewart; John Travolta; the Bostonian Gardner family; the painterly Wyeths; Marshall Field's heiress Marina Rust; the Rockefellers **$8 MILLION BUYS YOU:** A ramshackle camp with 3,000 feet of shoreline and views of Blue Hill Bay, protected anchorage, full-tide granite dock, two deep-water moorings for large vessels, and a boathouse **LOCAL COSTUME:** See "Into the WASP's Nest," p. 132.

NEWPORT, Rhode Island

THE DRAW: In Newport, Gilded Age excess and retrograde Republicanism mingle over cucumber sandwiches. The summer resort's female grandees are a prickly lot, making the rounds at the local National Society of the Colonial Dames of America and the Daughters of the American Revolution with frightening seriousness. Though Newport was once known for its whimsy—the place where Mrs. Stuyvesant Fish threw a dinner party for a monkey in white tie and tails—a stiff upper lip (and gin on the breath) is all but requisite for entry into the local clubs. Some of the newcomers on Ocean Drive have been summering there for 40 years, so don't expect a welcome wagon. Your neighbors will know your bloodlines better than you do. **IN RESIDENCE:** Hugh Auchincloss III; Old Guard matrons with names like "Oatsie" and "Britty" **$12.7 MILLION BUYS YOU:** A 14,440-square-foot castle on the highest point on Ocean Avenue with eight bedrooms, nine bathrooms, state-of-the-art home theater, and billiards room **LOCAL COSTUME:** See "Into the WASP's Nest," p. 132.

ST. MICHAELS, Maryland

THE DRAW: The legendary duck and goose hunting on the sleepy Delmarva Peninsula draws D.C. power brokers of the strong, silent type. Former tobacco plantations dot the banks of the Chesapeake, allowing members of the red-tie club to play at being landed gentry on weekends. It's a mere 90 minutes from Washington by car (30 by Chinook), and local joints like Albright's Gun Shop, Justine's Ice Cream Parlor, and the Tidewater Inn bolster its timeless all-American allure. **IN RESIDENCE:** VP Dick Cheney; ex-Defense Chief Donald Rumsfeld (his estate is called "Mount Misery"); ex-GOP spinmeister Tony Snow **$16.5 MILLION BUYS YOU:** A Colonial Revival mansion with grand hall, formal lawns, 3,300 feet of waterfront, tennis courts, and boathouse **LOCAL COSTUME:** (for him) Filson vests, Orvis khakis, L.L. Bean duck boots, Haliburton golf shirts, Brooks Brothers anything; (for her) Talbots casuals, boxy J. McLaughlin sheaths; Lands' End mom jeans, Crocs (unabashedly)

MONTECITO, California

THE DRAW: On the southern side of Santa Barbara, Montecito has a champagne socialist vibe. Lefty moguls and "low-key" celebs cherish the red-tiled roofs of their faux-Moorish villas and the thrill of seeing one another shop at the farmers' market. Since the 1930s, Hollywood types have been loving the breezy hospitality of the San Ysidro Ranch, where Vivien Leigh and Laurence Olivier were married, and Jack and Jackie Kennedy made a honeymoon pit stop. **IN RESIDENCE:** Oprah Winfrey; Beanie Baby daddy Ty Warner; Kevin Costner; Steve Martin **$29.5 MILLION BUYS YOU:** A 10,000-square-foot 1906 compound with

INTO THE WASP'S NEST

Dressing the Part from Nantucket to Newport

Generations of "summering" up and down the Eastern seaboard can teach you a thing or two about style. Below, the essential packing list:

FOR HER

- **Peter Elliot sailor shirt**
- **J. McLaughlin capri pants with little embroidered pineapples**
- **Ralph Lauren cashmere cable-knits in French turquoise, Grand Prix pink, and tangerine**
- **Tory Burch terry beach caftan**
- **Jack Rogers sandals**
- **Vera Bradley travel case**
- **Lilly Pulitzer psychedelic sundress**
- **Salmon Cove polos in Newport, Hampton, or Sanibel colors**
- **Matching Manuel Canovas swimsuit and cover-up**
- **Eric Javits folding large-brimmed hat**

FOR HIM

- **Vilebrequin swimming trunks**
- **Smathers & Branson "Bonefish" needlepoint belt**
- **Checked J. Press boxer shorts**
- **Madras Bermudas from Cape Madras**
- **Paul Stuart brass-buttoned navy blazer**
- **Nantucket Reds from Murray's Toggery Shop**
- **Tod's driving shoes**
- **Sperry Top-Siders in navy**
- **Stubbs & Wootton needlepoint slippers**
- **Loro Piana summer-weight cashmere V-neck**

Persian-inspired gardens, two terraced pools, and 125 varieties of palm tree **LOCAL COSTUME:** (for him) linen shirts, Mason's cargo pants, Patagonia vests, New Balances; (for her) Donna Karan hippie skirts, turquoise accented belts, James Perse tees; (for both) Cabernet mustaches

SAN JUAN ISLANDS, Washington

THE DRAW: Complete privacy. Of the 742 islands, most are uninhabited and only four are served by ferries—not a problem if you've got a sea plane. Microsoft's Paul Allen made waves on Lopez Island when he evicted a historic summer camp to make room for his 385-acre estate. **IN RESIDENCE:** Reclusive tech billionaires; Oakley eyewear magnate James Jannard **$25 MILLION BUYS YOU:** A 30-acre compound overlooking dramatic Peavine Passage, with 120-foot dock and boathouse **LOCAL COSTUME:** (for him) Charvet button-downs, Edun jeans, Sebago Campsides; (for her) Armani twin sets, headbands, Ellen Tracy capris; Birkenstocks

CAREYES, Mexico

THE DRAW: An eight-mile stretch of forgotten beach dotted with clifftop villas, it was developed by an Italian architect as a secluded retreat for his since-deceased playboy pals like Brit financier Sir Jimmy Goldsmith, Prince Egon von Furstenberg, and Fiat don Gianni Agnelli to get their party on. Assembled glameratti converge on the sleepy bistro Playa Rosa and trade Kate Moss gossip at the polo grounds. With only 42 villas, and no village to speak of, dinner party invites are a must. **IN RESIDENCE:** Supermodel Heidi Klum and singer Seal; elder statesman Henry Kissinger; various polyglot Mexican magnates **$12.5 MILLION BUYS YOU:** A gated 14-bedroom spread with open living rooms, gym, wine cellar, massage studio, and private screening room **LOCAL COSTUME:** (for him) Gucci swim trunks, sarongs from Kenya, short-sleeved shirts from Tommy Bahama; (for her) Marni peasant skirts, handmade Brazilian pareos, mirrored aviators

ST. BARTS, French West Indies

THE DRAW: Reached via terrifying ten-minute flight from St. Martin, the achingly chic colony known as the "French Hamptons" is the Caribbean's Filthy Richest isle. Much of the action takes place in Gustavia Harbour, winter home to the world's longest giga-yachts. After dark, the brash and the beautiful overdress for dinner at Creole haunt Maya's (a favorite of Joan Didion and Diddy alike), or mingle with the world-weary supermodels at the Hotel Eden Rock. **IN RESIDENCE:** Art dealer Larry Gagosian; Harrison Ford; David Letterman; Ron Perelman, et al. **$22 MILLION BUYS YOU:** An airy colonial villa on five mountaintop acres with infinity pool overlooking the beach **LOCAL COSTUME:** (for him) Flip-flops, Lacoste polo shirts, Paul Smith khaki shorts, Loro Piana cashmere sweaters (draped over the shoulders); (for her) Calypso sundresses, Kenzo tunics, Missoni bikinis, Jimmy Choo sandals

HARBOUR ISLAND, Bahamas

THE DRAW: For those who prefer puttering in a golf cart to preening aboard a stinkpot, countrified Harbour Island may be the antithesis of St. Barts. But don't be fooled: It's stuffed with just as many ducats. You can't serve a shuttlecock without hitting one of the Forbes 400. **IN RESIDENCE:** Island Records rex Chris Blackwell; Blockbuster billionaire Wayne Huizenga; J.Crew's Mickey Drexler **$4.6 MILLION BUYS YOU:** A three-bedroom blufftop house in the Narrows, with screened sleeping porches **LOCAL COSTUME:** See "Into the WASP's Nest," p. 132.

THE VINEYARD . . . REALLY?

Classic Resort Rivalries

ARGUING WHY ONE'S FAVORED HIDEAWAY IS SUPERIOR TO ANOTHER IS A FAVORITE PAStime of the leisure class. Here, five debates you'll eventually take sides on:

ST. MORITZ v. GSTAAD

GSTAAD HAS FILTHY RICH FINISHING school Le Rosey, the cozy Olden Inn, the slight edge on attracting obscure titled Euros, and Valentino. St. Moritz has a proper runway, the ultrasnooty Corviglia Ski Club, Sir Norman Foster, and more tangible signs of excess. Both have dinosaurish grand hotels called the Palace. Which one wins out? It all depends on where your pretensions lean. St. Moritzians dismiss Gstaad as an overreaching little hamlet. Gstaadites turn up their noses at St. Moritz, saying it's all just a bit "too much."

NANTUCKET v. THE VINEYARD

JACKIE O MADE MARTHA'S VINEYARD A haven for Democrats. With its wide open spaces and the sullen endorsement of celebrity introverts like Carly Simon and James Taylor, the island has always had something of a rich hippie vibe, ritzy Edgartown aside. Nantucket is farther out in the Atlantic, which allegedly discourages day-trippers. While both have their fair share of T-shirt shops, in Nantucket the preservationists hold greater sway, giving it a more homogeneous New England feel. Billionaires are welcome on both.

PORTO ERCOLE v. PORTOFINO

SINCE THE LEGENDARY HOTEL IL Pellicano first opened its doors in 1965, the American jet set has been coming to the Tuscan seaside town of Porto Ercole, a convenient spot for yachts to pause en route from St. Tropez to Capri. Portofino, on the Italian Riviera to the north, was a humble fishing village until the hard-partying Duke and Duchess of Windsor set up camp. Porto Ercole fans see it as more civilized and "exclusive." (There are theme park versions of Portofino in Japan and Florida, for crissake!) That said, come summer, it's still chockablock with Hollywood royals.

CAP-FERRAT v. CAP D'ANTIBES

FOR SHEER EXCLUSIVITY, CAP-FERRAT wins hands down, which is why the Rothschilds built there at the turn of the century. In comparison, the walled city of Antibes and neighboring Juan-les-Pins can seem a tad ... pedestrian. But then there's the Hotel Eden Roc, which lures stars from Cannes with its Jazz Age splendor. Plus, there's the practical fact that Antibes' deep-water port can hold multiple gigayachts at a time. Although both Caps have been colonized by the Russians, old-timers in each claim the other is "practically St. Petersburg."

ASPEN v. VAIL

WISTFUL FOR THEIR WILDER NIGHTS at the Hotel Jerome, Aspenites are fiercely loyal to their considerably older mining town, citing (at length) its pedigree as the western hub of '60s counterculture. (Vail wasn't even incorporated until '66.) They wouldn't be caught dead skiing anywhere but Ajax Mountain. Vailians, a generally quieter lot, are quick to denigrate Aspen's revolving roster of gauche celebs posing slopeside for the paps in borrowed Bogner (do Posh and Becks even *know* how to slalom?). Inevitably, Aspenites will counter that Vail is merely a Disney *manqué* of a proper ski town. And, oh, those endless lift lines!

BETTER OFF MED

Learning to Love the French Riviera

OLDSTERS LOVE WAXING NOSTALGIC FOR an imagined era when the French Riviera was an uninterrupted string of impossibly quaint fishing villages. But given that the moneyed have been coming to the Côte since the days of Belgian King Leopold II, it's only natural that the likes of Bill Gates, Russian oligarch Roman Abramovich, P. Diddy—and now you!—would eventually follow, fighting for dock slips and inflating real estate values.

To the uninitiated, the Riviera can seem like an impenetrable and bizarre pastiche of filthy rich clichés. Much of it isn't even pretty. Beyond all the monstrous, '70s-style apartment blocks in Monaco, the scratched Lucite, and the tinted windows, there are *hypermarchés* in Antibes so sprawling you'd think you were in Houston. And never mind the traffic, which can make Hamptons gridlock seem tolerable. If all that isn't damning enough, the returning tribes actually seem to enjoy how very '80s it all is. The unapologetic gilt of the Monte Carlo casino, the Gucci-suited goons with earpieces and submachine guns, the choreographed fountains, and the saccharine Euro-pop clubs all conspire to make you feel like Reagan's still in office.

But whether they love it or loathe it, the Filthy Rich keep returning, griping happily over salades niçoises at Les Caves du Roy about those other people ruining the Riviera. Another Methuselah of Cristal, please!

FRENCH CONNECTION
Where the Filthy Rich Frolic

CHOOSE YOUR OWN ADVENTURE
Hot-ticket travel agents

Booking the Louvre for an evening is a snap, care of **Paris Privé; Frank Zanchi** at **Bellini Travel** can arrange an intimate concert for you and yours at La Fenice in Venice; Leo Tolstoy's granddaughter **Tania Illingworth** will gladly book out the Hermitage for a peaceful, tourist-free visit. The bottom line? It will cost you (and then some) to see the wonders of the world without the pesky school groups and amateur photographers. But a handful of highly esteemed boutique travel agencies like those below are in the game of anticipating your every desire.

If you have $2.5 million to drop on a couple of weeks' vacay, the British company **Based on a True Story** will gladly arrange a one-of-a-kind expedition for you, organizing elephant polo with the Maharajah of Jaipur, perhaps, or jetting you via Gulfstream to ride with Western Mongolia's nomadic horsemen. With a guarantee of absolute anonymity, BOATS' "facilitators" will wrangle icebreakers for Antarctic exploration, stage a private Dakar rally across the Sahara, build you a bespoke-tented camp in Tanzania, arrange an introduction to a remote Amazonian tribe, or set up base camp for you in Iceland, complete with luxury, *en suite* igloos. To custom-tailor your ideal holiday, the team also sources yachts, helicopters, local healers, chefs, and masseuses to tend to your every whim. For an additional fee, a *National Geographic*–caliber lensman will record your priceless memories and turn them into a couture coffee-table tome upon your return.

- **PARIS PRIVÉ**
  parisprive.com
- **BELLINI TRAVEL**
  bellinitravel.com
- **TANIA ILLINGWORTH**
  theultimatetravelcompany.co.uk
- **BASED ON A TRUE STORY**
  basedonatruestory.com

JET SET CONFIDENTIAL

Whom You'll Meet Along the Way

SPEND TIME IN ANY EXCLUSIVE WATERING HOLE AND you're likely to come across some colorful characters. Head to Europe, and you'll meet a tribe of loaded riffraff so *faaahbulous*, so eccentric, so inexplicably shady, that it's imperative you be briefed before departure. Behold, the United Nations of ne'er-do-wells:

THE RUSSIAN OLIGARCH

STOMPING GROUNDS: Courchevel in France; Monaco; Belgravia in London **IDENTIFYING MARKS:** Nehru-collared button-down shirts; stone-washed Levi's; crude prison tat from early '90s stint in the gulag **DIRTY LITTLE SECRET:** Met wife number three, Miss Estonia 2001, at a brothel in Bratislava

THE ITALIAN PLAYBOY

STOMPING GROUNDS: St. Barts; the Costa Smeralda in Sardinia **IDENTIFYING MARKS:** Melon-colored flat-front trousers; white linen shirt unbuttoned to the navel; overgelled, mahogany-dyed hair; sun spots **DIRTY LITTLE SECRET:** The three paternity suits tucked behind the visor of his Ferrari F40

THE BRAZILIAN SUPERMODEL

STOMPING GROUNDS: Punta del Este in Uruguay; Tangier in Morocco; Cannes in France **IDENTIFYING MARKS:** Transparent Cavalli caftan with fringe detail; "dream journal"; metallic bikini; Michael Kors wedges **DIRTY LITTLE SECRET:** She's carrying the Italian Playboy's child

THE ENGLISH ARISTOBRAT

STOMPING GROUNDS: Careyes in Mexico; Formentera in Spain; the Maldives; Mauritius **IDENTIFYING MARKS:** "Ethnic" necklaces from a hippie in Ibiza; Matthew Williamson tunic; tangled blonde hair with dark roots **DIRTY LITTLE SECRET:** Functional illiteracy (She can barely read *Hello!*)

THE SAUDI PRINCE

STOMPING GROUNDS: On his retrofitted battleship in Antibes harbor; shopping for falcons in Dubai **IDENTIFYING MARKS:** Baby fat; multiple platinum rings; diamond-studded cell phone with contact info on the best escort agencies in 28 capitals; white snakeskin loafers **DIRTY LITTLE SECRET:** He's only 271st in line for the throne

THE TIPPING POINT

Keep Your Friends Close and Their Servants Closer

DURING YOUR WEEKEND AT SACRÉ BLEU, Felix and Mimi von Klimer's legendary Cap Ferrat estate, Clive and his staff consistently kept you a South Sider north of ignominy, washed and ironed your underwear, chilled your beach towels, and bribed Truffles not to soil the Aubussons with spoonfuls of steak tartare. So don't think you're off the hook with a gushing thank-you note and potted orchid for the hostess. The moment you exit the driveway, Clive's footmen will be scouring your bedside table for that all-important envelope—and they better find it. Why on earth would you tip someone else's staff, you ask? The rationale for this tradition (inherited from cash-poor English aristos) is that servants have to work that much harder when guests are afoot. And if you hope to be invited back, there's no getting around it, lest you be labeled a tightwad, or worse. He may have looked busy, but Clive heard what you said about Mimi's drinking in the loggia, and is perfectly happy to tattle if tested.

Whatever you do, avoid the slippered footsteps of Lord Conrad Black. After realizing that both he and his wife had tipped a friend's staff, he allegedly called his host to ask that one envelope be returned.

WHAT TO LEAVE

TIP = (NUMBER OF STAFF × NUMBER OF BEDROOMS) × LENGTH OF STAY IN DAYS + YOUR AGE

+ $100	+ $200	+ $300	+ $500	+ $1,000
if you ruined something worth under $1,000	if you ruined something worth over $1,000	if you made a drunken ass of yourself	if there was crying, drugs, or bodily fluids involved	if you've ever appeared on the Forbes 400

HOW TO BUY AN ISLAND

Your Own Floating Metaphor in Four Easy Steps!

ASK ANY 10-YEAR-OLD WHAT HE'D DO WITH A BILLION DOLLARS, AND CHANCES ARE "buy an island" would be high on his list. Since some dreams never die (and islands don't cost a billion), it's time to get serious. But where to start? You're not some Robinson Crusoe–style lunatic. You want Pratesi sheets and gourmet groceries and scantily clad servants who speak goddamn English. With hundreds of thousands of potential islands on which to build your private kingdom, it's important to make a plan.

❑ SELECT A REGION
It won't be hard—you have only two choices: The Caribbean or the South Pacific. The former has lured Filthy Rich islomaniacs since the 1930s, and is overpriced accordingly. The latter offers more in the way of natural beauty, but fewer buying options. In fact, only Fiji allows foreigners to own islands outright. (What are you so afraid of, Tahiti?) Of course, you could always join the bargain hunters down in Panama and Belize. But then again, who would come visit . . . I mean, aside from capsized drug runners and capitalist-hating kidnappers?

❑ HIRE A BROKER
Cheyenne Morrison is the only man on earth worth speaking to in this regard. The world's foremost private-island broker, he typically has 200-plus listings sprinkled across the seven seas, from $1 million fixer-uppers to $70 million aquatic fortresses. Go with the fortress.

❑ FLY IN THE TROOPS
Before you cut any checks, you'll want to fly in your design team for a final walk-through. In terms of filthy rich islands, makeup mogul Francois Nars's Polynesian utopia Motu Tane is the one to beat. When not in use, he rents it for $25,000 to $43,000 a night, "international phone calls and massages not included." He used celebrated Parisian Christian Liaigre for his interiors and landscaping legend Pascal Cribier for the grounds. How funny! That's exactly who you had in mind!

❑ SEAL THE DEAL
In one lump sum, no excuses. There's nothing sadder than a private-island owner with a mortgage.

ALONE AT LAST

Where the Stars Find Solace

MAGO ISLAND

MEL GIBSON

A $15 MILLION CHECK MADE OUT TO A Japanese hotel chain scored Mad Mel a 5,400-acre Fijian retreat complete with sugar plantation, 35 residents, 400 cattle, and 300 goats. Also included: outraged local Yavusa Vuaniivi tribesmen who say their ancestors own the land.

LITTLE HALL'S POND CAY

JOHNNY DEPP

MEASURING JUST A MILE LONG, LITTLE Hall's was a snip at $3.6 million. Located inside a nature preserve in the Exumas, it came with a basic cottage, tiki hut, generator, and not much else. The press-shy actor has said he was inspired by his reclusive pal Marlon Brando, who purchased a Tahitian isle after filming wrapped on *Mutiny on the Bounty*.

DISAPPEAR HERE
Musha Cay

MUSHA CAY

DAVID COPPERFIELD

WHEN A DEVELOPER REFUSED TO SELL IT to him, the tricky illusionist formed a shell company and bought this Bahamian Bali Hai for $45.5 million. With a full-time staff of 30 and room for 24 guests, he rents it out for $392,000 a week. Bill Gates, Steve Martin, and Oprah Winfrey have all felt the magic.

ISLAND ESSENTIALS

❑ **SEAPLANE**
Although you could always chopper in from the nearest airport, wouldn't an amphibious assault be much more fabulous? Jimmy Buffett seems to think so. His preferred ride, the Grumman Goose, is no longer in production, but reconditioned models can be had for under a million.

❑ **CARETAKER**
Considering you'll be there three weeks a year at most, and that your patch of paradise is isolated and accessible from all sides, it's crucial you hire some security. Lucky for you, they even have their own newsletter! Think about hiring a couple so he doesn't die of loneliness.

See Directory, p. 146, for contact details.

THE TROPICAL DIVIDE

LIVING THE BOHO DREAM

THERE ARE THE SHAMELESSLY LUXE places on earth (the Costa Smeralda, in Sardinia, for instance), and then there are the spots, often hidden in Third World countries, where the Filthy Rich follow pioneering artists and fashion-types in search of "authentic" experiences, a lingering colonial service culture, and a bending of the societal norms they must adhere to in their everyday lives. To the naked eye these boho enclaves may appear to be full of drop-outs, druggies, and other shady types. But for every dreadlocked party kid or heroin cartel, there's a gated, guarded compound fit for the adventurous billionaire who likes to "keep it real."

TULUM, Mexico

SUGAR-FINE SAND AND A surplus of supermodels on yoga retreats and swimsuit catalog shoots typify this hippy-dippy eco-resort on what's known as the "Mayan Riviera." Jet-set escapists flock here in winter to rid themselves of tan lines, smoke lots of excellent pot, and for Zamas, the premier beach shack bar for griping drunkenly about how "tourists" have completely ruined Cancún. **BE SEEN:** Star-spotting at laid-back Italian bistro Posada Margherita; braving the dirt road to Punta Allen in a pick-up truck to scope out the perfect site for your jungle eco-lair.

IBIZA AND FORMENTERA, Spain

THE PHOENICIANS WERE on to something when they settled on the dry shores of these Balearic islands. Beyond the madding crowd jostling for neon wristbands at the clubs in San Antonio, Ibiza is a sun-drenched red island dotted with olive trees and jagged coves ideal for discrete assignations. Filthy Rich kids temper nights dancing at Pacha with lazy days lounging in spare clifftop villas. Formentera is even quieter and lures tastemakers like Marni's Consuela Castiglione and Philippe Starck. **BE SEEN:** Lounging at Las Banderas; supping Rioja at Blue Bar on Formentera.

MARRAKECH, Morocco

WHERE TALITHA GETTY made the caftan famous. Eurotrash with a taste for the exotic jet in for a few nights at a tricked-out private riad, for the belly dancers at Le Comptoir, and for the hint of jasmine in the air at Yves Saint Laurent and Pierre Bergé's Jardin Majorelle. As on the Côte d'Azur, a soundtrack of mellow house music drifts in and out of this pink city's trendier haunts, occasionally drowning out all the French accents. The perfect spot for dandy types looking to pick up an opium addiction. **BE SEEN:** Lounging with a hookah at Palais Rhoul; in the pool at Riad el Fenn.

LAMU ISLAND, Kenya

LOCATED OFF OF THE eastern coast of Africa, Lamu has been a merchant outpost for thousands of years, and its resulting mélange of Arab and African culture is a refreshing rebuke to loaded bohos who think they've seen it all. A UNESCO-pro-

SECRET AGENT

You won't find Bill Fischer in the Yellow Pages

Operating more like a private concierge than your average ticket hustler, Fischer charges a one-time $100,000 initiation fee and an annual $25,000 before he's even picked up the phone. Call him the antibudget travel agent. Of course, you get what you pay for . . . quite literally. Fischer can score a reservation anywhere, book the unbookable, and make imaginative arrangements beyond your wildest dreams. Ask Steve Schwarzman for his number at the next Robin Hood Foundation gala. Not that he'd ever tell you.

tected 14th-century town dominates the island, where homes are made of coral stone and the beaches are impossibly white and empty. **BE SEEN:** Awaiting the next Brangelina sighting while drinking mint tea at the Baytil Ajaib inn.

PUNTA DEL ESTE, Uruguay

PUT ON THE MAP AS A South American winter colony (their summer season begins, conveniently, in December) by Brigitte Bardot, Omar Sharif, and the Rat Pack, today Punta is filled with "Uru-trash," rich-kid surfers, Buenos Aires aristocrats, and Brit "intellectuals" like Martin Amis. **BE SEEN:** Sipping sundowners at José Ignacio beach; dining on grilled fish in the garden at La Bourgogne; at L'Auberge.

FLORIPA, Brazil

"FLORIPA"—AS SANTA Catarina is affectionately known for its main city, Florianopólis—draws São Paulo and Rio's fattest cats, who chopper in to this seemingly low-maintenance island every weekend. But paradise has a price: A beach villa on the isle can run you $10 million. Safe from the crime-riddled metropolis, Brazil's elite come here to party with designer Carlos Miele and supermodels Gisele Bündchen and Caroline Trentini. **BE SEEN:** Topping up your tan at Praia de Cafe; surfing Praia Mole.

SHELTER SKELTER

Where to stash your cash.

LIECHTENSTEIN

COME FOR THE TAX DODGE: 75,000 companies have brushed up on their German just to call this petite nation home. Favorable tax codes make it a popular cache for Russian and Italian mob bosses. STAY FOR THE: Breathtaking vineyards with panoramic views of the Swiss Alps.

LIBERIA

COME FOR THE TAX DODGE: What's a little civil war amid extreme poverty? Liberia may not be everyone's definition of "haven," but it gives nonresident corporations carte blanche and offers nifty "flags of convenience" for shifty shipping companies. STAY FOR THE: Year-round temperatures in the mid-80s.

MARSHALL ISLANDS

COME FOR THE TAX DODGE: This island nation in the Pacific won't ask to see your financial statements when you register your business here, and they won't make you pay pesky taxes either. STAY FOR THE: Sea turtles; crystal clear lagoons.

MONACO

COME FOR THE TAX DODGE: W. Somerset Maugham dubbed it the original "sunny place for shady people." Prince Albert is nominally attempting to clean up the books, but the fact remains that his minute principality has 8,000 residents and 130,000+ hush-hush bank accounts. STAY FOR THE: 007-style gambling at the Casino and floating party scene during the Grand Prix.

DIRECTORY

SECOND, THIRD, AND FOURTH HOMES

CHRISTIE'S GREAT ESTATES
Tel.: 505-983-8733
ChristiesGreatEstates.com

FIRST PALM BEACH PROPERTIES
Philanthropist Thomas "T.Q." Quick's agency has the island wired.
230 S. County Road
Palm Beach, FL 33480
Tel.: 561-655-0379

MASON & MORSE RANCH COMPANY
The best in the West. Giddyap!
214 Eight Street, Suite 100
Glenwood Springs, CO 81601
Tel.: 970-928-7100
Ranchland.com

RIVIERA PRESTIGE INTERNATIONAL
The keys to the Côte.
7 Promenade des Anglais
Le Royal Luxembourg
06000 Nice, France
Tel.: 33 4 97 03 45 03

SIBARTH REAL ESTATE
Honesty, integrity . . . $24 million three-bedroom villas.
"La maison Suédoise"
Rue Samuel Fahlberg, Gustavia
97133 St. Barts
French West Indies
Tel.: 59 590 29 88 91
SibarthRealEstate.com

SOTHEBY'S INTERNATIONAL REALTY
Tel.: 866-899-4747
SothebysRealty.com

PRIVATE ISLAND BROKERS

CHEYENNE MORRISON
Coldwell Banker Morrison's Private Islands
P.O. Box 478
Port Douglas
Queensland 4877
Australia
Tel.: 61 7 4099 3939
ColdwellBankerAustralia.com.au

VLADI PRIVATE ISLANDS
Ballindamm 7
Hamburg D-20095, Germany
Tel.: 49 40 33 89 89
Vladi-Private-Islands.de

URBANE OUTFITTERS

CAPE MADRAS
The finest summer plaids on the planet.
P.O. Box 6306
Cape Elizabeth, ME 04107
Tel.: 207-799-0017
CapeMadras.com

ERIC JAVITS
Top-shelf toppers.
433 Fifth Avenue
Suite 500
New York, NY 10016
Tel.: 800-374-4287
EricJavits.com

FABUCCI
Flattering swimsuits for curvy doyennes.
9200 Sunset Boulevard, PH 22
Los Angeles, CA 90069

J. PRESS
Where addicts cop their seersucker.
262 York Street
New Haven, CT 06511
Tel.: 203-772-1310
JPressonline.com

THE KIKOY COMPANY
Sarongs and kikoys for your inner Peter Beard.
Tatu Buildings, Sulby Covert
Welford Road, Sibbertoft
Leicestershire
LE16 9UJ, UK
Tel.: 44 18 5888 0888
Kikoy.com

LILLY PULITZER
Sundresses in every shade of sherbet.
C. Orrico
336 South County Road
Palm Beach, FL 33480
Tel.: 561-659-1284
LillyPulitzer.com

MURRAY'S TOGGERY SHOP
For authentic Nantucket Reds.
62 Main Street
Nantucket Island, MA 02554
Tel.: 508-228-0437
NantucketReds.com

SALMON COVE
Polo shirts for Protestants.
474 North Lake Shore Drive
Suite 2710
Chicago, IL 60611
Tel.: 631-418-8511
SalmonCove.com

SMATHERS & BRANSON
Needlepoint-loving Bowdoin grads keep it real.
5202 River Road
Bethesda, MD 20816
Tel.: 301-229-9436
SmathersAndBranson.com

TOD'S
The nubby soul of summer.
650 Madison Avenue
New York, NY 10022
Tel.: 212-644-5945
Tods.com

TORY BURCH
Mainlining the Main Line since 2005.
47 Newtown Lane
East Hampton, NY 11937
Tel.: 631-907-9150
ToryBurch.com

VERA BRADLEY
Travel bags with trippy prints.
Vera Bradley at Jefferson Pointe
4110 West Jefferson Boulevard
Fort Wayne, IN 46804
Tel.: 260-434-1900
VeraBradley.com

VILEBREQUIN
Whimsical swimming trunks for father and son.
14 rue Gambetta
83990 Saint-Tropez, France
Tel.: 33 04 94 96 33 60
Vilebrequin.com

CARETAKERS

THE CARETAKER'S GAZETTE
Place an ad in the industry bible.
3 Estancia Lane
Boerne, TX 78006
Tel.: 830-755-2300
Caretaker.org

SEAPLANES

GOOSE CENTRAL
Your Grumman Goose hunt starts here.
Geocities.com/AlaskanGoose/

TRAVEL AGENTS

BELLINI TRAVEL
7 Barb Mews
London W6 7PA, UK
Tel.: 44 020 7602 7602
BelliniTravel.com

DIANE HILLIARD
Hilliard & Olander
226 East Myrtle
Stillwater, MN 55082
Tel.: 651-275-8960
HilliardOlander.com

TANIA ILLINGWORTH
The Ultimate Travel Company
25-27 Vanston Place
London SW6 1AZ, UK
Tel.: 44 020 7386 4646
TheUltimateTravelCompany.co.uk

INDAGARE TRAVEL
Custom travel advisory service.
138 East 78th Street, 4B
New York, NY 10075
212-988-2611
Indagare.com

LISA LINDBLAD TRAVEL DESIGN
27 East 95th Street
New York, NY 10128
Tel.: 212-876-2554
LisaLindblad.com

BARBARA A. GALLAY
Linden Travel Bureau
909 Third Avenue
New York, NY 10022
Tel.: 800-846-3226
LindenTravel.com

MARY ANN RAMSEY
Betty Maclean Travel
M & I Building
800 Laurel Oak Drive
Suite 200
Naples, FL 34108-2713
Tel.: 800-865-8111
BettyMacleanTravel.com

PALLAVI SHAH
Our Personal Guest
21 East 33rd Street
New York, NY 10016
Tel.: 212-319-1354
OurPersonalGuest.com

PARIS PRIVÉ
116, boulevard Pereire
Paris 75017, France
Tel.: 33 0 1 42 56 27 59
ParisPrive.com

PRISCILLA ALEXANDER
Protravel International
515 Madison Avenue
New York, NY 10022
Tel.: 800-227-1059
ProTravelInc.com

NANCY AND JIM STRONG
Strong Travel Services
8214 Westchester Drive
Suite 670
Dallas, TX75225
Tel.: 214-361-0027
StrongTravel.com

VALERIE WILSON TRAVEL, INC.
475 Park Avenue South
New York, NY 10016
Tel.: 800-776-1116
WTI.com

HOTELS

As you flit around the globe, be sure to bunk with the Inn crowd at these tycoon-approved classics.

THE AMERICAS

BELLAGIO
3600 Las Vegas Boulevard South
Las Vegas, NV 89109
Tel.: 888-987-6667
BellagioResort.com

THE BEVERLY HILLS HOTEL
9641 Sunset Boulevard
Los Angeles, CA 90210
Tel.: 800-283-8885
TheBeverlyHillsHotel.com

BLANTYRE
16 Blantyre Road
Lenox, MA 01240
Tel.: 413-637-3556
Blantyre.com

THE CARLYLE
35 East 76th Street
New York, NY 10021
Tel.: 212-744-1600
TheCarlyle.com

CHATEAU MARMONT
8221 Sunset Boulevard
Hollywood, CA 90046
Tel.: 323-656-1010
ChateauMarmont.com

FIFTEEN BEACON
15 Beacon Street
Boston, MA 02108
Tel.: 877-982-3226
XVBeacon.com

HOTEL BEL-AIR
701 Stone Canyon Road
Los Angeles, CA 90077
Tel.: 800-648-4097
HotelBelAir.com

THE INN AT LITTLE WASHINGTON
Middle and Main Streets
Washington, VA 22747
Tel.: 540-675-3800
TheInnAtLittleWashington.com

LITTLE NELL
675 East Durant Avenue
Aspen, CO 81611
Tel.: 888-843-6355
TheLittleNell.com

THE MERCER
147 Mercer Street
New York, NY 10012
Tel.: 212-966-6060
MercerHotel.com

THE PENINSULA
9882 South Santa Monica Blvd.
Beverly Hills, CA 90212
Tel.: 800-462-7899
BeverlyHills.Peninsula.com

THE RALEIGH
1775 Collins Avenue
Miami Beach, FL 33139
Tel.: 305-534-6300
RaleighHotel.com

THE ST. REGIS
2 East 55th Street
New York, NY 10022
Tel.: 800-759-7550
StRegis.com

STEIN ERIKSON LODGE
7700 Stein Way
Park City, UT 84060
Tel.: 800-453-1302
SteinLodge.com

EUROPE

THE BERKELEY
Wilton Place
Knightsbridge, London
SW1X 7RL, UK
Tel.: 44 20 7335 6000
TheBerkeleyHotelLondon.com

CLARIDGE'S
Brook Street
London W1K 4HR, UK
Tel.: 866-599-6991
Claridges.co.uk

THE DORCHESTER
53 Park Lane, Mayfair
London W1K 1QA, UK
Tel.: 44 20 7629 9988
TheDorchester.com

GEORGE V
31 rue Pierre Charron
Paris 75008, France
Tel.: 33 149 52 7000
GeorgeVParis.com

GRAND HOTEL DU CAP-FERRAT
71 Boulevard du Général de Gaulle
06230 Saint-Jean-Cap-Ferrat
Paris, France
Tel.: 33 49 37 65 050
Grand-Hotel-Cap-Ferrat.com

HOTEL BYBLOS
Avenue Paul Signac
83990 Saint-Tropez, France
Tel.: 33 49 45 66 800
Byblos.com

HOTEL CALA DI VOLPE
Costa Smeralda
Porto Cervo
Costa Smeralda, Sardinia, Italy
Tel.: 39 0789 97 6111
HotelCalaDiVolpe.com

HÔTEL COSTES
239 rue St-Honoré
75001 Paris, France
Tel.: 33 1 42 44 50 00
HotelCostes.com

HOTEL DE RUSSIE
Via del Babuino 9
Rome 00187, Italy
Tel.: 39 06 32 88 81
HotelDeRussie.it

HÔTEL DU CAP-EDEN-ROC
Boulevard JF Kennedy
06601 Antibes, France
Tel.: 800-566-5356
EdenRoc-hotel.fr

HOTEL LA SCALINATELLA
8 Via Tragara
Capri Town, Capri
Italy 80073
Tel.: 39 081 837 0633

HÔTEL LE BRISTOL
112 Rue Fbg St. Honoré
75008 Paris, France
Tel.: 33 1 5343 430
Hotel-Bristol.com

PLAZA ATHÉNÉE
25 avenue Montaigne
Paris 5008, France
Tel.: 33 866 732 1106
Plaza-Athenee-Paris.com

THE RITZ
15 Place Vendôme
75001 Paris, France
Tel.: 33 1 43 16 30 30
RitzParis.com

CARIBBEAN

EDEN ROCK
Baie de St. Jean
FWI-97133 St. Barthélemy
French West Indies
Tel.: 877-563-7105
EdenRockHotel.com

PARROT CAY
Box 164, Providenciale
Turks and Caicos Islands
Tel.: 649-946-7788
ParrotCay.como.bz

ROUND HILL
John Pringle Drive
P.O. Box 64
Montego Bay, Jamaica
West Indies
Tel.: 876-956-7050
RoundHillJamaica.com

SANDY LANE
St. James, Barbados
BB24024, West Indies
Tel.: 866-444-4080
SandyLane.com

ASIA

CHIVA-SOM RESORT
73/4 Petchkasem Road,
Prachuab Khirikham
77110 Thailand
Tel.: 66 3251 1154
Chivasom.com

LE MÉRIDIEN BORA BORA
Motu Tape BP 190
Bora Bora, French Polynesia
Tel.: 689-60-5151
StarwoodHotels.com/Lemeridien

THE PENINSULA
Salisbury Road
Kowloon, Hong Kong, SAR
Tel.: 866-382-8388
HongKong.Peninsula.com

RAFFLES
1 Beach Road
Singapore 189673
Tel.: 800-637-9477
Raffles.com

ANYWHERE

FOUR SEASONS
Tel.: 800-819-5053
FourSeasons.com

ANYWHERE, IN A PINCH

THE RITZ-CARLTON
Tel.: 800-542-8680
RitzCarlton.com

CHAPTER SEVEN / TYCOONS ON THE MOVE

FLOAT SOME & JET SOME

"It is absolutely excessive. No question about it. But it's amazing what you can get used to."

—LARRY ELLISON, ON HIS 454-FOOT GIGAYACHT, *RISING SUN*

LOOK AT YOU GO—A MEMBER OF THE most mobile tribe in human history and you never even have to drive! Soon, you'll be zipping around town in the back of a bombproof fortress, jetting off to Nice on an hour's notice, and cruising down to Cuba for the hell of it. And to think you once flew *standby*.

Yes, it's exhausting to be perpetually on the move, but recent advances in filthy rich transport will ease the pain, allowing you to venture wherever you want, whenever you want, in the grand style you're accustomed to. Never again will you funnel lotions into 2.5-ounce bottles or be patted down like a common perp. (You've got a polo match to get to, goddamnit, and the sheikh hates waiting.)

Considering that you'll be burning at least $5,000 an hour in your private jet (or, PJ, so as not to offend the less fortunate) and probably 30 times that just to gas up your gigayacht, you'll want to maximize the emotional return on your investments. In the design phase, this means any over-the-top whims you've been too embarrassed to indulge on terra firma are back in play. Always dreamed of having your own professional recording studio despite an utter lack of talent? Rock on, cap'n! This is just the sort of flourish that will give your boat 'zazz in the eyes of your fellow yachtsman.

Perhaps as penance, the Filthy Rich prefer understated cars during the work week, which means no Italian jobs or vintage Rolls-Royces, and certainly no limos (unless you're okay with strangers assuming you're a capitalist pig before they've even heard what you do for a living).

As the most public symbols of your exceptional wealth and taste, for better and for worse, how you roll speaks volumes.

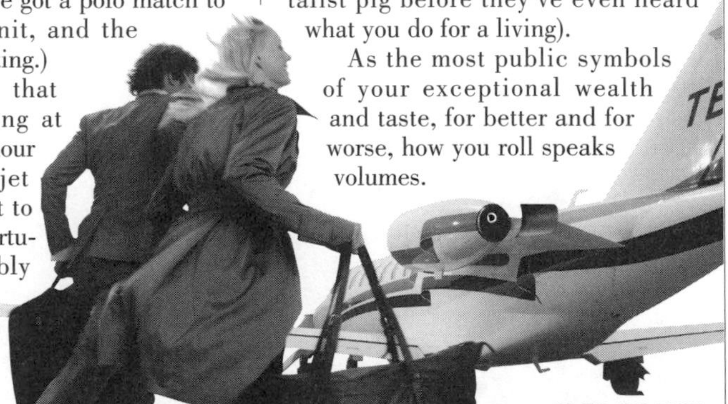

UP, UP, AND AWAY

BY LAND

CAR AND STRIVER

Whip-Smart Rides for Backseat Drivers

WITH SO MANY MODELS ON THE MARKET, YOU'D THINK THERE'D BE A DECENT RANGE of acceptable autos. Like countless arrivistes before you, you would be wrong. In a time when gym teachers lease yellow Hummers, the very rich opt for either menacingly incognito or tastefully anonymous. Indeed, you'd glance past most of these cars unless you'd seen their sticker prices. A proper wealth wagon comes fully loaded in the color of your choice (as long as it's black), and is purchased outright, never leased.

CADILLAC ESCALADE

CURB APPEAL: Perhaps the only thing the President and half of hip-hop agree on: The Escalade's tanklike ability to dominate the road compels even Hollywood egomaniacs to buy them. And Giles will just *adore* the rearview camera when he's parking this beast. **WHAT IT SAYS:** "Step aside, scumbag, coming through." **LESSER OPTIONS:** GMC Suburban or Yukon Denali

MERCEDES G-WAGEN

CURB APPEAL: Its angles are a bit Nazi-ish for some tastes, but Nicole Richie doesn't seem to mind, nor does the Pope, whose eponymous "mobile" was built on its chassis. **WHAT IT SAYS:** "After Pilates class, I may invade Poland." **LESSER OPTION:** Range Rover

MAYBACH 62

CURB APPEAL: Sensing a market for cars that cost twice as much as the average home, Mercedes-Benz dipped deep into its archives in 2002. Every year since, 1,000 picky plutocrats have made the pilgrimage to Sindelfingen to specify a handful of the over 2 million options available on the Maybach—from the burl of the dashboard wood to the fabric on the fully reclining back-

seats. It takes two weeks to build each one by hand, and no two are exactly alike. **WHAT IT SAYS:** "My other car is a Sikorsky chopper." **LESSER OPTION:** Rolls-Royce Phantom

LEXUS LS HYBRID

CURB APPEAL: The carbon-conscious from Malibu to Montecito rejoiced when Lexus unveiled this overpriced, marginally more fuel-efficient version of its bestselling sedan. *Finally,* an excuse to junk all those glorified golf carts! (Or, uh, recycle them or something.) **WHAT IT SAYS:** "Please don't ask me about my other six cars." **LESSER OPTION:** The indignity of the Prius

MERCEDES S-CLASS

CURB APPEAL: The S stands for *Sonderklasse,* which is German for "special class," so already you have something in common. The most popular luxury sedan in the world, it's the taxicab of the Filthy Rich. Sure, BMW makes better cars for *driving,* but Benz is the ultimate riding machine. **WHAT IT SAYS:** "The whole Maybach thing's a bit much, wouldn't you say?" **LESSER OPTION:** BMW 7 Series

WEEKEND WHEELS

ASTON MARTIN VANQUISH S

CURB APPEAL: A limited-edition dose of British refinement, it hits 200 mph with just the slightest of taps. Monogrammed slippers not included. **WHAT IT SAYS:** "Bonds. Junk Bonds."

BENTLEY AZURE CONVERTIBLE

CURB APPEAL: A collector's piece since 1919, only 400 of these land yachts are assembled each year. There's nothing like feeling the summer breeze through your wispy white comb-over. **WHAT IT SAYS:** "I own several pairs of yellow pants."

FERRARI

CURB APPEAL: Because at one point or another, every Filthy Rich man must be "that guy." **WHAT IT SAYS:** "I am Paulo. You like to dance?"

DRIVEN TO DISTRACTION

Filthy Rich Autophiles

THE SULTAN OF BRUNEI

THE WORLD'S FLUSHEST monarch owns between 3,000 and 5,000 vehicles; no one's sure. In 1998, a British car magazine ran illicit photos of his garage revealing a peculiar taste for custom station wagons fashioned out of Bentleys and Ferraris. **OWNS:** You name it, he's got one. Or six. For starters, there's his Lamborghini Diablo Jota, Bugatti EB110, Jaguar XJR-15, over 500 Rolls-Royces, and every winning car driven by a Formula One World Drivers Champion since 1980.

4-WHEEL DRIVE
Extreme Collector
Jay Leno

JAY LENO

MIDDLE AMERICA'S favorite late-night jokesmith owns over 85 vintage cars and 70 motorcycles, which he stores in a 17,000-foot garage in Burbank, California. According to Leno lore, he drives a different one each day. **OWNS:** Mattel put out a line of Hot Wheels based on his collection, which includes a 1951 Hudson Hornet, Porsche Carrera GT, 1906 Baker electric car, and 1906 Stanley Steamer (he's a sucker for fixer-uppers).

JERRY SEINFELD

THE RETIRED FUNNYMAN'S Porsche fixation requires its own townhouse on Manhattan's Upper West Side. **OWNS:** Over 300 Porsches—including a coveted 959, which he snagged for $700,000. Only 268 were ever built, and none were even street-legal until fellow 959 owners Paul Allen and Bill Gates pressured President Clinton to sign a "show and display" law easing emissions and crash-test standards in 2003. True story.

CUSTOM RIDES FOR MOVING TARGETS

As the world goes mad and the wealth trench widens, standard security options are no longer sufficient. So jittery tycoons—including more than 40 world leaders and, ahem, **Posh** and **Becks**—ship their vehicles to Carat Duchatelet, a Belgian defense contractor with a sideline in kidnapping and assassination prevention. Its patented "armored shells," in concert with an array of à la carte add-ons (self-sealing fuel tanks, oxygen supply systems, minesweepers . . . the odd gun turret), protect passengers from threats big and small.

BY AIR

INTO THIN AIR

Cracking the Jumbo Jet Set

"You have the pilots at your throat about vacation, that their wife is pregnant, why can't they have New Year's Eve off? It's on and on and on."
—GOVERNOR ARNOLD SCHWARZENEGGER, ON THE PERILS OF GULFSTREAM OWNERSHIP

THE FAA PREDICTS 22,000 PRIVATE JETS will be operating in the U.S. by 2020. When that many people are on to something, can it still be considered a luxury? You can probably tell where this is headed...

Hell, even notorious tightwad Warren Buffett gets it. When the Oracle of Omaha bought his first PJ in 1989, he dubbed it the "Indefensible" and mocked it in a shareholders' report. He christened his second purchase, in 1995, the "Indispensable"; today, he owns NetJets (see p. 157). Timber billionaire Tim Blixseth took his love a little further, naming his dogs Learjet and G2. It's a simple fact—when you're as busy and in demand as you are, you simply don't have the patience to push aside strangers, watch minimum wagers rifle through your Valextra, or make small talk with "road warriors" in stale airport lounges. Time is money, and it would be irresponsible to fritter it away.

JETIQUETTE

To bolster your karmic rating, it's customary to offer lifts to the less fortunate whenever possible. In Palm Beach, St. Barts, and Aspen, bumming PJ rides is practically a sport. Should you ever find yourself stranded, simply wait on the edge of the tarmac with your luggage until someone you know strolls by. When they do, just be sure to keep in mind the following passenger faux pas:

- **Telling strangers in the terminal whose plane you're on**
- **Wearing sweats**
- **Delaying takeoff**
- **Approaching the flight deck uninvited**
- **Forgetting to send a thank-you note**
- **Tipping (they're not flying for you, idiot)**
- **Offering to pay for the fuel or flight time**
- **Comparing any aspect of the PJ with other PJs (particularly your own)**

INITIAL ASCENT

Picking Out Your PJ

DASSAULT FALCON 7X

DETAILS: Falcon owners love to brag about the military pedigree of this fighter jet tricked out for corporate titans. It can fly 5,950 miles with eight passengers and three crewmembers and hit a maximum speed of Mach .90. Twenty-eight windows line the fuselage to maximize natural light.

Price: $41 million

CESSNA CITATION X

DETAILS: It only seats seven and the cabin's a bit crammed, but, at 600 miles per hour, it's the fastest PJ out there. (At Mach .92, it approaches the speed of sound.) The Citation is well suited for U.S. travel, since it can fly 3,300 nautical miles

SUPERSIZE ME
When a Gulfstream Won't Do

The trouble with small jets is that you live large. Which is why you might want to buy a retired commercial airliner and have it refitted. Some frequent flyers who traded up:

JOHN TRAVOLTA Boeing 707: The "Jett Clipper Ella" (for his son, Jett, and daughter, Ella) has its own runway leading up to the door of the actor's Florida compound, Jumbolair.

SERGEY BRIN & LARRY PAGE Boeing 767: Designed to hold 224 passengers, it's been retrofitted for 50.

DONALD TRUMP Boeing 727: You might be surprised to learn that a 30-foot-long Trump logo is emblazoned on the fuselage.

SHELDON ADELSON Boeing 767: The richest man you've never heard of uses his to shuttle his family back and forth between Las Vegas and his various gambling meccas in Asia.

PAUL ALLEN Two Boeing 767s: Never one to be outdone, Allen is the proud owner of not one, but two of the largest jumbo jets ever made. The man's got a lot of friends, apparently.

WING AND A PRAYER
Captain Travolta Prepares for Take-off

without refueling (New York to L.A., with a pit stop in Palo Alto), but you'll need a bigger rig for intercontinental jaunts.

Price: $20.5 million

BOMBARDIER CHALLENGER 605

DETAILS: Canadian outfit Bombardier turned people onto PJs in the first place with its swanky (if crash-prone) Learjet, which ruled the skies through the '60s and '70s. Its latest bestseller offers three floor plans to seat 9 to 12 passengers, and can fly 4,045 nautical miles at a maximum speed of Mach .82.

Price: $26.7 million

GULFSTREAM G550

DETAILS: Behold, the Gulfstream against which all others are measured. Maxing out at 9 miles per minute (Mach .885) and a cruising altitude of 51,000 feet, it can travel up to 6,750 nautical miles (JFK to Narita) on a single tank of gas. Its 96-foot cabin seats 14 to 18 passengers, depending on legroom.

Price: $47 million

GOEING, BOEING...GONE

All Aboard "The Flying Palace"

The Airbus A380 is the world's largest passenger jet and, thanks to a recent impulse buy, the most expensive plane ever purchased for personal use. Its mystery owner–a particularly Dionysian Gulf State royal–shelled out $300 million for the so-called Superjumbo as soon as it hit the market. It can travel 9,000 miles without refueling (Honolulu to Rio), but is far too large to land at small airports, so his highness will need something a bit more manageable should he ever head to Telluride. In an economy-class configuration, it can seat 853 passengers, but you can bet his natural gas reserves it won't be set up quite that way.

Whoever he is, he's given jet-set designer Edése Doret a $150 million budget to finish the A380's 6,640-square-foot cabin. His grand vision includes a combination screening/sitting room, wet bar, custom bookcase (to display a scale version of the owner's jumbo yacht, naturally), 14-seat dining room, double-decker lounge with low tables, Persian rugs, and an elaborate mural of the desert. You know, to keep the hippie vibe going.

PRICE: $300 MILLION

RUNWAY REPORT

Tips for Touching Down in Style

SHOCKING AS IT SOUNDS, your capital-sapping puddle jumper will arrive with nary a hook to hang your blazer on. You must now spend $3 to $30 million painting, furnishing, and customizing it.

To start with, you'll want all the latest airborne-office gadgetry (WiFi, plasma TVs, iPod docks, what have you), and a comfy perch to watch the clouds go by. If it's big enough, you'll also want a screening room, and a bedroom for overnight flights and daytime assignations.

The Google guys famously hung hammocks in their 767, though that's probably a bit paramilitary for most tastes. One group of very frequent flyers, a family of Gulf-state royals, had closed-circuit cameras mounted on the wings of their jet so they could enjoy the view without craning their necks. Nike's Dassault Falcon 2000EX is painted to resemble the sole of a running shoe.

You might also consider an exercise nook, a Jacuzzi (too heavy for most jets, but Tom Cruise's G-IV has one), or solid-gold floor tiles (why the hell not?). Donald Trump has a sauna on his 727—and 24-carat gold-plated seatbelt buckles. In general, you'll find weight restrictions to be your greatest limiting factor, followed by the panty-waists at the FAA. Taste, as you've probably gathered, is not an issue.

CASTING YOUR CREW

- **PILOT** "Top Gun" grad with soothing baritone; Midwestern discretion; ability to land on short, sandy airstrips in subtropical locales
- **COPILOT** All of the former, but less grizzled
- **FLIGHT ATTENDANT** (Preferably three.) Disarmingly sexy; able to mix martinis at a 45-degree angle; impeccable bedside manner; ability to keep her mouth shut

IT'S EASY BEING GREEN

The Magic of "Carbon Offsets"

FLYERS WHO FEEL GUILTY ABOUT THEIR CO_2 output, but have no intention of altering their lifestyles even one iota, now have an option: the carbon offset. It's quite simple, really. For every cubic meter of ozone-depleting gases your various jets spew forth, you pay some crunchy type to remove an equal quantity of carbon from the atmosphere. As this is physically impossible, your "offsets" will typically be put toward a long-term project like Amazonian reforestation, or the landscaping of a windmill farm in Palm Springs. But don't worry about the pesky details. For your purposes, it's a zero sum equation: You pollute the environment jetting back and forth to St. Barts all winter, then you pay someone to make it all better. With your green conscience cleansed, be sure to brag about how "carbon neutral" you are. It's the new "antifur."

MILE HIGH CLUBS

Where Moguls Learn to Share

"Life is too short to stand in line."
—AVION PRIVATE JET CLUB MOTTO

While awaiting delivery of your PJ, you might consider fractional ownership–but only out of absolute necessity. Ever since fly-by-night operations like Jumpjet began offering sliver-sized shares to suburban dermatologists, the industry has suffered a bit of an image crisis in certain filthy rich circles. But that's neither here nor there. Fact is, you're jetless, and it's not like you're going to fly commercial.

There are two ways to go about securing a fraction. The easiest option is to buy a prepaid card, which allots you a chunk of flying time. Sounds great until you get to the part about blackout dates, advance booking, and three-hour departure windows. Unless you enjoy paying hundreds of thousands of dollars to be treated like a FedEx package, this method is not for you.

The far superior option is to buy a slice of a specific PJ, or several slices of multiple PJs, to ensure you always have the right plane for the right occasion. NetJets is the industry leader, but buying shares in Air Royale, Avion, CitationShares, or Flexjet is acceptable. Just remember that all PJs are not created equal. Through NetJets, a sixteenth share of a Hawker 400XP will run you about $406,250, whereas a sixteenth share of a Gulfstream G550 will set you back $2.6 million. (Guess which is cooler.)

MAN OVERBOARD
A Classic Stinkpot

BY SEA

TO HULL WITH IT

Boating with the Big Fish

"I promise you, it's not about size, it really isn't."
—BARRY DILLER, ON HIS 305-FOOT SAILBOAT, *EOS*

WHETHER YOU ACTUALLY WANT ONE or not, you *will* buy a yacht. You must. You're simply not Filthy Rich until you've conquered the high seas. It's not just the megamillion-dollar purchase price; it's the implied priorities. A serious stinkpot shows people you value your privacy, appreciate the outdoors, and have so much cash you can piss it away like last night's Lafite.

When J. P. Morgan launched his 98-meter *Corsair II* in the early 1900s he ignited a century-long love affair with floating wood. Now, everyone wants a boat. And they want them big. Today, there are 7,000 boats over 80-feet long floating worldwide, and another 700 under construction. Orders for gigayachts over 150-feet long have doubled just in the past decade.

To get a respectably sized vessel from one of the world's better boatyards—Trinity Yachts, Feadship, Blohm + Voss, Benetti, or Lürssen—expect to wait at least two years, though it will likely take longer than that. You could, of course, buy a used one, but only if it has provenance, like the *Christina O*, Grecian playboy Ari Onassis's fabled panty-dropper (sadly it isn't for sale).

Whatever you do, don't ponder your purchase for too long. It will only make you question your sanity. Just hold your breath and walk the plank.

ALL HANDS ON DECK

AT THE BARE MINIMUM, YOU'LL NEED TO HIRE THE FOLLOWING CREW MEMBERS. OR, BETter yet, have the captain do it. (You'll need *someone* to blame.)

CAPTAIN

British or French; a spinner of yarns; closet alcoholic; merciless with the paps; sleeping with the Second Cook

FIRST MATE

All of the above, minus the bulbous gut and cancerous nose; an avid surfer/diver/boozer

ENGINEER

Degree from University of Istanbul; brilliant; reclusive; chubby

CHIEF STEWARDESS

Swedish, Kiwi, or South African; very blonde; very tan; very thin; very white; happiest in a bikini; 25 to 35

DECKHAND

Czech, Australian, or South African; perfectly bronzed and sculpted; constantly shirtless; cheeky; flirtatious; screwing your daughter

STEWARDESS

(At least two) WASP; busty; 18 to 25

HELLO, SAILOR! A Typical Deck-Hand

LAUNDRESS

Filipina; cheery; silent; capable of removing Pinot Noir from any linen garment

HEAD COOK

Yours, from home. Worked at a four-star restaurant; trained under a famous chef; can squeeze a five-course meal out of a single zucchini

SECOND COOK

Sexy; Brazilian; knows her way around a potato peeler; makes a mean tapioca

CAT

Short-haired calico picked up in Corsica; the Engineer's first mate; goes by "Cat"

NAMING YOUR BOAT

Traditionalists insist it's bad luck to use the same moniker twice (*Splurge I* and *Splurge II*) or to change a boat's name. Ignore these bores, change names on a whim, and number your boats as you buy them. (The Forbes family is on their fifth *Highlander.*) Women's names are always up for grabs (*Lady Anne*), but since your personal life changes with the tide, it's better to go mythical (*Méduse*). You can choose a name that makes sense only to you (*Tatoosh*), or one that evokes omnipotence (*Octopus*). Just be sure you can say it with a straight face. (Clearly, *Skat* owner Charles Simonyi doesn't speak German.)

SPLASHING OUT

It's What's Inside That Counts

YOU MAY HAVE REFINED TASTE WHEN it comes to your houses, but rest assured, you will leave it onshore. To set your boat apart from all the other $20 million wonders, you'll first need the imprimatur of a boldface designer. Popular choices include Fulvio de Simoni, Lazzarini Pickering Architetti, and Zuccon International Project Studio.

Out on the water, anything goes, and don't let them tell you otherwise. Newspaper tycoon Duane Hagadone told his team, "Give me some sizzle!" and ended up with an 18-hole golf course on the deck of the *Lady Lola;* snake-obsessed fashion guru Roberto Cavalli's Wally Boat has leather floors, python armchairs, and goat-skin walls.

Whatever motif you go with, just be sure to showcase as much wood as possible. It helps remind everyone that they're actually on a boat. As always, trust your instinct. Don't worry if everything looks heinous the first time around. There's absolutely no shame in getting your yacht "refitted" (gutted, redesigned, and redecorated) on a biannual basis. In fact, it's expected.

HEAD OF ITS CLASS
A Master Bath

CAPTAIN'S CRUNCH

Boating by the Numbers

A yacht is a hole in the water into which you pour money, a destitute tycoon once said. These days, they're so ruinously expensive even the Gettys rent theirs out (granted, for $320,000 a week). Think of it this way: For $20 million, you could either buy an emerging software startup from your teenage neighbor, or 140 feet of teak and steel. ($75 million gets you another hundred feet.) Then there's the annual operating cost, typically 10 percent of the purchase price. Oh, and fuel: It costs around $785,400 for the 224,400 gallons of gas needed to top up the tank on Paul Allen's *Octopus*. When you tally it all up, it would make more sense to lob a grenade at your Bugatti. At least you'd get the insurance.

PHOENIX RISING
Your Very Own Super Sub

TOYS AHOY!

Must-Have Accessories

PHOENIX 1000 SUBMERSIBLE

If your boat is the toy you show the world, your 213-foot sub is just for you. Literally. U.S. Submarines has built only one of these 5,000-square-foot sea monsters, and is looking for a buyer. If $20 million is more your speed, they also offer the 118-foot Seattle 1000.

PRICE: $65 million

EUROCOPTER AS 350 B3

Choppers are expensive, loud, dangerous, difficult to fly, and utterly indispensable. This model is a mid-range copter with seating for four.

PRICE: $2.4–$4 million

ANOTHER YACHT

Known as a "shadow boat," your second yacht acts as a floating garage-cum-entertainment center. It's where you house your screening room, helicopters, cars, Jet Skis, motorcycles, submarines, and unruly guests. Shadow Marine customizes 150- to 280-foot versions.

PRICE: Upon Request

N971AE

TOP CHOP
The Eurocopter

O. LORDY
The Christina and Her Tender

YACHT SPOTTING

Boats You Need to Know

Dubai

525 FEET (2006)

OWNER: Dubai ruler Sheikh Mohammed bin Rashid Al Maktoum **WOW FACTORS:** Nearly the length of two football fields, it's rumored to have a flight deck, submarine hold, and disco, but rarely leaves Dubai, so no one's sure. **WHERE TO SPOT:** Jebel Ali, Dubai

Prince Abdul Aziz

482 FEET (1984)

OWNER: King Abdullah of Saudi Arabia **WOW FACTORS:** Interior by Buckingham Palace favorite David Hicks, glass-topped retractable pool cover, private hospital, and 65-person crew. **WHERE TO SPOT:** Malta; Marbella, Spain

Atlantis II

380 FEET (1981)

OWNER: The Niarchos family **WOW FACTORS:** Twelve guest suites, 28-seat dining room, 40-seat movie theater, and swimming pool. The paps are obsessed with this boat. **WHERE TO SPOT:** Port Hercule, Monaco

EOS

305 FEET (2006)

OWNER: Media mogul Barry Diller **WOW FACTORS:** Its $200 million price tag, for starters. Interiors maven François Catroux made sure he spared no expense. The silverware alone cost $200,000. A triple-masted schooner, it's the world's largest sailing vessel. **WHERE TO SPOT:** Cannes; St. Barts

Christina O

323 FEET (1943, REFITTED IN 2001)

OWNER: Greek businessman John Paul Papanicolaou **WOW FACTORS:** At the touch of a button, the pool bottom rises and becomes a dance floor. The stools in "Ari's Bar" were originally covered in whale foreskin. **WHERE TO SPOT:** Marseilles, France; Santorini, Greece

Limitless

315 FEET (1997)

OWNER: Limited Brands CEO Les Wexner **WOW FACTORS:** Credited with kicking off the gigayacht trend, it features a 41-foot-wide deck swathed in 3,000-square-feet of teak. **WHERE TO SPOT:** Palma, Mallorca

Talitha G

247 FEET (1929, REFITTED IN 1993)

OWNER: The Gettys **WOW FACTORS:** A celebrity charter favorite (Tom Cruise, Hugh Grant), the late J. Paul Getty's refitted classic is the filthy richest stinkpot on the high seas, from its working fireplaces, to its antique elevator, to its old-world canvas awnings. A tasteful 12-guests max. **WHERE TO SPOT:** Corfu, Greece; Panama City, Panama; the Maldives

Privacy

155 FEET (2004)

OWNER: Golf phenom Tiger Woods **WOW FACTORS:** $150,000 scuba system and inflatable decompression chamber. **WHERE TO SPOT:** Star Island, Florida

The Highlander V

151 FEET (1986)

OWNER: The Forbes family **WOW FACTORS:** The fifth Forbes yacht has 14 "heads" and a Bell Jet Ranger III helicopter. **WHERE TO SPOT:** New York City

TESTING THE WATERS

Try Before You Buy

To kill time while your yacht is under construction, it's perfectly acceptable to charter. Consider the 408-foot *Savorona* with its Turkish bath built from 260 tons of hand-carved marble **($455,000 per week)**. If you're looking for something more intimate, the crew on the 230-foot *Absinthe* will ferry you up to Alaska for a bit of off-yacht heli-skiing **($252,000 per week)**. If kids are in the picture, you could do worse than the pirate-themed, 265-foot *Bart Roberts*, complete with 400-gallon piranha tank. After tucking in the twins, the stripper pole–accented dance floor could be just the thing to spice up your failing marriage (**$350,000 per week**). For a more classical stinkpot experience, try the *Reverie*, the *Turama*, or the *Alysia*, which tops out at **$1,000,000 per week**. You might also consider befriending the Latsis clan. The Greek shipping dynasty's invitation-only club, PrivateSea, is essentially a high-end boatshare, with membership capped at 100. Anywhere from **$200,000 to $1.4 million** buys you access to a variety of charters, the world's better yacht clubs, and VIP tickets to events like the America's Cup. (Not that you need their help.)

SERIOUS SHIP
The Alysia

OFF THE DEEP END

Larry Ellison vs. Paul Allen vs. Roman Abramovich

WHO SAYS DUELING IS DEAD? ORACLE chief Larry Ellison, Microsoft cofounder Paul Allen, and Russian oligarch Roman Abramovich are engaged in a three-way battle royale to build the biggest, baddest stinkpot yet. In 2000, Allen launched the **300-foot *Tatoosh*,** only to be upstaged by Abramovich's **370-foot *Le Grand Bleu*.** (It has a 72-foot sailboat on deck, should the mood

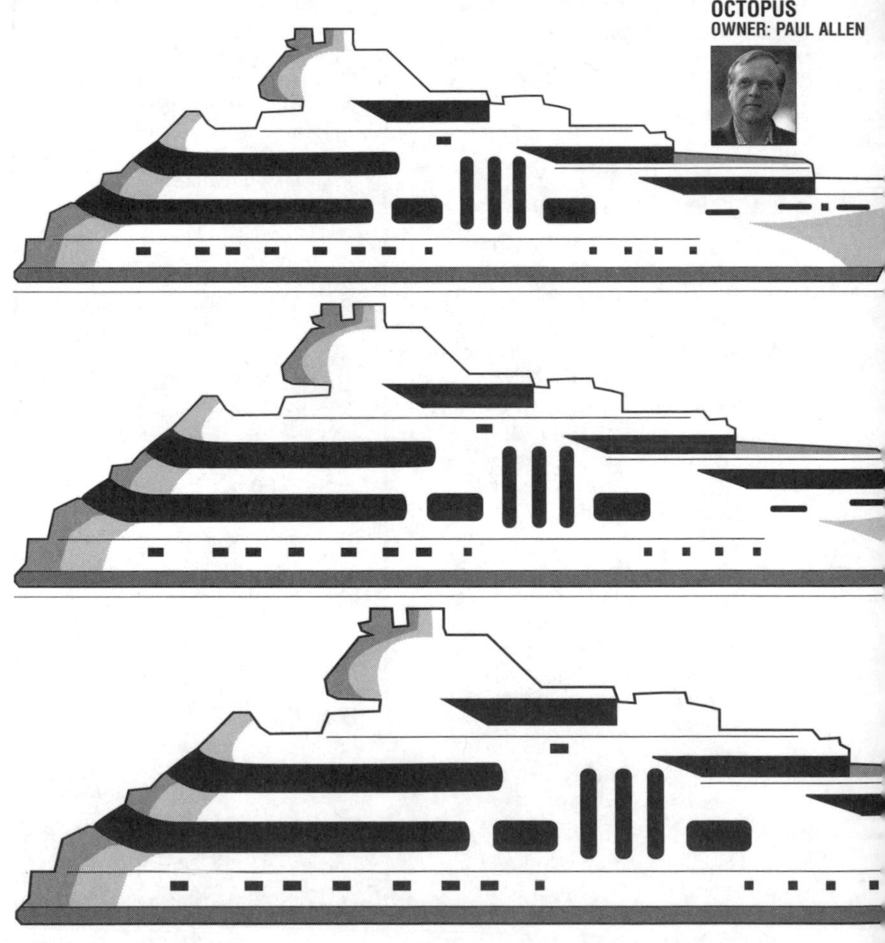

strike him.) Adding insult, Abramovich promptly one-upped himself with a second boat, the **377-foot *Pelorus*** (it's supposedly bulletproof).

In 2003, it was Allen's turn to leave Abramovich in his wake with the $250 million, **414-foot *Octopus*,** a six-story dork fantasia with a glass-bottom living room, basketball court, helipad, and recording studio. He also flashed the coolest toy yet: The lower deck's docking station conceals a yellow submarine.

By the time Abramovich got around to launching his **282-foot *Ecstasea*** with its dual helipads and Chinese-themed interior, he hardly made a ripple.

414 FT

Meanwhile, the famously competitive Ellison was biding his time, spending his days talking shop at the Lürssen shipyard—the same one that had recently launched the *'Pus*. Originally, Ellison had ordered up a **392.5-footer,** but then decided on an impromptu upgrade. Looking very much like a floating condominium, Ellison's five-story, 80-room ***Rising Sun*** was launched in 2004. At **454 feet,** it's almost 60 feet longer than he had initially planned and 40 feet longer than *Octopus*. Coincidence?

But the race isn't over yet. Abramovich is about to roll out the ***Eclipse*,** which is designed to do just that. A 525-foot, **$300-million** floating city, it will be the largest privately owned boat in the world. Until Allen and Ellison decide to upgrade.

454 FT

RISING SUN
OWNER: LARRY ELLISON

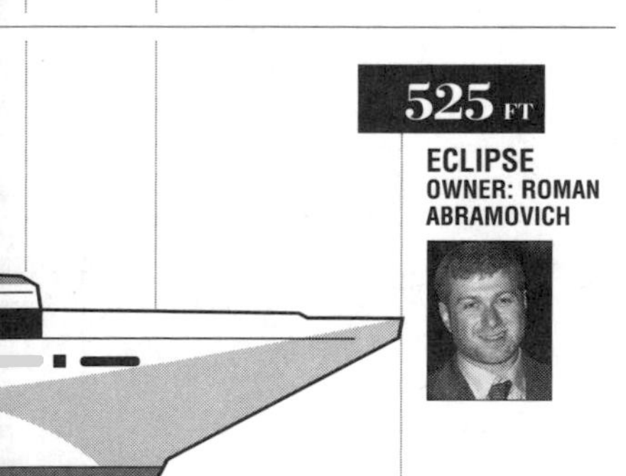

CAVEAT EMPTOR

THE PROBLEM WITH GOING GIGA

Bigger is always better . . . except when it's not. Since Paul Allen dropped $250 million on *Octopus* and Larry Ellison put $200 million into *Rising Sun*, both men have discovered there isn't anywhere to park them. Most ports simply aren't deep enough to accommodate floating mansions. So, instead of docking next to their fellow plutocrats, they find themselves paying $25 million in annual maintenance fees to anchor (or, in the case of the *'Pus*, hover anchorless with the help of some fancy-pants gadgetry) next to oil tankers and trash barges. When Allen and his *'Pus* hit the French Riviera, he has to stay several miles offshore, and chopper in his dinner guests. It's only a matter of time until the yacht clubs catch up with the gigayachts, but until then, these guys are out to sea.

WALLYPALOOZA!

The Cult of the Wally Boat

IN 1994, LUCA BASSANI EMERGED FROM the port of Monte Carlo with a new kind of craft he called the Wally Boat. Flying in the face of the "white hull" school of yacht design, it was lightweight and carbon-colored, with high-tech gizmos galore, a loft-style interior, and mid-century modern-esque Italian furnishings. Its breakthrough bells and whistles—electronic sail controls, retractable propellers, lines that run under the deck to avoid entangling the crew—made it possible for a crew of 4 to do the work of 10 or 20. It was also insanely fun to sail.

And so it began. Today, there's a Wally for everyone, from the 36-foot WallyNano, which can be sailed solo (and loaded on your gigayacht), to the Wally 143, Bassani's answer to the Love Boat-style stinkpot.

At the Maxi Rolex Cup in Sardinia these days, Wallys comprise about a third of the entrants. Not bad for a kid from Monaco.

SEXY BEAST
The Wally 143

HOW WASPS STAY AFLOAT

Since debuting in 1994, the 36-foot Hinckley Picnic Boat has taken pride of place alongside Nantucket Reds in the hearts of New England blue bloods and their imitators. Inside its hand-built wooden exterior is a jet-propelled engine that maxes out at 28 knots. But all anyone really talks about is the patented "Jetstick," which allows for stationary 360-degree turns and parallel docking. (Yes, it's gin-and-tonic-proof.) The latest model, which can be outfitted with a gas grill or icebox, but not both, will set you back between $500,000 and $750,000–all for a vessel you can't spend the night on.

RUNS ON TRISCUITS
The Hinckley Picnic Boat

YOU GOTTA REGATTA

Sailing Is a Summer Sport—Unless You're Loaded

JANUARY

KEY WEST RACE WEEK
(Key West, Florida)
Top off your tan while bagging a trophy at this five-day spectacle launched in the 1980s.

VALLARTA RACE
(San Diego, California)
Race to Mexico with intrepid members of the San Diego Yacht Club—including multiple generations of the Scripps family, who've been doing it since 1953.

MARCH

ST. MAARTEN HEINEKEN REGATTA
(St. Maarten)
While purists decry the commercialism, more than 250 yachts join the fun in Simpson Bay.

APRIL

ANTIGUA CLASSIC YACHT REGATTA
(Antigua)
The Filthy Rich have been sipping Mount Gay while riding the Caribbean breeze since the first race back in '67.

NEWPORT TO ENSENADA RACE
(Newport Beach, California)
Join the throng of elite sailors (449 entries in 2007) for this race to Mexico, which once lured Humphrey Bogart and newsman Walter Cronkite.

MAY

LEUKEMIA CUP REGATTA
(San Diego, California)
Hit this San Diego Yacht Club regatta after the Newport to Ensenada for a charitable sail with some of the world's best.

JUNE

AMERICA'S CUP MATCH (varies)
Billionaire boatsmen from all over the globe come to whip it out and see whose is biggest. The oldest and most prestigious trophy in international sports, "Auld Mug" is the Holy Grail of sailing.

NEWPORT BERMUDA RACE
(Newport, Rhode Island)
Launched in 1906, this preppy rite of passage must be completed in 56 hours if you want to take home the Lighthouse trophy.

BLOCK ISLAND RACE WEEK
(Block Island, Rhode Island)
Old salts and new money flock to this 185-nautical-mile race, first held in 1946.

JULY

EDGARTOWN YACHT CLUB REGATTA
(Edgartown, Massachusetts)
The apex of Vineyard yachting since 1923.

AUGUST

NEW YORK YACHT CLUB CRUISE
(Newport, Rhode Island)
Pull on your Breton Red trousers for this annual week of races and beer blasts.

SEPTEMBER

BLUE NOSE REGATTA
(Grosse Pointe, Michigan)
Self-mocking old-money types have been gathering at the Grosse Pointe Yacht Club to race on Lake Saint Clair since 1924.

OCTOBER–DECEMBER

Your work here is done. Time to hit the slopes!

ALIVE WITH PLEASURE
Newport to Ensenada

DIRECTORY

AUTO DEALERS

THE COLLECTION
Porsche, Ferrari, Maserati, Aston Martin, Lotus . . .
200 Bird Road
Coral Gables, FL 33146
Tel.: 305-444-5555
TheCollection.com

MANHATTAN MOTOR CARS
Bentley, Lamborghini, Porsche, Rolls-Royce, Spyker.
270 Eleventh Avenue
New York, NY 10001
Tel.: 888-808-6068
ManhattanMotorcars.com

ASTON MARTIN OF NEW ENGLAND
Vicar of vintage Aston Martins.
85 Linden Street
Waltham, MA 02452
Tel.: 781-547-5959
AstonMartin_Lotus.com

FLETCHER JONES MOTOR CARS
Top shop for Maybach and Mercedes.
3300 Jamboree Blvd.
Newport Beach, CA 92660
Tel.: 949-718-3014
MbzSales.com

WIDE WORLD OF CARS
BMW, Ferrari, Maserati . . .
125 East Route 59
Spring Valley, NY 10977
Tel.: 845-425-2600

LAMBORGHINI OF ORANGE COUNTY
Premier supplier of Italian cop magnets.
2441 S. Pullman Street
Santa Ana, CA 92705
Tel.: 714-546-4000

BRITISH AUTO SPECIALISTS
Jaguar, Land Rover, MG, Triumph . . .
2216 Solona Street
Fort Worth, TX 76117
Tel.: 817-589-7974
BritAuto.net

RARE & VINTAGE RIDES

THE AUTO COLLECTIONS
World's largest classic car showroom.
3535 Las Vegas Blvd. South
Las Vegas, NV 89109
Tel.: 702 794-3174
AutoCollections.com

CLASSIC SHOWCASE
On-site restoration specialists.
913 Rancheros Drive
San Marcos, CA 92069
Tel.: 780-747-9947
ClassicShowcase.com

COPLEY MOTOR CARS
Vintage Land Rover and Mercedes.
37 Chestnut Street
Needham, MA 02492
Tel.: 781-444-4646
CopleyMotorCars.com

DRAGONE CLASSIC MOTOR CARS INC.
Family-run autophile emporium.
1797 Main Street
Bridgeport, CT 06604
Tel.: 203-335-4643
DragoneClassics.com

THOMAS HAMANN
Serious collectors only.
1117 East Putnam Avenue
Riverside, CT 06878
Tel.: 203-918-8300
HamannClassicCars.com

HERITAGE CLASSICS
Best showroom in L.A.
8980 Santa Monica Blvd.
West Hollywood, CA 90069
Tel.: 310-657-9699
HeritageClassics.com

EAST COAST ROVER
Vintage Land Rover sales and restoration.
East Coast Rover Co.
13 Merrill Drive
Rockland, ME 04841
Tel.: 207-594-8086
EastCoastRover.com

RACE CAR DEALERS

GRAND PRIX CLASSICS
Historic racing cars.
7456 La Jolla Blvd.
La Jolla, CA 92037
Tel.: 858-459-3500
GrandPrixClassics.cp

FINE SPORTS CARS
Replica racing cars.
8640-3 Villa La Jolla Drive
Suite 3
La Jolla, CA 92037
Tel.: 619-625-3838
FineSportsCars.com

ARMORED CARS

CARAT-DUCHATELET
Pimp your ride.
U.S. office
9917 East Bell Road, Suite 120
Scottsdale, AZ 85260
Tel.: 480-948-9035
Carat-Duchatelet.be

PRIVATE JETS

BOMBARDIER
800 Rene-Levesque Blvd. West
Montreal, Quebec
Canada H3B 1Y8
Tel.: 541-861-9481
Bombardier.com

CESSNA
P.O. Box 7706
Wichita, KS 67277
Tel.: 800-4CESSNA
Cessna.com

DASSAULT
Teterboro Airport
P.O. Box 2000
South Hackensack, NJ 07606
Tel.: 201-440-6700
Dassault-Aviation.com

GULFSTREAM
500 Gulfstream Road, M/S C-10
Savannah, GA 31407
Tel.: 912-965-5555
Gulfstream.com

JET BROKERS

GENERAL AVIATION SERVICES
Sales, brokerage, acquisitions, and consulting.
430 Telser Road
Lake Zurich, IL 60047
Tel.: 847-726-5000
GenAv.com

FRACTIONALS & CHARTERS

AIR ROYALE INTERNATIONAL
Charter away.
9100 Wilshire Blvd.
Suite 420, West Tower
Beverly Hills, CA 90212
Tel.: 310-289-9800
AirRoyale.com

AVANTAIR
Exclusive provider of the Piaggio Avanti P.180—the first flying hybrid.
4311 General Howard Drive
Clearwater, FL 33762
Tel.: 727-539-0071
AvantAir.com

AVION PRIVATE JET CLUB
Priced per seat, a step above first class.
335 North Maple Drive
Suite 208
Beverly Hills, CA 90210
Tel.: 310-281-4888
FlyAvion.com

CITATIONSHARES
Joint venture between Cessna and TAG Aviation. Zip around in small planes; 9 passengers max.
5 American Lane
Greenwich, CT 06831
Tel.: 203-542-3000
CitationShares.com

FLEXJET
Bombardier joins the fractional frenzy.
3400 Waterview, Suite 400
Richardson, TX 75080
Tel.: 800-FLEXJET
FlexJet.com

NETJETS
Air Buffett
581 Main Street
Woodbridge, NJ 07095
Tel.: 877- 356-5823
NetJets.com

PRIVATE JET SERVICES GROUP
Jumbo jets for let.
5 Batchelder Road
Seabrook, NH 03874
Tel.: 603-929-9300
PJSGroup.com

JET COMPLETION CENTERS

LUFTHANSA TECHNIK
German for baller.
Lufthansa Technik AG
Weg Beim Jäger 193
22335 Hamburg, Germany
Tel.: 49 40 5070 3514
Lufthansa-Technik.com

DECRANE AEROSPACE
"For business, VIP and head-of-state aircraft."
8425 Pulsar Place, Suite 340
Columbus, OH 43240
Tel.: 614-848-7700
DecraneAerospace.com

JET INTERIORS

A.I.M.S. INTERNATIONAL
Acoustics and sound reduction.
507 West Ninth Street
Wilmington, DE 19801
Tel.: 514-497-0491
AimsInternational.us

EDÉSE DORET INDUSTRIAL DESIGN
Sky's the limit.
Studios in New York, Texas, England, Ireland, France, Germany, Kuwait, and Sri Lanka
Tel.: 212-928-5431
EdeseDoret.com

SHIPYARDS

BENETTI
In the biz since 1873.
55049 Viareggio
Italy
Tel.: 39 0584 3821
BenettiYachts.it

BLOHM + VOSS
Nearly demolished at the end of WWII. Built Savarona, Enigma, Lady Moura.
Hermann-Blohm-Str. 3
Hamburg D-20457, Germany
Tel.: 49 40 3119 0
BlohmVoss.de

FEADSHIP
Launches five major yachts annually.
U.S. office
801 Seabreeze Boulevard
2nd floor Yachting Center
Suite E, Bahia Mar
Fort Lauderdale, FL 33316
Feadship.nl

LÜRSSEN YACHTS
German shipyard that birthed Paul Allen's Octopus, Barry Diller's Eos, Larry Ellison's Rising Sun.
Fr. Lürssen Werft GmbH & Co. KG
Zum Alten Speicher 11
Bremen-Vegesack 28759, Germany
Tel.: 49 421 6604 166
Lurssen.com

TRINITY YACHTS
Megayachts made in America.
13085 Seaway Road
Gulfport, MS 39503
Tel.: 228-276-1000
TrinityYachts.com

WALLY
8 Avenue des Ligures
MC98000 Monaco
Tel.: 377 9310 0093
Wally.com

YACHT INTERIORS

FRANÇOIS CATROUX
20 rue du Faubourg St. Honoré
Paris 75008, France

SMALL BOATS

THE HINCKLEY COMPANY
Home of the Picnic Boat.
Rhode Island Sales Office
One Little Harbor Landing
Portsmouth, RI 02871
Tel.: 401-683-7005
HinckleyYachts.com

YACHT BROKERS

BURGESS
16/17 Pall Mall
London SW1XSLU, UK

Tel.: 44 20 7766 4300
BurgessYachts.com

DAHM INTERNATIONAL
17, Boulevard Albert 1er
MC-98000 Monaco
Tel.: 377 93 50 25 86
Dahm-International.com

FRASER YACHTS
Full-service yacht specialists.
1800 Southeast 10th Avenue
Suite 400
Fort Lauderdale, FL 33316
Tel.: 954-463-0600
FraserYachts.com
Other locations:
London: 44 20 7016 4480
Milan: 39 02 45 47 09 12
Monaco: 377 93 100 450
Newport Beach: 949-673-5252
New Zealand: 64 9 421 1020
San Diego: 619-225-0588
Seattle: 206-382-9494

YACHT ACCESSORIES

EUROCOPTER
The chopper your helipad's been longing for.
Tel.: 800-873-0001
Eurocopter.com

SHADOW MARINE
Order a mini-yacht (or two) to trail your boat.
1535 SE 17th Street
Suite B201
Fort Lauderdale, FL 33316
Tel.: 954-779-7099
ShadowMarine.com

U.S. SUBMARINES
Next-level toys for extremely bored billionaires.
Offices in Paris, Dubai, Seattle, and Portland
Tel.: 208-687-9057
USSubs.com

YACHT CLUBS

Bad Ass Burgees.

BOSTON YACHT CLUB
Founded in 1866 by Dartmouth alums; 500 members; in its heyday BYC members designed and built ten America's Cup defenders.
1 Front Street
P.O. Box 487
Marblehead, MA 01945
Tel.: 781-631-3100
BostonYachtClub.net

CHICAGO YACHT CLUB
Founded in 1875; two clubhouses: Monroe Station and Belmont Station.
400 East Monroe Street
Chicago, IL 60603
Tel.: 312-540-0312
ChicagoYachtClub.org

EDGARTOWN YACHT CLUB
Founded in 1905; created the Vineyard as you know it.
1 Dock Street
Edgartown MA 02539
Tel.: 508-627-4361
EdgartownYC.org

GROSSE POINTE YACHT CLUB
Founded in 1914; has a bowling alley.
788 Lake Shore Road
Grosse Pointe Shores, MI 48236
Tel.: 313-884-2500
GPYC.org

INDIAN HARBOR YACHT CLUB
Founded in 1889; 15-year waiting list. No cutting.
710 Steamboat Road
Greenwich, CT 06830
Tel.: 203-869-2484
IndianHarborYC.com

NEW YORK YACHT CLUB
Founded in 1884; the queen of clubs; before the Newport clubhouse opened in 1988, it was landlocked in Midtown.
37 West 44th Street
New York, NY 10036
Tel.: 212-382-1000
and
New York Yacht Club
Harbour Court
5 Halidon Avenue
Newport, RI 02840
Tel.: 401-846-1000
NYYC.org

SAN DIEGO YACHT CLUB
Founded in 1886; two-thirds of members own boats, the rest are just posing.
1011 Anchorage Lane
San Diego, CA 92106
Tel.: 619-221-8400
SDYC.org

SAN FRANCISCO YACHT CLUB
Founded in 1869, it's the oldest club on the West Coast.
98 Beach Road
Belvedere, CA 94920
Tel.: 415-435-9133
SFYC.org

SEATTLE YACHT CLUB
Founded in 1892; 3,000 members; newbies can be initiated as early as age ten. (It keeps the bloodlines pure.)
1807 East Hamlin Street
Seattle, WA 98112
Tel.: 206-325-1000
SeattleYachtClub.org

ST. FRANCIS YACHT CLUB
Founded in 1927 in the shadow of the Golden Gate.
On the Marina
San Francisco, CA 94123
Tel.: 415-563-6363
STFYC.com

YACHT CREWS

THE CREW NETWORK
Largest global database of prescreened yacht crew.
1800 SE 10th Avenue
Suite 404
Fort Lauderdale, FL 33316
Tel.: 954-467-9777
CrewNetwork.com
Other locations:
France: 33 4 97 21 13 13
New Zealand: 64 9 302 0178
Barcelona: 34 93 225 9132
Mallorca: 34 971 40 28 78
San Diego: 619-523-8723
Italy: 39 0584 38 01 547

CHAPTER EIGHT / GET A HOBBY

PLAYGROUNDS & PASTIMES

"'What'll we do with ourselves this afternoon?' cried Daisy, 'and the day after that, and the next thirty years?'"

—F. SCOTT FITZGERALD, ***THE GREAT GATSBY***

SOME TYCOONS, LIKE THE SPARTAN Warren Buffett, are said to be happiest with the simple things in life. (Just a book and a lightbulb, as his ex-wife once put it.)

But most are more dedicated materialists, liberally indulging their spoiled inner children at any given chance. They spend their nonworking hours snapping up NBA franchises and failing newspapers, amassing museum-quality art collections, and playing high-goal polo. Selfless types devote their resources to supporting needy causes, such as ballet and Harvard. Self-interested know-it-alls throw their money into politics. The self-deluded dabble in Hollywood.

Even the most middle-class interests get taken to the extreme. Bill Gates collects first editions—by Da Vinci. Curious about journalism, real estate mogul Mort Zuckerman bought *U.S. News & World Report* and installed himself as editor. Sufficiently entertained, he went on to buy the New York *Daily News*. Clearly, it's important to think big.

SHOOTING THE BREEZE

In other words, it may look like child's play, but as with many filthy rich endeavors, it's not. This poses a problem if, at heart, you don't care a whit about installation art, grouse shooting, or rare Methuselahs of wine. And, truth be told, many moguls secretly detest all three. But when they imagine their grandiose future obits, they'd much rather be remembered as winning sportsmen, Medici-like patrons of the arts, and admired philanthropists than as underage-model-chasing bores who loved throwing greenbacks in the air at Club 55.

Assuming you, too, prefer the sound of the former, it's time to get busy.

SPOILED SPORTS

Filthy Rich Fun and Games

IT'S NO ACCIDENT THAT THE KID PICKED last in dodge ball—the shrimp accustomed to skulking on the sidelines with the mathletes—is often the one who scales the Forbes 400. It's for this reason that plutocrats so often enjoy golf, a genteel game that doesn't require breaking a sweat and involves a suitable amount of expensive equipment. Pricey gear, paired with far-flung destinations, should be the logical throughline when selecting an appropriate sport to take up. Your peers are much less likely to chase a soccer ball around a field than to go fly-fishing in the Andes—a trip that requires chartering an ice-breaking ship, several helicopters, and scores of guides and translators, not to mention all the custom flies. Besides, you look silly in shorts.

Many, of course, still prefer the sidelines. London-based Russian oligarch Roman Abramovich bought the Chelsea Football Club. (After all, paying $29.99 for a soccer ball isn't nearly as much fun as plunking down $280 million.) And he's not the only one. Private equity rainmaker Tom Hicks and his partner, George Gillett Jr. scooped up the Liverpool Football Club for $920 million; tycoon Malcolm Glazer snagged Manchester United for $1.5 billion; billionaire investor Phil Anschutz has also gotten in on the beautiful game, importing David Beckham to play for his team, the Los Angeles Galaxy. Even übernerd Paul Allen has tried to shed the geek mantle, buying the Portland Trail Blazers and the Seattle Seahawks, as well as sponsoring an America's Cup yacht to the tune of $10 million. As a rule: Those who can't play, purchase.

But caveat emptor: Before you go out and invest in a local bowling team, outfitting it with a state-of-the-art alley and Prada-designed shoes, you should know that certain sports, no matter how pricey, will always be viewed with suspicion.

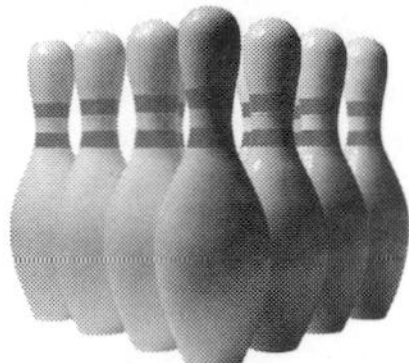

SPORTS TO STEER CLEAR OF

- Drag racing
- Bowling
- Rodeo
- Roller derby
- Tractor pull
- Gymnastics
- Volleyball
- Bass fishing
- NASCAR
- Motocross
- Monster truck
- Hockey

THE REEL WORLD
Mogul vs. Nature

FLY-FISHING

FILTHY RICH ANGLERS RACK UP MORE air miles than any other sports obsessives, since their chosen obsession necessitates multiday journeys to impossibly remote habitats in search of the Big One. (This has nothing to do with wanting to get away from their wives.) If Hemingway's your thing, it's worth heading to Kiribati (1,300 miles from Hawaii in the South Pacific) to experience firsthand the muscular

PREFERRED PLAYGROUNDS

Freshwater fly-fishing
- *Nimmo Bay*, British Columbia
- *Big Hole River*, Montana
- *Itchen*, *Avon*, and *Test* rivers, England
- *Talachulitna River*, Alaska
- *Tongariro River*, New Zealand

Bonefishing
- *Ascension Bay*, Yucatán Peninsula, Mexico
- *Christmas Island*, South Pacific
- *Ambergris Caye*, Belize

THE AMERICA'S CUP

The America's Cup has changed dramatically since 1977 when an overtanned businessman named Ted Turner victoriously skippered his own yacht, *Courageous*, before pitching up pickled at the trophy ceremony. Today, the ships are still helmed (in the financial sense) by wealthy patrons, but they're far less likely to actually sail them than to be awkward 18th wheels to their 17-member professional crews. It was not always thus. The 156-year-old Cup has its origins as a gentlemanly competition: J. P. Morgan, Harry Vanderbilt, and Sir Thomas Lipton all made their mark on the sport. But the cost is staggering, and gearing up for the races has become a form of "mine is bigger than yours" for some of the richest men in the animal kingdom—most notably, Larry Ellison. His team has an annual budget of $95 million, but even that wasn't enough for him to snag "Auld Mug" in Valencia in 2007. Poor guy.

HOT PURSUIT
The S.S. Ellison

camaraderie that develops best while poling across tropical flats in panga boats in search of pugnacious bonefish. Or tear a page from Ted Turner's playbook and jet down to Patagonia, were he's purchased thousands of acres of Argentine wilderness to ensure he'll always have a river to himself. Whether freshwater streams or saltwater lagoons are your thing, spending tens of thousands of dollars on trips to isolated fishing lodges, accessible only by helicopter or seaplane, is your ticket into an elite fraternity of wise, wealthy and, above all, *manly* moguls. Pitting man against nature, fly-fishing is a sport in which cunning and skill are as indispensable as $1,000-a-day guides and a Buddha-like reserve in the face of vicious mosquitoes. In exchange, you earn the right to dress like Papa.

SKILLS TO PERFECT

The Double Haul. If you can't cast your line more than 50 feet, you won't be landing many trophies. If you want to chopper-fish in New Zealand or bonefish the Yucatán with the big boys, you'll first need to master this difficult move (it's all in the wrist), which will allow you to cast consistently and gracefully, even in a headwind.

The Triple Crown. Land an angry bonefish, a leaping tarpon, and an oddly shaped, stubbornly elusive permit on a single fly in the same day.

ESSENTIAL GEAR

- ***Orvis Tailwater waders ($379)***
- ***Bjarne Fries Katana bamboo fly rod ($3,500)***
- ***R. L. Winston bamboo fly rod ($3,000)***
- ***Sage Elite fly rod for sailfish and marlin ($1,455)***
- ***Polarized sunglasses by Maui Jim Kahuna ($349)***
- ***Umpqua fly selections for trout, striped bass, and tarpon ($580)***

TEED UP Richie McMoneypants

GOLF

At first glance, golf may seem to be one of the more democratic of elitist sports. After all, there are public courses aplenty and droves of middle managers enjoying a regular 18 holes at their local. That said, in its most rarefied form, the perverse Scottish tradition of traipsing around in the rain to put a ball in a tiny cup is satisfyingly expensive and exclusive. Since you'll need to belong to multiple clubs (to keep up appearances), annual dues can reach into the millions. Advanced duffers will also want to be able to say "been there, done that" about the hundreds of top-grade greens found worldwide. With a round of golf for nonmembers costing upwards of $1,000 at the better clubs (not including tips for the caddies and the postmatch Cohibas), covering all

PREFERRED PLAYGROUNDS

- *St Andrews Old Course* and *Gleneagles*, Scotland
- *Royal County Down* and *Ballybunion*, Ireland
- *Bandon Dunes*, Oregon
- *Pebble Beach*, California
- *Cypress Point*, California
- *Augusta*, Georgia

LOCKED AND LOADED
The Bull-shot

5 parts hot beef bouillon | **2 parts vodka** **pinch celery salt** | **Tabasco sauce** **salt and pepper**

Mix soup and spirits, add celery salt, a few drops of Tabasco sauce, and salt and pepper to taste. Sip out of a sterling silver thermos while driving home in a vintage Land Rover.

---

your bases can get pricey. Generally, you'll want to play new courses over a period of two days; hence the need for five-star accommodations. And forget work: You'll need to travel year-round to find the optimal conditions: 70 degrees in southern environs and 60 degrees in Scotland and Ireland. You might not need all the high-priced doohickeys that supposedly improve your game, but it wouldn't be nearly as much fun without them.

SKILLS TO PERFECT

Reading the Green. Determining the path that your ball will travel by analyzing the contour and texture of the fairway.
The Vardon Grip. This overlapping grip allows your hands to work in unison during the swing.

ESSENTIAL GEAR

- ***Osborn & Robert needlepoint belt ($285)***
- ***Maruman golf drivers ($2,000)***
- ***Titleist graphite irons ($1,100)***
- ***Louis Vuitton golf bag ($8,400)***
- ***Escalade golf cart ($16,000)***
- ***Custom John Lobb golf shoes ($4,000)***

SHOOTING & STALKING

IF YOU WANDER INTO THE WOODS IN Arkansas or the bleaker parts of the Midwest, you'll find pickups full of Joe Six-Packs itching to shoot the hell out of Bambi. To set themselves apart, the Filthy Rich hew to the European hunting traditions. And while there is fine shooting and stalking in Canada (as well as Austria and the Czech Republic), serious hunters head to the Scottish moors or take aim at wild boar and partridge in the Spanish countryside. A day's grouse shooting or deer stalking in the craggy Highlands can easily run upwards of $40,000 for a party of eight. But be warned: Shooting holidays from glossy brochures are viewed with revulsion by the titled lot who dominate the sport. The English shooting season runs from the "Glorious Twelfth" of August through February 1. Befriend the right Brit and you'll spend this time chasing wild grouse, pheasants, and other decorative game, while enjoying the cachet that comes from being invited to kill animals alongside the right people. Expect pomp and circumstance galore: the wizened gamekeeper, the teenage "beaters," the blue-blooded dogs nipping at your heels.

SKILLS TO PERFECT

Bagging a Tall Bird. Shooting a bird flying at a height of 100 feet or more.
The Lead. Lining up your shot so that the hapless bird flies into the pellet blast.

PREFERRED PLAYGROUNDS

- *Scotland* (for grouse)
- *Dorset, Gloucestershire,* or *Devon,* England (for pheasant)
- *The King of Spain's estates* (for partridge and wild boar)

TROPHY FEES FOR AFRICAN GAME

Bull elephant: **$12,000** and up
Lion: **$5,500** and up
Leopard: **$3,500** and up
Sable: **$2,500** and up
Blue wildebeest: **$1,250** and up
Giraffe: **$1,000** and up
Warthog: **$350** and up
Porcupine: **$200** and up

ESSENTIAL GEAR

(cont'd from p. 175)

- ***Bespoke Holland & Holland "Royal Double" rifle ($260,000)***
- ***Ghurka pocket flask ($175)***
- ***Bespoke Dege & Skinner "Phitwell" three-piece tweed shooting suit ($5,200)***
- ***Mud-splattered green Range Rover ($95,000)***
- ***Hunter Sovereign Wellington boots ($450)***
- ***Holland & Holland thermos ($1,355)***

HIGH CAMP
A 4-Star Hut

BIG GAME HUNTING

As *OUT OF AFRICA* AUTHOR KAREN Blixen put it, "There is something about safari life that makes you forget all your sorrows and feel like you've drunk a half bottle of champagne." Indeed, though you'd think the wildlife protection lobby would have something to say about half-cocked huntsmen running around with semiautomatic weapons, in Africa today tycoons looking to channel Teddy Roosevelt can cap off a day taking potshots at elephants with as much champers as they can stomach. At luxurious tented camps in Zimbabwe, Tanzania, and South Africa, well-heeled hunters can still dine amidst fine antiques on guinea fowl casserole served by locals in starched white uniforms. Camouflage and neon orange are seriously frowned upon; traditional khaki is preferred. Once you've scored a "trophy," your game will be skinned and field cured in preparation for its future as terribly chic taxidermy, then shipped home to your den in a handsome crate (see p. 48). Expect to pay a minimum of $10,000 for a five-day safari, excluding trophy fees, airfare, import licenses and tariffs, shipping, and tips.

SKILLS TO PERFECT

Nailing the Big Five. Bagging an elephant, a rhino, a lion, a leopard, and a buffalo on one safari.

ESSENTIAL GEAR

- ***Bespoke Holland & Holland "Royal Deluxe" Side by Side Shotgun ($250,000)***
- ***Iridium 9505A satellite phone ($1,500 plus $6 a minute to check your voicemail from the bush)***
- ***Garmin Nüri handheld GPS ($750)***
- ***Tag Safari buffalo skin soft rifle bag ($459)***
- ***Beretta Sahariana safari jacket ($250)***
- ***F. M. Allen Swarovski binoculars ($2,110)***
- ***Proguanil antimalarial medication ($15 copay)***
- ***James Purdey & Sons leather cartridge belt ($400)***

PREFERRED PLAYGROUNDS

- *Makalolo Plains* and *Save Basin* in Zimbabwe
- *Rift Valley* in Tanzania, Botswana, South Africa, and Zambia

FIELDS OF GOLD
A Bit of Stick and Ball

POLO

THE ORIGINAL "SPORT OF KINGS," HIGH-goal polo is still the poshest game around. Dating from about 600 B.C., it began as a military training exercise for nomadic tribes of Central Asia. British soldiers stationed in India stumbled upon it in the 1860s, imported it to the U.K. and lent it a whiff of colonial glamour. Since then, it's been hard to think of polo without imagining pristine emerald grounds, clotted cream and strawberries, and buckets full of bubbly. But behind the Ralph Lauren tableau lies a bone-crushing contact sport, in which players are routinely maimed, and millions are at stake. Owning polo farms in Wellington, Florida, and England is a

PREFERRED PLAYGROUNDS

- *Wellington,* Florida
- *Santa Barbara,* California
- *Calgary,* Canada
- *Cowdray Park Polo, Midhurst, West Sussex, Guards Polo Club, Windsor Great Park, Berkshire,* England
- *Sotogrande,* Spain
- *Tortugas* and *Ellerstina,* Argentina
- *St. Moritz* and *Gstaad,* Switzerland

HOW TO SPEAK POLO

Stick and Ball

A practice session to work on your shots, undertaken on special fields so as not to scruff up the real deal.

Chukka

A seven-minute playing period (seven and a half in England). Significant because, in high-goal polo, there are six chukkas. Players change ponies every chukka, and any proper player comes to the field with at least eight mounts.

Divots

The holes made on the field by all those pounding hooves. Spectators tramp them down at halftime—plutocrat watching at its most extreme.

must: You need 70 to 100 flat acres for a proper one, and each 20-acre field will cost half a million to prep. A "string" of ponies (eight horses) will run you $800,000 (flying them overseas several times a year not included). And that's just for starters. Truly dedicated players have additional "reserve" ponies in training, and sink hundreds of thousands of dollars into breeding their best ones. But while the animals are pricey, it's the swath of short, studly Argentine players you need to hire to play alongside you that might give you pause. With the top players in the world commanding annual salaries of $2 million, your team, trainers, vets, horses, and grooms can easily cost $10 million or more a year—a snap for bigwigs like Swiss financier Urs Schwarzenbach, or polo-loving American moneyman Peter Brant.

SKILLS TO PERFECT

Line-Man-Ball. The mantra players use to remind themselves to travel in the lane in which the ball has been hit and avoid potentially horrifying collisions.

Take the Man. Removing your opponent from the line of play by knocking your horse into his to throw him off course.

ESSENTIAL GEAR

- ***Eight Argentine polo ponies ($800,000 and beyond)***
- ***Patey polo helmet ($300)***
- ***Custom Sumatran polo mallets ($195 each)***
- ***Casablanca knee guards ($250)***
- ***La Martina zip-up polo boots ($475)***
- ***Hermès polo saddle ($3,500)***

SHOW JUMPING

A WHOLE 'NOTHER TRIBE OF FANATICAL equestriennes to wrap your head around. The "hunter/jumper" set start young. In certain preppy circles on the East and West Coast, it's common to buy a child a small $300,000 pony before she's mastered her ABCs. This sets her up for a lifetime obsession with yet another stratospherically expensive sport, as she moves on to a medium and then a large pony before finally graduating to a proper horse. A Grand Prix–level horse will set you back about $2 million, while training, boarding, shipping, and entry fees for a season run around $100,000 per horse . . . any old horse. At the end of it all, you might wish you'd encouraged little Tatiana to take up ice-skating. On the plus side, she'll have great posture and mix in good circles while tackling the hunter, jumper, and equitation categories. The truly mad take up eventing, where they scale natural obstacles at top speeds, risking their very erect necks in the process. The more subdued opt for dressage, where equine ballet replaces jumps. World-class dressage horses can cost up to $4 million a piece.

SKILLS TO PERFECT

Double Clear. Completing a jumper course without knocking down any elements and then completing the final jump-off without knocking down any elements.

ESSENTIAL GEAR

- ***McGuinn Farms custom tack trunk ($960)***
- ***Devoucoux saddle in buffalo hide ($4,380)***
- ***Custom Der-Dau riding boots in baby calfskin ($1,500)***
- ***Hermès broadcloth horse blanket ($1,073)***
- ***Tailored Sportsman or Pikeur breeches ($310)***
- ***Grand Prix–caliber horse ($2 million)***

PREFERRED PLAYGROUNDS

- *Winter Equestrian Festival, Wellington,* Florida
- *Spruce Meadows,* Calgary
- *Aiken,* South Carolina
- *Hampton Classic, Bridgehampton,* New York
- *Lake Placid,* New York

THE HEIRESS DIVISION

The strongest riders inevitably take up the precipitously expensive sport shortly after learning to walk. Jackie Kennedy first straddled a pony at age two, and was competing in the Hampton Classic before her tenth birthday. Up-and-coming faces (with familiar last names) include Paige Johnson, daughter of BET founder Bob Johnson; Brianne Goutal, the fragrance heiress; and Alison Firestone of the tire dynasty. Below, some of the other exquisitely groomed fillies leading the pack:

GEORGINA BLOOMBERG

ZARA PHILLIPS

GEORGINA BLOOMBERG

The daughter of media mogul-turned-politico Mike has already mastered the junior circuit and graduated to the U.S. Show Jumping Team. She also sponsors a charity called the Rider's Closet, donating used breeches and boots to aspiring equestrians less fortunate than she.

ZARA PHILLIPS

Queen Elizabeth II's eldest granddaughter made her first splash in horsey circles when she embarked on a very public romance with National Hunt jockey Richard Johnson. More recently, she snagged the gold medal for eventing at the 2006 FEI World Equestrian Games.

ATHINA ONASSIS DE MIRANDA

ATHINA ONASSIS DE MIRANDA

The world's most famous heiress (to some $800 million of her grandfather Aristotle Onassis's fortune) wed Brazilian show jumper Doda Miranda in 2005 and has since declared her interest in competing for a spot on Greece's Olympic equestrian team.

SHOPAHOLIC HALL OF FAME

WHEN TOO MUCH IS NEVER ENOUGH

The Pack Rat Publishing King

IT'S NO SECRET THAT WILLIAM RANDOLPH Hearst, the penny-newspaper baron, was a bit of a spendthrift. But his obsession with priceless clutter is a cautionary tale for credit-card-happy moguls everywhere. Never content in the same place for long, he owned seven gargantuan castles sprinkled around the globe. Each was packed to the rafters with a museum's worth of exotic antiques and *objets d'art;* paintings covered every available speck of wall space. San Simeon, Hearst's California fantasia, boasted the largest private zoo in the world, with herds of American bison, zebras, camels, yaks, giraffes, kinkajous, jaguars, 300 white fallow deer, and one lone elephant.

Although exceptionally gifted at spending, he often couldn't keep track of the things he had bought, or find space to display them. Ancient artifacts, purchased in bulk from European dealers (who had pilfered the castles of down-on-their-luck aristocrats for their best customer), never saw the light of day. Multistory warehouses in New York and San Francisco were chockablock with unimaginable treasures. A glass-bottomed yacht Hearst commissioned wound up in storage, having never touched water.

His collections ran the gamut: 19th-century Navajo textiles, 6th-century Greek amphorae, Spanish religious statuary, and Depression-era folk art, to name just a few. Forced to downsize after World War I, he unloaded some of his never-before-seen possessions through Gimbel's department store. The 1941 sale catalog details over 20,000 curiosities, among them a sideboard that once belonged to Charles Dickens, a waistcoat worn by George Washington, and a Bible of Thomas Jefferson's. There were multiple suits of armor and hundreds of medieval crosses, but for every chalice Hearst parted with, there were another three just like it in storage.

The moral of his story? If you can't fit it into one of your seven gargantuan castles, you probably don't need it.

CONSUMPTION JUNCTION
San Simeon

MASTERPIECE THEATER

The Importance of Being Arty

PRESUMABLY YOU EARNED YOUR BILlions because you live for the kill. Losing out on a profitable deal makes your blood boil. Coming in second? Disaster.

Congratulations! You're ready to start collecting art. If you thought paintings were just a passing concern for the decorator, think again. Ever since the Medici princes commissioned their first fresco the upper tier of the art world has been the domain of the ludicrously loaded. If you own a serious house, you need serious "works." But even with the liquidity to blow $7 million on a Basquiat for the billiards room, you'll have to steel yourself for a fight. There are only so many Richard Princes to go around. You're competing with the major museums and an international mafia of collectors who, thanks to their intrepid art dealers, know a painting is about to go to market before its owner knows he's ready to sell. At auctions you'll be up against cachet-hungry Russians and hedge-funders who aren't going to drop their paddles when they hear $50 million.

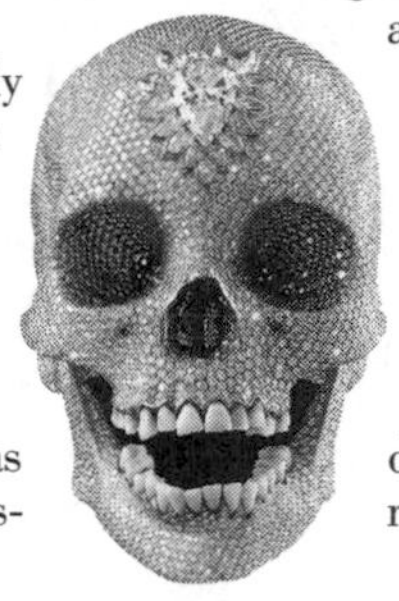

DAMIEN HIRST'S "FOR THE LOVE OF GOD," a life-size platinum cast of a human skull covered in 8,601 diamonds, sold for $100 million in 2007.

To be a true player, you need to know your stuff. Aspiring super-collectors typically don't start with a priceless Rothko. First, they dip their feet in at a contemporary art fair, like Frieze in London, schmooze one of the junior dealers at the Gagosian Gallery, and figure out who owns what. But lest you think this is just a game, it's worth noting that the art market has outperformed Wall Street for several years going. Yes: That scribbled canvas could one day be more valuable than your entire stash of Berkshire Hathaway.

FOUR WORKS THAT BROKE THE BANK

Adele Bloch-Bauer (1907) This Klimt classic shattered all records when cosmetics kingpin Ron Lauder made it the **$135 million** centerpiece of his Neue Galerie.

Study from Innocent X (1962) This painting by Francis Bacon, influenced by a Velasquez from 1650, went for **$52.6 million** at auction—twice as much as any of his previous work.

Green Car Crash (1963) This Andy Warhol silk screen sold for a shocking **$71.7 million.** Seven bidders fought over it before a telephone bidder from China took it home.

White Center (Yellow, Pink, Lavender on Rose) (1950) by Mark Rothko sold for **$72.8 million** in 2007, setting a new record for contemporary art.

IN VINO PLUTOCRAS

Because You're Far Too Loaded to Drink Bad Wine

ALTHOUGH DIEHARD OENOPHILES TEND TOWARD THE pompous, a working knowledge of the wine landscape and a well-stocked cellar are prerequisites for any real social interaction. In recent years, interest in collecting has spiked dramatically, turning everyone and his mother into an amateur sommelier. Should you develop that peculiar thirst, just remember that even the ultrarare "trophy" wines fetching tens of thousands of dollars on the auction block can get you drunk. Hoarding the good stuff is so middle class.

THE STELLAR CELLAR

A SYBARITE'S SHOPPING LIST

BORDEAUX

Out of the many spectacular chateaux and vintages found in the world's largest fine wine region, here are the three worth sipping:

❑ *Chateau Petrus (Pomerol), 1998*
$2,499/bottle

❑ *Chateau Latour (Pauillac), 2000*
$1,599/bottle

❑ *Chateau Haut-Brion (Pessac-Léognan), 2000*
$870/bottle

BURGUNDY

The best come from the Côte d'Or region—with the Comte de Nuits to the north and the Côte de Beaune (the heartland for white burgundies) to the south.

❑ *Domaine Comte Georges de Vogue Bonnes-Mares (Chambolle-Musigny), 2005*
$1,000/bottle

❑ *Domaine Jean Marc Boillot Batard Montrachet (Montrachet), 2005*
$465/bottle

CULT CABERNET

Getting your hands on certain California Cabs can land you on a wait list as long as the one for an Hermès Birkin.

❑ *Screaming Eagle*
Still the most sought after, it can easily cost **$1,000 a bottle.** If you can find it.

❑ ***Your Name Here***
Crushpad, a San Francisco–based winery, will create a wine to your specifications, for about **$10,000 a barrel** (roughly, $35 a bottle).

CHAMPAGNE

If you're going to pop the cork, might as well drink the best. In pink, naturally:

❑ *Louis Roederer Cristal Brut Rosé, 1999*
$550/bottle

GO WEST, YOUNG MAN

How to Lose Your Shirt in Hollywood

Ever since Howard Hughes strolled up to the premiere of *Hell's Angels* with Jean Harlow on his arm and his name in lights, Hollywood has held an irresistible allure for the exceptionally loaded. Spending your fortune bankrolling other peoples' movies that will, in all likelihood, head straight to DVD, sure seems like a stupid hobby. But isn't it worth it for the corner banquettes, stacks of glossy invites, and access to nubile young talent? A certain type of billionaire seems to think so.

Take real estate scion Steve Bing. When he inherited a sizable chunk of change (some $600 million) on his 18th birthday, he took off for La La Land. In the decades since, he's written a few scripts *(Missing in Action, Kangaroo Jack)*, produced a few movies *(Get Carter, The Big Bounce)*, and inked a deal with Warner Bros. He may not be giving an Oscar speech anytime soon, but being "in the business" has certainly been a boon to his private life, enabling him to enjoy what would otherwise be inconceivable dalliances with A-listers like Elizabeth Hurley (the mother of his son) and Nicole Kidman.

Name a billionaire bachelor who wouldn't want that kind of hobby? For the would-be movie mogul, the first step is to set up a production company—the grander sounding, the better. The ever-modest Bing dubbed his Shangri-La Entertainment. Greek shipping heir Paris Latsis and Prince Abdul Azim, son of the Sultan of Brunei, have their own companies, too. Will they make great films? Probably not. Will they make *any* films? Only time will tell. But in the meantime, they're having a whole lot of fun.

So, go ahead, get dazzled by the klieg lights. Find your very own Jean Harlow. Just don't expect to make your money back.

BOX OFFICE BINGO
An "Executive Producer"

COLLECT THEM ALL!

Other Objects Worth Hoarding

BONING UP
T. Rex Fetches Top Dollar

DOLLS

DEMI MOORE

MOORE REPORTEDLY HAS THE LARGEST collection in the world of lifelike dolls by designer Jodi and Richard Creager, which retail at $2,500–$10,000 apiece. When she was married to action star Bruce Willis, a rumor went around that he had bought her another house to store all her fancy figurines.

NORMAN ROCKWELL PAINTINGS

STEVEN SPIELBERG

THE DIRECTOR'S LIFELONG FASCINATION with the all-American artist left him with enough paintings to stock the Norman Rockwell Museum in Stockbridge, Massachusetts. But the provenance of one of them, *Russian Schoolroom*, sparked controversy in 2007. Though Spielberg purchased the painting from an aboveboard gallery, the $700,000 work had been stolen from another one.

DINOSAUR BONES

NICOLAS CAGE

THE ACTOR RECENTLY OUTBID FELLOW bone collector Leonardo DiCaprio for a 32-inch-long Tyrannosaurus rex skull, paying $276,000 for the 67-million-year-old fossil. The T. rex head joined a human one that Cage has dubbed "Vince."

ROCK MEMORABILIA

PAUL ALLEN

BILL GATES'S FORMER PARTNER CREATED the Experience Music Project to channel his insatiable fixation on rock 'n' roll history. His collection now includes over 80,000 artifacts. His favorites are said to be Eric Clapton's "Brownie" guitar, which he strummed on "Layla," and Bob Dylan's Martin from his days as a broke Village busker.

SLAVE MEMORABILIA

OPRAH WINFREY

LIKE WHOOPI GOLDBERG, MIKE TYSON, and Bill Cosby, Oprah is said to hold one of the most significant private collections of items pertaining to the darkest chapter in American history. Working with Quincy Jones, she is leading the charge to establish an African American history museum on the mall in Washington, which would house items like slave chains, segregation signage, and photographs of the civil rights movement.

FABERGÉ EGGS

VICTOR VEKSELBERG

IN 2004, THE RUSSIAN BUSINESSMAN bought Malcolm Forbes's collection of 180 Fabergé eggs and miniatures for an estimated $90 million, just before they were to come under the gavel. The Coronation Egg, an Easter gift from Tsar Nicholas II to his wife in 1897, is the finest piece in the collection, said to be worth around $30 million alone.

RARE MANUSCRIPTS

BILL GATES

THE MICROSOFT COFOUNDER'S EXTENSIVE library includes the Codex Leicester, a 72-page manuscript of Leonardo da Vinci's diagrams and notes, he bought for $30.8 million at Christie's in 1994.

DA VINCI LODE
The Codex Leicester

WHERE THE WILD THINGS ARE

A Zoo of One's Own

Hedge-funder Michael Steinhardt has stocked his Bedford, New York, estate with some unusually furry–and feathered–companions: African crested porcupines, $2,000-a-head flamingos, a South American rodent known as a capybara, Madagascan ring-tailed lemurs, albino wallabies, and a pair of spider monkeys named Fred and Ginger. His personal menagerie also boasts three zonkeys (zebra-donkey crossbreeds), which may explain why invites to his annual end-of-the-summer fête are so coveted.

In keeping a private zoo, Steinhardt follows a venerated filthy rich tradition. Napoléon's wife, Josephine, turned her mansion, Malmaison, into an exotic aviary. Irénée du Pont amused himself at his Cuban estate with a pack of trained iguanas. Anheuser-Busch honcho August Busch played circus ring-leader at his Missouri spread with an elephant, several camels, and a small herd of buffalo.

Then there's publishing exec Fred Drasner. In addition to several Nubian goats, he keeps camels at his Millbrook, New York, estate. He even created a custom saddle for his favorite, Lawrence, so he could ride him down to the ultrastuffy Millbrook Hunt Club and hiss at the local swells.

HEY, BIG SPENDER

The Development Office Is On Line One (and Two, and Three, and . . .)

IF THE DISGRACEFUL GAP BETWEEN YOUR LIFESTYLE AND THAT OF THE OTHER 99.9999 percent of people on this planet has you wondering where you'll be spending eternity, fear not: There's a billion-dollar industry solely devoted to helping you unleash your inner altruist. Having co-opted the strategies of Fortune 500 companies, today's top-tier nonprofits operate with cold-blooded precision, identifying, stalking, and snaring their prey like seasoned hunters. Consider yourself in the crosshairs.

CACHET-ING IN

FOUR NONPROFITS THAT NEVER FLY COACH

HARVARD

WITH THE LARGEST ENDOWMENT OF any academic institution in the world, and the second largest of any nonprofit (behind the Bill & Melinda Gates Foundation), Harvard clearly has a knack for squeezing fat checks out of the Filthy Rich. Yes, it's the oldest American university and its countless esteemed and wildly successful graduates aren't exactly known for being impoverished. But those tens of millions pouring in each year aren't all the result of misty-eyed remembrances of bong sessions at the Delphic. Even nongraduates have been known to donate to the school whose name is synonymous with greatness. Sounds creepy, but it's true. In the mid-'80s, college dropout turned corporate raider Ivan Boesky (whose speech at Stanford inspired Gordon Gekko's "Greed Is Good" soliloquy in *Wall Street*) so coveted the prestige a membership at the Harvard Club of New York conveyed that he decided to buy one. With a few deftly timed donations to the university's School of Public Health, he was noshing Cobb salad in the Grill Room like he'd always dreamed. Classy!

KENNEDY CENTER

THE JOHN F. KENNEDY CENTER FOR THE Performing Arts in Washington is a "living memorial" to the 35th president and the site of more scheming than the NSA. For especially overachieving members of the filthy rich strata, a seat on the board represents the pinnacle of political and social power. How could an underattended opera house—the first public arts facility built and subsidized by the federal government (through the National Park Service)—engender so much intrigue? New board members can be appointed only by sitting presidents, who typically employ the positions for patronage. Board hopefuls have been known to spend years and hundreds of thousands of dollars in donations (both to the Center and the appropriate political coffers) in the hope of being tapped. Mercifully, once you're on, you're on. Appointments are for life, and the board can be expanded only through an act of Congress.

MEMORIAL SLOAN-KETTERING CANCER CENTER

THE CENTER'S UPPER-CLASS BONA FIDES were cemented in 1945 when tycoon Alfred P. Sloan Jr. and Charles F. Kettering, vice president and director of research for General Motors, inspired by the government's success building the A-bomb, endowed a plan to use modern industrial research techniques to cure the Big C. Ever since, Sloan-Kettering's board and the hospital's frequent fund-raising galas have featured a revolving cast of New York City's moneyed elite, whose hefty donations have turned the institute into the country's leading cancer treatment and research center.

BILL & MELINDA GATES FOUNDATION

THOUGH IT WAS ALREADY THE WORLD'S richest nonprofit by a long shot, the Gates Foundation was pushed into another galaxy by Warren Buffett's 2006 decision to double its endowment. With over $38.7 billion at its disposal, the foundation has plenty of cash to burn before it needs your money. Still, it's a testament to what a little dough can do: It currently provides 99 percent of the funds deployed worldwide toward eradicating polio.

'SOFT POWER
Bill and Melinda

BIG MEN ON CAMPUS

A LOOK AT NAMING RIGHTS

THE PRIVILEGE OF ATTACHING ONE'S surname to something in perpetuity is the A-bomb in the fund-raiser's arsenal. Typically reserved for those who pledge 50 percent or more of a project's budget, they are not doled out lightly.

As a rule, the donation must be in excess of a million dollars, the donor must have a lengthy history with the institution, and his or her name must be (mostly) free of negative connotations. Increasingly, however, the only rule is the golden one,* and the likelihood of getting your name cast in bronze will be in direct proportion to how badly your cash is needed. In some cases, just giving the biggest single dollar amount, known as the "lead gift," is enough.

Academic and religious institutions are by far the most accommodating, and also the most desirable. No matter your countless misdeeds, how better to prove your unimpeachable character than by underwriting your local JCC?

Still, naming rights are far from a science, as the following cases illustrate:

S.I. NEWHOUSE SCHOOL OF PUBLIC COMMUNICATIONS

LOCATION: Syracuse University, Syracuse, New York
DONOR: Condé Nast press baron S. I. Newhouse Sr.
Before he gobbled up *Vogue*, *Vanity Fair*, and just about every other glossy rag on the newsstands, the late S. I. Newhouse cared about journalism. Or wanted his friends to think he did. **COST: $15 MILLION**

KOHL CENTER

LOCATION: The University of Wisconsin-Madison
DONOR: Supermarket mogul and U.S. senator Herb Kohl.
After years of selling them groceries, the Wisconsin alum gave Badger fans a state-of-the-art venue in which to drunkenly harass opposing Big Ten teams. **COST: $25 MILLION**

THE MASTER

LOCATION: The jungles of Colombia, South America
NAMED: 1998
DONOR: Amateur ornithologist Bernard Master.
The scientist who discovered the unnamed species donated his naming rights to British charity BirdLife International, which auctioned them off to raise funds for a 3,000-acre nature preserve. **COST: $105,000**

TISCH CHILDREN'S ZOO

LOCATION: Central Park Zoo, New York, New York
DONOR: Laurence "Larry" Tisch, former CEO of CBS television and co-owner of Lorillard Tobacco.
A fellow board member who had pledged $3 million to the zoo dropped out over Tisch's ties to the evil weed, forcing the late billionaire to cover the entire project himself. **COST: $4.5 MILLION**

FRANK H. ROGERS ATOMIC TESTING MUSEUM

LOCATION: Las Vegas, Nevada
DONOR: Jim Rogers, owner of Sunbelt Communications.
Rogers, who operates NBC and Fox affiliates in nine western states, named the museum for his father, who helped develop the site. Wherever Dad is, we're sure he must be glowing. **COST: $2 MILLION**

* *He who has the gold rules.*

GAME OVER
The Astros Clean House

DU PONT? NEVER HEARD OF HIM

When the name game turned to mud

- After Enron imploded in 2002, the Houston Astros hastily removed all traces of the disgraced energy giant, which had recently negotiated a 30-year naming rights agreement for the team's home stadium. After buying out the contract, the team's owners renamed it Astros Field until Coca-Cola struck a deal to dub it Minute Maid Park.

- In 1986, Villanova University unveiled the Du Pont Pavilion basketball arena, paid for primarily by John du Pont, troubled scion of the chemical and carpet dynasty. Shortly after he was found guilty of the 1996 murder of Olympic wrestling gold medalist Dave Schultz, the school stripped his name off the facility, and renamed it the Pavilion.

- Almost immediately after it opened in 2004, the University of Missouri's Paige Sports Arena, which had been dedicated to the daughter of two big-league donors, had to be renamed. The spoiled student had been caught cheating and her parents were feeling less charitable than usual. Someone named Mizzou took the honors instead.

- The NFL's Tennessee Titans were similarly screwed in 2002 when Adelphia Communications went belly-up after its founder was indicted for investor fraud and other chicaneries. Luckily, a single missed payment on its naming-rights deal with the team allowed the Titans to bow out of their agreement and remove the company's logo from their stadium. It's now known simply as the Coliseum.

A BRIEF HISTORY OF MEDIA MOGULDOM

"I didn't go into journalism to make money—a wise decision."
—MORT ZUCKERMAN

JOSEPH PULITZER

(1847–1911)

TOYS: *St. Louis Post-Dispatch; New York World*
The original muckraker, Pulitzer encouraged operatic stories in his city daily, the New York *World,* an innovation that helped make it the biggest paper in the nation. But sensationalism is only part of his legacy: Having built his fortune peddling tripe to the masses, he bankrolled Columbia University's prestigious journalism school and the Pulitzer prizes.

STOP THE PRESSES!

The Benefits of Buying Ink by the Barrel

A modern plutocrat's value isn't just measured in stocks and bonds. It's charted daily in the gossip columns, business sections, and society pages of our nation's free press. A sensitive lot, more than a few tycoons find this constant attention troubling. Not all of it, mind you–just the negative stuff. Which is why so many cash-rich control freaks try their hand at publishing. If you can't beat 'em, buy 'em! How else to explain the sudden rush of neophytes into the dying newspaper biz? Sure, the *Metropolis Gazette* is a hopeless money pit, the aspiring Murdoch thinks, but it's *my* hopeless money pit! The real satisfaction, of course, comes from knowing you own the very journalists who would otherwise be nipping are your heels. Signing a newspaper's payroll has a funny way of making unseemly stories disappear into thin air.

Plus, there's a social bonus: invites to those summer media softball games in Sag Harbor!

RUPERT MURDOCH

(b. 1931)

TOYS: *The Wall Street Journal; The Times* (London); *New York Post;* Fox News; MySpace

One of the 21st century's preeminent power brokers, Murdoch conquered Australia and England before arriving on American shores in 1973. Today, the right-wing kingmaker is the *bête noire* of lefties the world over, who deride his expanding empire as an arm of the Grand Old Party. But forget red state, forget blue state—the only color Rupe cares about is green. Before *The O'Reilly Factor,* the guy green-lighted *The Simpsons.* Next stop? China!

MORT ZUCKERMAN

(b. 1937)

TOYS: *The Atlantic Monthly; U.S. News & World Report; New York Daily News*

After making his fortune erecting skyscrapers in Boston, he made his name in the '80s as a hard-charging media prince. A frequent presence on the Upper East Side dinner party circuit (along with buddies Barbara Walters and Sir Harry Evans), he has since leveraged his print journalism hobby into a third career as a know-it-all Sunday morning talk show pundit.

JARED KUSHNER

(b. 1981)

TOYS: *New York Observer*

The new, peach-fuzzy face of media moguldom, this boyish real estate scion snapped up the well-read Upper East Side tattle sheet for under $10 million in 2006. In short order, he unveiled a fresh tabloidy format and linked up with sexy real estate heiress Ivanka Trump. Synergy!

WILLIAM RANDOLPH HEARST

(1863–1951)

TOYS: *San Francisco Examiner; Seattle Post-Intelligencer; Cosmopolitan; Town & Country; Good Housekeeping; Harper's Bazaar*

Before he collected medieval monasteries and Assyrian antiques, rich kid Hearst went after newspapers and magazines, seizing the tabloid mantle from his chief rival, Joseph Pulitzer. The "Father of Yellow Journalism" threw his weight around whenever possible, using his papers to drum up support for his little pet causes, like the Spanish-American War.

CONRAD BLACK

(b. 1944)

TOYS: *The Daily Telegraph; Chicago Sun-Times; The Jerusalem Post; New York Sun*

Everyone's favorite Canadian-born English lord learned the hard way that a newspaper's coffers aren't your personal petty cash drawer, when he was convicted of fraud in 2007 for misappropriating $6.1 million from his holding company, Hollinger International.

ROBERT MAXWELL

(1923–1991)

TOYS: *Daily Mirror; Sunday Mail;* Macmillan Publishing

Czechoslovakian magnate Robert Maxwell (neé Jan Ludvik Hoch) made his fair share of enemies as he aggressively rolled up tabloid titles and newspaper holding companies across Britain in the '70s and '80s. Frequently tarred as a shady wheeler-dealer, he fell off his yacht and drowned in 1991 while vacationing in the Canary Islands; his daughter claimed he'd been murdered by "dangerous elements."

THE POWER GAME

"There are two things that are important in politics. The first is money, and I can't remember what the second one is."
—MARK HANNA, CAMPAIGN MANAGER TO WILLIAM McKINLEY

If gravitas is what you seek, dipping your tentacles into the political arena can be a hugely rewarding hobby. Politicians are quite useful, after all, and every one of them needs a piggy bank on speed dial. As someone who's used to getting your own way, you might even consider running for public office. (At least you'll know where your cash is being squandered.) Just follow the lead of these moneyed Machiavellis and you'll be playing the game in no time . . .

❑ MICHAEL BLOOMBERG
The Super Candidate
Tough-talking midget spent $160 million to become mayor of New York City, twice. Used his vaunted position to ban smoking, trans fats.

❑ ARIANNA HUFFINGTON
The Mouthpiece
Well-married face of limousine liberalism failed in her bid to govern California, but succeeded in dominating the Internet with her lefty must-read blog, the *Huffington Post.*

❑ RICHARD MELLON SCAIFE
The Puppetmaster
Secretive scion behind the Vast Right-Wing Conspiracy poured his many millions into the Arkansas Project, the driving force behind Bill Clinton's impeachment.

❑ GEORGETTE MOSBACHER
The Party Girl
When not hawking high-priced face creams for Borghese, this flame-haired cougar cochairs the RNC's finance committee. Her talent: Knowing people like you.

❑ SHELDON ADELSON
The Single-Issue Sultan
America's third richest plutocrat only picked up the hobby recently, scaring the bejeezus out of Democrats. If you're a friend of Israel, you're a friend of Shelly's.

❑ GEORGE SOROS
The Benefactor
Billionaire speculator spent $75 million trying to oust George W. Bush in the 2004 election. In the off-season, drops hundreds of millions on countless pet projects, like legalizing weed.

DIRECTORY

FISHING GEAR

LELAND FLY FISHING
463 Bush Street
San Francisco, CA 94108
Tel.: 415-781-3474
FlyFishingOutfitters.com

ORVIS
432 Boston Post Road
Darien, CT 06820
Tel.: 203-662-0844
Orvis.com

FISHING LODGES

FIREHOLE RANCH
P.O. Box 686
West Yellowstone, MT 59758
Tel.: 406-646-7294
FireholeRanch.com

JAGUAR REEF LODGE
P.O. Box 297
Hopkins, Stann Creek
Belize
Tel.: 800-289-5756
JaguarReef.com

NIMMO BAY RESORT
1978 Broughton Blvd.
Port McNeill, British Columbia
Canada V0N 2R0
Tel.: 800-837-4354
NimmoBay.com

TONGARIRO LODGE
83 Grace Road
P.O. Box 278
Turangi, New Zealand
Tel.: 64 7 386 7946
TongariroLodge.co.nz

GOLF DESTINATIONS

BALLYBUNION GOLF CLUB
Sandhill Road, Ballybunion
County Kerry, Ireland
Tel.: 353 68 27146
BallybunionGolfClub.ie

BANDON DUNES GOLF RESORT
57744 Round Lake Drive
Bandon, OR 97411
Tel.: 541-347-4380
BandonDunesGolf.com

CYPRESS POINT GOLF CLUB
3150 17 Mile Drive
Pebble Beach, CA 93953
Tel.: 831-624-2223

GLENEAGLES
Auchterarder
Perthshire PH3 1BR, Scotland
Tel.: 44 0 1764 662231
Gleneagles.com

PEBBLE BEACH
1700 17 Mile Drive
Pebble Beach, CA 93953
Tel.: 831-624-3811
PebbleBeach.com

THE ROYAL & ANCIENT GOLF CLUB
St Andrews
Fife KY16 9JD, Scotland
Tel.: 44 0 1334 460000
StAndrews.org.uk

ROYAL COUNTY DOWN GOLF CLUB
36 Golf Links Road, Newcastle
County Down
Northern Ireland T33 0AN
Tel.: 44 0 28 4372 3314
RoyalCountyDown.org

HUNTING OUTFITTERS

BERETTA
From safari jackets to firearms.
17601 Beretta Drive
Accokeek, MD 20607
Tel.: 800-636-3420
BerettaUSA.com

DEGE AND SKINNER
Tweed shooting suits are just the thing.
10 Savile Row
London W1S 3PF, UK
Tel.: 44 020 7287 2941
Dege-Skinner.co.uk

HOLLAND & HOLLAND
Buy an antique firearm with serious provenance.
31-33 Bruton Street
London W1J 6HH, UK
Tel.: 44 020 7499 4411
HollandAndHolland.com

SAFARI ARRANGEMENTS

ABERCROMBIE & KENT
1520 Kensington Road, #212
Oak Brook, IL 60523
Tel.: 800-554-7016
AbercrombieKent.com

F. M. ALLEN
962 Madison Avenue
New York, NY 10021
Tel.: 212-737-4374
FMAllen.com

HHK SAFARIS
P.O. Box CH273
Chisipite, Harare
Zimbabwe
Tel.: 263 4 499165 *or* 499875
HHKSafaris.com

MICATO SAFARIS
15 West 26th Street
New York, NY 10010
Tel.: 212-545-7111
Micato.com

POLO & EQUESTRIAN GEAR

C.M. HADFIELD'S SADDLERY
300 Business Park Way, #B100
Royal Palm Beach, FL 33414
Tel.: 800-854-7433

DER DAU
1885 McDonald Avenue
Brooklyn, NY 11223
Tel.: 718-336-4513
DerDau.com

MAISON GOYARD
For bespoke polo equipment trunks in their signature leather.
233, rue St. Honoré
Paris 75001, France

Tel.: 33 01 42 60 57 04
Goyard.com

LA MARTINA
Avenue Santa Fe
Buenos Aires, Argentina
Tel.: 54 11 4576-0010/2
LaMartina.com

McGUINN FARMS
Custom trunks and accessories.
14600 Mustang Trail
Fort Lauderdale, FL 33330
Tel.: 954-434-5848
McGuinnFarms.com

POLISTAS
12-13 Burlington Arcade
Piccadilly
Mayfair, London W1J 0PH, UK
Tel.: 44 020 7495 6603
Polistas.com

ART CONSULTANTS

BARBARA GUGGENHEIM
Wife of Hollywood super-lawyer Bert Fields. Clients: Warren Beatty; Tom Cruise
Guggenheim Asher Associates
139 South Beverly Drive, #214
Beverly Hills, CA 90212
Tel.: 310-275-2133
GuggenheimAsher.com

ART DEALERS

ACQUAVELLA GALLERIES
Clients: Paul Allen; Steve Wynn
William Acquavella
18 East 79th Street
New York, NY 10075
Tel.: 212-734-6300
AcquavellaGalleries.com

LARRY GAGOSIAN
Clients: Newhouse; David Geffen
Gagosian Gallery
980 Madison Avenue
New York, NY 10021
Tel.: 212-744-2313
Gagosian.com

MARC GLIMCHER
Clients: Steve Jobs; Ivan Reitman
Pace Wildenstein Gallery
32 East 57th Street, 2nd floor
New York, NY 10022
Tel.: 212-421-3292
PaceWildenstein.com

MARIAN GOODMAN
Clients: Euros; anyone who wants a Richter.
Marian Goodman Gallery
24 West 57th Street
New York, NY 10019
Tel.: 212-977-7160
MarianGoodman.com

JAY JOPLING
Clients: Lily Safra; Andrew Lloyd Webber
White Cube
48 Hoxton Square
London N1 6PB, UK
Tel.: 44 020 7930 5373
WhiteCube.com

ANTIQUARIAN BOOKS

BAUMAN RARE BOOKS
535 Madison Avenue
New York, NY 10022
Tel.: 212-751-0011
BaumanRareBooks.com

BIBLIOCTOPUS
120 South Crescent Drive
Beverly Hills, CA 90212
Tel.: 310-271-2173
Biblioctopus.com

KENNETH W. RENDELL GALLERY
Credited with stocking Bill Gates's library.
989 Madison Avenue
New York, NY 10021
Tel.: 212-717-1776
KWRendell.com

WINE AUCTIONEERS

ACKER MERRALL & CONDITT
160 West 72nd Street
New York, NY 10023
Tel.: 212-787-1700
AckerWine.com

D. SOKOLIN
12 Foster Avenue
P.O. Box 1206
Bridgehampton, NY 11932
Tel.: 800-946-3947
Sokolin.com

WINE AUCTION

SONOMA PARADISO
250 D Street
Santa Rosa, CA 95404
Tel.: 707-522-6444
SonomaParadiso.com

CALIFORNIA CULT WINES

BLANKIET ESTATE
P.O. Box 2100
Yountville, CA 94599
Tel.: 707-963-2001
Blankiet.com

BRYANT FAMILY VINEYARDS
1567 Sage Canyon Road
St. Helena, CA 94574
Tel.: 314-231-8066

COLGIN CELLARS
P.O. Box 254
St. Helena, CA 94574
Tel.: 707-963-0999
ColginCellars.com

DALLA VALLE VINEYARDS
P.O. Box 329
Oakville, CA 94562
Tel.: 707-944-2676
DallaValleVineyards.com

HARLAN ESTATE
P.O. Box 352
Oakville, CA 94562
Tel.: 707-944-1441
HarlanEstate.com

SCREAMING EAGLE
P.O. Box 12
Oakville, CA 94562
Tel.: 707-944-0749
ScreamingEagle.com

CUSTOMIZED WINE

CRUSHPAD
Drink yourself silly.
2573 3rd Street
San Francisco, CA 94107
Tel.: 415-864-4232
CrushpadWine.com

CIGARS

CLUB MACANUDO
Where Rudy Giuliani met wife 3.
26 East 63rd Street
New York, NY 10065
Tel.: 212-752-8200
ClubMacanudo.com

NAT SHERMAN
A mecca for cigar aficionados.
12 East 42nd Street
New York, NY 10017
Tel.: 800-692-4427
NatSherman.com

CHAPTER NINE / BILLIONAIRE BREEDING HABITS

TO HEIR IS DIVINE

"I've never lived in a building that didn't have my name on it."
—IVANKA TRUMP

EVEN WITH ALL YOUR HOUSES, ART, clothes, friends, and club memberships, there will eventually come a time when you realize something's missing—a vague feeling of emptiness you can't quite shake—until one day, perhaps while thumbing through the Bergdorf catalog in search of an answer, it hits you: You need an heir.

If you regularly share a bed with someone of the opposite sex, getting your hands on some suitable offspring shouldn't be a problem: The Filthy Rich make babies the same way everyone else does; they just do it on nicer sheets. And lately they do it more often. It's become something of a status symbol to have a large brood—the more, the merrier. It's what you do with them once they've hatched that's the challenge.

Although raising a child of privilege has never been easy, it's getting more harrowing by the moment. As with so many other social diseases, Paris Hilton is largely to blame. When the hotel heiress flashed her business from atop a banquette near the end of the last century, it was a rallying cry to spoiled sybarites everywhere: Go forth and party, my fellow heirheads. You have nothing to lose but your dignity.

Where flagrant materialism, functional illiteracy, and mindless hedonism were once things to be ashamed of, they are now the height of fashion. With the right connections at VH1, they might even make your kid a superstar.

Brace yourself: The age of the überbrat is upon us. And it's only going to get worse.

"BENTLEY FOR BABIES"
The Silver Cross

GREAT EXPECTATIONS

A Pregnancy Primer

HAVING A BABY IS SERIOUS BUSINESS, and a great way to land a signature kids line with your favorite designer. With access to experimental fertility treatments and $100,000 Ivy League egg donors, the Filthy Rich are never too old to start reproducing. If and when you decide to spawn, you'll have a slew of new people in your life—a delivery nurse, nutritionist, massage therapist, prenatal yoga instructor—and another fabulously expensive thing to adore. Just remember: While tax deductible, a child is not a depreciating asset, per se. Time to hire some help and stock up.

AND BABY MAKES SEVEN! A Filthy Rich Mommy's Dream Team

BABY SHOWER POWER

The Care Necessities

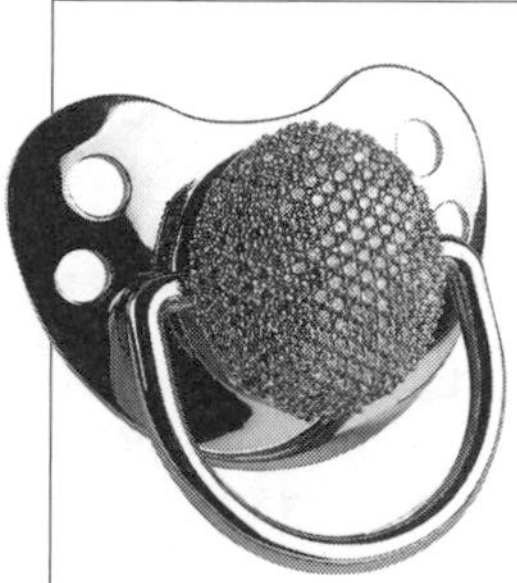

Personalized Pacifier

❑ Diamond binky with 278 pavé diamonds **$17,000**

❑ Harry Allen "bank in the form of a pig" **$195**

❑ Silk shantung baby sling from Oopa Baby **$298**

❑ Carrs of Sheffield brush and comb set **$345**

❑ Smythson of Bond Street baby book **$362**

❑ Georg Jensen baby rattle **$650**

❑ Life-size plush baby elephant **$700**

❑ Goyard diaper bag **$3,000**

❑ *Where the Wild Things Are,* by Maurice Sendak (first edition) **$10,000**

❑ One share of Berkshire Hathaway **$138,500** (approx.)

❑ Home sonogram machine (as purchased by Tom Cruise) **$200,000**

THE PERFECT BUMP

Like all first-time mothers, moneyed moms-to-be tend to behave as though they're the first woman ever to be impregnated. But not all of their bumps are created equal. A filthy rich bump is tight, pert, and shaped like a basketball—giving people the impression you gained exactly the baby's weight, and nothing more. Once it's delivered, you have exactly two months to reclaim your pre-pregnancy figure before your friends start whispering. Bonus points for a faster recovery.

WHAT'S IN A NAME?

As with luxury brands, the Filthy Rich are constantly on the run when it comes to children's names. Some socialite on a Gulfstream decides to name her kid Bella, and then—plop!—it trickles down into flyover country. Exactly how this happens, no one's quite sure, though TV plays a role. (Remember Dylan on *90210*? Met any baby Dylans at the club lately?) Thankfully, it's the surname that really counts. And if the mother's maiden name packs more punch, so be it. It's understandable why dissolute oil heir Brandon Davis (née: Brandon Zarif) or Margherita Missoni (née: Margherita Maccapani) would prefer mom's moniker. On the whole, today's übertycoons give their kids the same boring names as the rest of America, although there are a few exceptions:

OLD MONEY

FOR BOYS	FOR GIRLS
Chip (Charles)	**Binky (Barbara)**
Dash (Dashiel)	**Eleanor**
Jock (Jack, John)	**Georgina**
Tad (Theodore, Ted)	**Penny (Penelope)**
Topper (Christopher)	**Polly**
Trey	**Priscilla**
Trip (as in, the III)	**Tattie (Theodora)**
Warren VIII	**Weezie, Weeza (Louise, Louisa)**

NEW MONEY

FOR BOYS		FOR GIRLS	
Carter	**Jack**	**Audrey**	**Hermione**
Casper	**Jasper**	**Ava**	**Imogen**
Chase	**Julian**	**Bella**	**Jasmine**
Coleman	**Justin**	**Bronwyn**	**Lydia**
Cooper	**Leo**	**Chloë**	**Olivia**
Deacon	**Max**	**Daphne**	**Phoebe**
Frederick	**Milo**	**Ella**	**Sienna**
Harris	**Taylor**	**Elle**	**Sophia**
Hunter	**Toby**	**Gloria**	**Violet**

HOLLYWOOD

And then, there are those names in a class all their own—the Pilot Inspektors, the Suris, the Scouts. The only rule here is that no one—at least no one anyone gives a damn about—can have a kid with the same name. If you work in entertainment of any sort, particularly if you're an actor or musician, you are free to improvise. A few suitably bizarre suggestions:

FOR BOYS			FOR GIRLS		
Ajax	**Motown**	**Salinger**	**Alaska**	**Innocenta**	**Silver Lake**
Bandit	**Kojak**	**The Snizz**	**Agony**	**Kumquat**	**Tamazapam**
Blip	**Kool**	**Sukot**	**Calamine**	**Nurse**	**Tellurida**
Bristle	**Mittens**	**Quickness**	**Fizzle**	**Ovaltine**	**Yoni Michel**
Captain	**Neutrino**	**Tourist**	**Garnish**	**Palladium**	**Yuba**
Coolness	**Muzzle**	**Whistler**	**Gomorrah**	**Paper**	**ZZZ**
Curtain	**Pringle**	**8-Ball**	**Honeypot**	**Prancer**	**(pronounced "Z")**

BABY BALLERS

Filthy Rich Before Their Time

CHRISTINA ONASSIS

There's a downside to inheriting zillions, and it isn't just the taxes. Someone had to die.

HOWARD HUGHES

b. December 24, 1905

When Howard was 19, his father died and left him the monolithic Hughes Tool Company, which held the patent for a drill bit used by every oil company in the world. Naturally, he did as any kid would—he dropped out of Rice University, married his heiress sweetheart, Ella, and took off for Hollywood to make movies featuring scantily clad babes and death-defying stunts. Later, he went insane.

HOWARD HUGHES

CHRISTINA ONASSIS

b. December 11, 1950

The only daughter of billionaire Aristotle Onassis spent her childhood on her namesake yacht dressing her dolls in custom Dior. In a span of two years in the late '70s, she lost her brother, mother, and father to various tragedies, making her—at 25—the only heir to Ari's $500 million fortune. She married four times before her death from a drug-related heart attack at age 33.

ALBERT VON THURN UND TAXIS

ALBERT VON THURN UND TAXIS

b. June 24, 1983

German Prince Albert II inherited over $2 billion at the tender age of eight. The money is a lot older than he is, dating back to the Roman Empire's postal service. (Stamps were expensive back then.) These days he lives in a castle surrounded by acres and acres of private forest. And ladies: He's single.

ARMY OF ONE
Fifth Avenue's Finest

THE NANNY STATE

Mother's Little Helpers

KNOW THE FIRST THING ABOUT CHILD CARE? OF COURSE YOU DON'T. SO IT'S TIME TO HIRE some people who do. Just imagine how much better a parent you'll be when someone else is waking up in the middle of the night, changing diapers, dealing with bath time, and teaching Bronwyn how to walk. What a weight off your shoulders.

WEST CARIBBEAN NANNIES

SMALL CHILDREN WILL respect and adore your nurturing surrogate, plus they'll pick up a little French. (*J'adore Dior!*) Bonus: West Caribbean nannies usually have families of their own and zero desire to sleep with your husband.

AUSSIE NANNIES

WHEN YOUR KIDS start getting active, it's time to hire a full-time playmate. Nannies from Down Under are famously fun-loving, energetic, and less attractive than their French or Scandinavian counterparts. Plus, there's that universally appealing accent.

AMERICAN NANNIES

YOU'RE MORE THAN welcome to hire an all-American nanny—particularly a pretty one with a great personality, a top-tier education, and a lifelong interest in early child development—but it isn't recommended.

EASTERN EUROPEAN NANNIES

If your children start acting out, lean on the former Eastern Bloc to keep them in line. Unemotional and hard-as-nails, these girls are very good at controlling kids, although their overall affect can be a tad Slavic. Also, they have killer bodies when they're young.

BRITISH AGENCY NANNIES

In the U.K., the Council for Awards in Children's Care and Education and the Royal Society of Health certify nannies, so you know if you're getting a legit Mary Poppins. Be warned, though: These buxom status nannies won't take any guff, particularly not yours.

MANNIES

Isn't it about time Mom did something for herself? The kids are old enough to be out on their own, but you could use a watchful eye after school and when you're traveling. He might as well be 25 and fun to look at. Part-time models and full-time surfers are particularly qualified.

THAT'S HOW WE STROLL

Prams for the Glam

No, you're not going to touch the thing. But that doesn't mean your baby won't be judged by its ride. Here are three for the road:

SILVER CROSS BALMORAL
$2,895

A "Bentley for Babies," the Silver Cross has been the stroller of choice for British aristos since the 1920s. Today, Hollywood royals like Madonna, Sarah Jessica Parker, and Catherine Zeta-Jones follow suit.

BUGABOO BY BAS KOSTERS
$2,000

Countless Upper East Side MILFs and celebs like Gwyneth Paltrow push the standard-issue $900 Chameleon, but only 1,000 have upgraded to the hand-stitched, white-leather model. Care to make that 1,001?

MACLAREN LIMITED LEATHER AND GOLD STROLLER
$3,800

The S&M styling of this black leather monstrosity is a hit with fashion slaves the world over. The lightweight carbon fiber frame offsets the 9-carat-gold paint job. But hurry! They only made 20, thank God.

PUSH IT REAL GOOD
The Maclaren

TEACH YOUR CHILDREN SWELL

"The only reason I always try to meet and know the parents better is because it helps me to forgive their children."

—LE ROSEY HEADMASTER LOUIS JOHANNOT

TO THE UNINITIATED, AMERICAN PREP SCHOOLS CAN SEEM LIKE CARBON COPIES OF each other. (Tiny student–teacher ratios, 100 percent college matriculation, sloppily dressed white kids, miles of wainscoting.) But once you toss aside the glossy brochures and pay attention to what really matters—reputation, gossip, and who went where—a clearer picture emerges.

DAY SCHOOLS

WHERE KIDS STAY IN THE PICTURE

IF YOU'RE THE TYPE OF PARENT WHO wants to watch his children grow up, your options are limited by geography. In most places, the Filthy Rich demonstrate their solidarity by backing one school. (You'll recognize it by the glitzy new athletic center, SUV-packed parking lot, and recently paved roads.) A look at the better-known prepatoriums:

ST. ALBANS

Washington, D.C.
4–12. BOYS ONLY.

VOTE FOR ME!

Anglophilia, Capitol-style. Admissions director Mason Lecky was No. 42 on a *GQ* list of "The 50 Most Powerful People in D.C." Alumni: Al Gore Jr., Jesse Jackson Jr., *Washington Post* chairman Don Graham, and Marriott Hotels honcho J. W. Marriott Jr. $28, 860 per year

BUCKLEY

Sherman Oaks, California
K–12. COED.

ALUMNI UPDATES COURTESY OF *US WEEKLY*

Oldest independent school in L.A. Former Griffins include Paris and Nicky Hilton, Nicole Richie, Kim Stewart, Alyssa Milano, Nicollette Sheridan, and Kim Kardashian. Log on to the headmaster's blog. Clearly, he has some explaining to do. $23,100–$26,000 per year

CHAPIN

New York, New York
K–12. GIRLS ONLY.

LADIES FIRST

Academic rigor in a charm school setting. Where Jackie O learned to curtsy. Alumnae: Sunny von Bülow, Vera Wang, Lilly Pulitzer, Casey Johnson, Ivanka Trump, Queen Noor of Jordan, socialite DJ Samantha Ronson, and Sigourney Weaver. $29,100 per year

COLLEGIATE

New York, New York
K–12. BOYS ONLY.

THE OLDEST IN THE NATION—AND THEY KNOW IT

First independent school in America. With just 213 students in the upper school, it's tooth-and-nail to secure a spot. *The Wall Street Journal* ranked it No. 1 in the world for college matriculation. Alumni: *New York Times* publisher Arthur Sulzberger Jr., Edgar Bronfman Jr., and actor David Duchovny. $29,100 per year

CROSSROADS

Santa Monica, California
K–12. COED.

PIPELINE TO THE IVIES . . . AND THE IVY

A funky experiment in progressive education, it's now the unofficial feeder school of Hollywood's ruling class. Signature programs include Mysteries, in which students reveal their innermost thoughts. Your kid may still do drugs—but it'll be at somebody famous's house! Past and present Crossroaders include Kate Hudson, Cisco Adler, and the spawn of Dustin Hoffman, Brian Grazer, Kiefer Sutherland, Larry David, and Meg Ryan. $22,030–$26,100 per year

DALTON

New York, New York
K–12. COED.

IT'S ALL DOWNHILL FROM HERE

Start soliciting recommendation letters now. Right now. Under the "Dalton Plan," children are treated as "social beings" whose spirits must be nurtured. VIP Daltonians include Anderson Cooper, Sean Lennon, and the kids of Mia Farrow, Rupert Murdoch, Robert Redford, and Bruce Wasserstein. $30,650–$31,200 per year

KID COUTURE

The Age of Foot-High Fashion

Before they can grip a credit card, many kids skip "goo goo, gaa gaa" and go straight to "Gucci." As such, little Sophie isn't going to be placated with Stride Rite and Baby Gap, never mind–*shudder*–"hand-me-downs" from her big sister. She knows exactly what she wants (hint: It looks a lot like what Mom's wearing), and will guilt her until she gets it. Thankfully, today's filthy richest adult designers–Vilebrequin, Dior, Gucci, Michael Kors, Marc Jacobs, La Perla, you name it—will be more than happy to help her.

FRANCIS W. PARKER

Chicago, Illinois
PK–12. COED.

"LINCOLN PARK IS THE CENTER OF THE UNIVERSE"

First prep school PTA in the country. Pay the pre-kindergarten tuition of $17,830 to reserve a spot early, or just apply to the Latin School. Former Colonels include Anne Heche, Daryl Hannah, and playwright David Mamet. $17,830–$23,890 per year

HARVARD-WESTLAKE

Los Angeles, California
7–12. COED.

AGENT SELECTED, MOTHER APPROVED

Hollywood neponistas and pint-size intellectuals only. Past Wolverines include Candice Bergen, Jake and Maggie Gyllenhaal, Hard Rock heir-head Harry Morton, Tori Spelling. $27,000 per year

HOCKADAY

Dallas, Texas
PK–12. GIRLS ONLY.

HOME OF THE "HOCKADAISIES"

Saddle shoes, plaid skirts required. White graduation dresses hang in alums' closets, next to their deb and wedding gowns. Alumnae: Barbara and Jenna Bush. $14,540–$20,770 per year

ST. JOHN'S

Houston, Texas
K–12. BOYS ONLY.

REJECTED GEORGE W. BUSH

Powerhouse lacrosse team. Retro plaid uniforms. Untucked shirts lead to detention. Like *A Separate Peace*, but with shitkickers and dip. Beloved rich-kid auteur Wes Anderson spoofed his experience here in *Rushmore*. $13,390–$16,825 per year

THE CONCERNED PARENTS' GUIDE TO TEXTING

Curious what darling Ava's been tapping on about at the dinner table? Below, a handy acronym decoder:

IHEAAD I Haven't Eaten Anything All Day

STNW Stop Typing, Nanny Watching

CMMC Checking Mom's Medicine Cabinet

DWMAP? Didn't We Meet at Promises?

PIPB/LGN Parents in Palm Beach. Let's Get Naked

WHA? Who Has Adderall?

OA Olsen Alert

N/A/H Name/Age/Headshot

TDS Total Day Student

CUIV See you in Vegas

YRICSTS! Yeah, Right, I Can See the Scars!

OSY On Stavros's Yacht

BMT Buy Me That

HBD Housekeeper Buying Drugs

MDAA My Dad's an Asshole

ADVANCE PLACEMENT
Mary Institute

LAKESIDE SCHOOL

Seattle, Washington
5–12. COED.

"MOMMY WROTE EXCEL"

"Without Lakeside there would be no Microsoft," said Bill Gates, explaining why he donated $40 million to the school's endowment in 2005. Filthy rich phenom Paul Allen and cell phone pioneer Craig McCaw also did time. $20,450–$21,000 per year

LATIN SCHOOL OF CHICAGO

Chicago, Illinois
5–12. COED.

NORTHWESTERN OR BUST

When Nancy Reagan attended, she performed in a play called *First Lady*. Other Romans include chewing gum scion William Wrigley Jr. and philanthropist Brooks McCormick. $20,675 per year

ST. MARK'S SCHOOL OF TEXAS

Dallas, Texas
1–12. BOYS ONLY.

THE LONE STAR SCHOOL

The Roosevelts donated a carillon, the Hunts a football stadium, the Rogers a pool—that leaves you the petting zoo. Hop to it. Past Marksmen include billionaire oilman Richard Bass, Ross Perot Jr., and Owen and Luke Wilson (the former was expelled for cheating on a geometry exam). $16,909–$20,931 per year

MARY INSTITUTE AND ST. LOUIS COUNTRY DAY SCHOOL

St. Louis, Missouri
JK–12. COED.

HEADLAND IN THE HEARTLAND

100-acre campus in ritzy suburb of Ladue. When Missourians ask, "Where'd you go to school?" they mean high school. It matters. Alumni: Betty Grable, Monsanto chairman Charles Sommers, and May Department Stores honcho Morton May. $15,450–$18,690 per year

NATIONAL CATHEDRAL

Washington, D.C.
4–12. GIRLS ONLY.

"MY DADDY CAN SUBPOENA YOUR DADDY"

Sister school of St. Albans. Choir is kind of a big deal. Alumnae: Al Gore's daughters (Karenna, Kristin, and Sarah), LBJ's daughters (Lynda and Luci), and various Rockefellers and Roosevelts. $28,905 per year

NOBLE AND GREENOUGH

Dedham, Massachusetts
7–12. COED.

NO BALLS, NO GLORY

187-acre campus snaked by the Charles River. Five-day boarding. Boys bunk in a castle filled with secret passageways and false doors. Weirdly good crew teams. Bitter Milton rival. Alumni: JFK, two Bay State governors, various important Brahmins with names like Saltonstall. $29,500 per year

PINGRY

Martinsville, New Jersey
K–12. COED.

CATCHALL FOR THE NEW YORK RUNOFF

Alumni told all in Jamie Johnson's *Born Rich.* Considered the best school in dirty Jersey. Former Bears include Q-tip scion Woody Johnson, S. I. Newhouse IV, and MediaOne mogul Amos Hostetter Jr. $21,750–$26,100 per year

SIDWELL FRIENDS

Washington, D.C.
PK–12. COED.

PLAY DATES AT 1600

Quaker utopia where White House kid Chelsea Clinton told the school nurse, "Don't call my mom, she's busy. Try my dad." Alumni include children of Al Gore, Richard Nixon, Teddy Roosevelt, Donald Rumsfeld, and Herbert Hoover. $26,790–$27,790 per year

SPENCE

New York, New York
K–12. GIRLS ONLY.

FAST TRACK FOR FAST GIRLS

If Spence were a woman, it would be Gwyneth Paltrow. So there. Girls learn to smash glass ceilings with smiles on their faces. Alumnae: mayoral spawn Emma and Georgina Bloomberg, rock royal Jade Jagger, Frick heiress Helen Clay Frick, and cereal scionette Marjorie Lake Post. $27,000 per year

SCHOOLS FOR SCOUNDRELS

Ship Out to Shape Up

A rebellious streak is perfectly normal; driving your Ferrari into the pool is not. Should your kids get truly out of hand, it may be time to send them to a therapeutic wilderness camp. (Reform schools are for poor people.)

COTTONWOOD DE TUCSON
Tucson, Arizona

Your precious will be surrounded by cacti and a team of therapists at Cottonwood, tucked into the foothills of the Sonoran Desert. Each day, students meet with a shrink, take martial arts classes, and complete an outdoor challenge. The experience culminates in Family Week. Try your best to show up. $45,000 for 45 days

NEW HORIZONS FOR YOUNG WOMEN
Springfield, Maine

Run by Barbara Walters' daughter, Jackie, who bounced back from her teenage years as a stoned Studio 54 bad girl to open her own camp for coddled hellions. Mirrors and makeup are strictly banned. That will teach them. $18,900 for 6 weeks; $28,350 for 9 weeks

BOARDING SCHOOLS

THE BEST PARENTING MONEY CAN BUY

THE KINDS OF BONDS THAT LAST A LIFEtime can only be made when teenagers terrorize one another in close quarters. As they always have, plutocrats who want the best for their children ship them off to a handful of elite boarding schools for indoctrination into the ruling class and lessons in covert substance abuse. (Later, their kids thank them for it.) While these schools are no longer the sole province of East Coast WASPs, they still run the show. Here are the heavyweights:

CHOATE ROSEMARY HALL

Wallingford, Connecticut
9–12. COED.

TUNE IN, TURN ON, GET A'S

A New York favorite. Filthy rich Choaties include Ivanka Trump, Glenn Close, JFK Jr., Amanda Hearst, and Michael Douglas. $39,360 per year

DEERFIELD ACADEMY

Deerfield, Massachusetts
9–12. COED.

FROM B-LIST TO A-LIST

Admitted girls in 1989 for the first time since the '40s. King Abdullah II Ibn Al Hussein of Jordan liked it so much he built his own clone, King's Academy, in Madaba, and hired away Deerfield's headmaster. Other alumni include Nelson Rockefeller Jr. and right-wing moneyman Richard Mellon Scaife. $37,756 per year

ST. GEORGE'S

Newport, Rhode Island
9–12. COED.

CUTE BUT DUMB

Caught F. Scott's eye in *This Side of Paradise*. Best squash courts in the country. Rife with prep traditions like the Pie Race and Headmaster's Holiday. Illustrious alumni include John Jacob Astor, William Henry Vanderbilt III, Bush family patriarch Prescott Bush, and pharma king Albert Merck. $36,550 per year

FOREIGN DESKS
For That European Finish

ETON
Windsor, England
Stiff Upper Everything

Est. 1440 by King Henry VI. Boys only. The only type of public school your kids should ever attend. (And that's because it's private. Tricky Brits!) Thirteen hundred boarders, ages 13 to 18. Stodgy uniform requires white tie, morning coat, and pinstripe trousers. Life goal: become House Captain. "Old Etonians" include Prince William, Prince Harry, and two-thirds of the British ruling class. $49,262 per year

INSTITUTE LE ROSEY
Rolle and Gstaad, Switzerland
The Filthy Richest of Them All

Est. 1880. Coed. Four hundred boarders, ages 7 to 18. The most expensive prep school in the world. Any "child who has been spoilt and who is used to his/her way of life" and "anyone who has a drug habit, in whatever form" is discouraged from applying. Lessons are taught in French and English. Daily 10:30 A.M. chocolate breaks. From January through March the student body packs up for Gstaad, and everyone skis from 2 to 5 P.M. Former "Roseans" include Strokes frontman Julian Casablancas, Alexandra and Egon von Furstenberg, Princess Marie-Chantal of Greece, Dodi Fayed, and the Aga Khan. $66,721 per year

GROTON
Groton, Massachusetts
8–12. COED.

HOME OF THE "SNOTTY GROTTIES"

172 perfect boys, 183 perfect girls. Where Calvinism, WASP ritual still reigns. Handshakes to end each day. Alumni: *Prep* author Curtis Sittenfeld, Franklin Roosevelt, William Paul Getty, many a Harriman, a museum's worth of Whitneys. $39,850 per year

HOTCHKISS
Lakeville, Connecticut
9–12. COED.

NO DRINKING. NO DRUGS. NO KIDDING. FUN STOPS HERE.

"No chance" policy toward substance abuse. Hardcore dress code. Twelve Steinway pianos on campus; four telescopes. Its cavernous theater puts most Broadway houses to shame. Aspiring jam banders dig the professional recording studio; future CEOs hone their schmoozing skills on the nine-hole golf course. Famous Kissies: Fords galore, *Time* magazine cofounder Henry Luce, candy capo Forrest Mars, Morgan Stanley founder Harold Stanley, and Boston Red Sox chairman Tom Werner. $33,310 per year

LAWRENCEVILLE
Lawrenceville, New Jersey
9–12. COED.

GOOD OL' SCHOOL

Just old boys passing lacrosse balls with old boys, until 1985 when girls were invited to play. House system, just like the Brits. Ex-Lawrencians include pollster George Gallup, Tinsley and Topper Mortimer, Michael Eisner, Lydia Hearst-Shaw, and Greek socialite Taki Theodoracopulos. $36,820 per year

IN LOCO PARENTIS

Checklist for Keeping Your Kids Popular

- Freshman Year -

❑ Cite vague **"security concerns"** to score Chloë a single room (freshmen are required to share), then dispatch your decorator to outfit it with a 50-inch plasma, seagrass carpeting, and canopy bed.

❑ Inure yourself to the outrageous **monthly bills** flowing from the campus grill and bookshop. Understand that she needs to bribe her way into the cool crowd with endless rounds of Diet Cokes and grilled cheeses. Also, casually charging a new pair of shorts every time she's late for field hockey practice is just how it's done.

❑ **FedEx six cases** of Diet Raspberry Snapple Iced Tea to her each month. The hockey team will be duly impressed when she spikes them with Absolut.

- Sophomore Year -

❑ Put Chloë **on the Pill.**

❑ **Take her out of school for** New York Fashion Week in September.

❑ Allow her to **bring three friends** on the boat over spring break in Turkey. The "legendary blow-out" that results when they discover that Italians, like the Filthy Rich, start drinking at age 12 will keep her in BFFs for the next two semesters.

- Junior Year -

❑ Top up **those donations** so Chloë can take her mind off her books and concentrate on things that actually matter, like landing a *Teen Vogue* internship.

❑ Pull her **out of school** for a semester to deal with her spiraling bulimia/coke addiction. While she's home, buy her some new boobs. The combined effects of surgery and extended convalescence will give her the confidence she needs come fall.

❑ Buy her a **Range Rover** and a parking spot where she can stash it off campus. Sure, it's against school rules, but how else is she gonna buy kegs?

- Senior Year -

❑ Let Chloë **booze on the PJ** back from Nice. When she's immediately busted by her RA for having Bordeaux breath, mumble something about "cultural differences," smile menacingly, and walk away.

❑ **Throw a party for 200** at "The Inn" to toast her graduation. Fly in Nobu to cater it.

❑ Have the Maine **cottage reshingled** and the lawns resodded. It needs to look smashing when she and 475 of her closest friends park their grad week party flotilla in the backyard. Shut off the sprinkler.

STROKE OF GENIUS
Andover

MIDDLESEX

Concord, Massachusetts
9–12. COED.

PUTS THE SEX IN ST. GROTTLESEX

Bested only by Andover in *Boston* magazine's annual rankings. Class I students must carve their own plaques. Prepsploitation flick *School Ties* filmed here. Alumni: Ur-WASP Henry Cabot Lodge, ex-Massachusetts gov. Bill Weld, New Mexico gov. Bill Richardson; and *40-Year-Old Virgin* Steve Carell. $40,780 per year

MILTON ACADEMY

Milton, Massachusetts
K–12. COED.

HOME OF THE '05 LOCKER ROOM ORGY. WILL. NEVER. LIVE. IT. DOWN.

James Taylor lived in Wolcott, dropped out. T. S. Eliot, Robert F. Kennedy, and Ted Kennedy made it through. $34,524 per year

ST. MARK'S

Southborough, Massachusetts
9–12. COED.

THAT SIDE OF PARADISE

Superbrat central. Slammed in print as dim and elitist by both Vladimir Nabokov (who sent his son there) and W. H. Auden (who visited in 1939, and sneered at its English pretensions). Tiny endowment keeps it from reclaiming prewar glory, when everyone's folks were in *Who's Who.* Moneyed St. Markers include Forbes and Pulitzers aplenty, Prince Hashim of Jordan, and a pair of Vanderbilts. $39,150 per year

ST. PAUL'S

Concord, New Hampshire
9–12. COED.

AMERICAN ETON

Still tops—even after the teacher-student sex scandals and trustee wars of the early aughts. Ideal for sixth-generation legacies with Yale/CIA aspirations. Posh Paulies include John Kerry, William Randolph Hearst, cartoonist Gary Trudeau, and J. P. Morgan. $40,850 per year

PHILLIPS ACADEMY

Andover, Massachusetts
9–12. COED.

"IT'S 'ANDOVER,' STUPID"

Oldest boarding school in the U.S. Hancock himself signed its articles of incorporation. Stupid mascot: Gunga the Gorilla. Alumni: George Bush Jr.

and Sr., Jeb Bush, JFK Jr., and John W. Kluge Jr. $37,200 per year

PHILLIPS EXETER ACADEMY

Exeter, New Hampshire
9–12. COED.

HARVARD, HERE I COME

Long live the Harkness Method, where students sit around a table and "exchange ideas" with their teacher. Alumni: *The World According to Garp* author John Irving (who can't stop writing about it), *American Psycho*'s Patrick Bateman, *Da Vinci Code* scribe Dan Brown, and Gore Vidal. $36,500 per year. It would be more, if it weren't for the $1 billion endowment.

MISS PORTER'S

Farmington, Connecticut
9–12. GIRLS ONLY.

THE FINAL WORD IN FINISHING

Aka "Farmington," where girls go to become ladies, and leave as lesbians (kidding!). Once an alpha factory, it's seen its stock fall with the rise of coeducation. Alumnae: Jackie O, Gloria Vanderbilt, Agnes Gund, Lilly Pulitzer, "Poor Little Rich Girl" Barbara Hutton, and Brenda Frazier. $38,520 per year

TAFT

Watertown, Connecticut
9–12. COED.

ALL IN THE FAMILY

William Howard Taft's brother got the ball rolling. Eighteen-hole golf course. Two hockey rinks. Ten fields. Mr. & Mrs. Mac run the show. Alumni: James Stillman Rockefeller, George Weyerhaeuser, financier John Vogelstein, and many, many Tafts—naturally. $37,400 per year

THACHER

Ojai, California
9–12. COED.

GIDDYAP!

California's oldest boarding school (admittedly, not saying much), aka "Casa de Piedra." Founder Sherman Thacher Day took Lord Palmerston's words to heart: "There's nothing so good for the inside of a man as the outside of a horse." First-year "Toads" must ride and maintain their own animals. Cowboy hats are worn without irony. Deadly serious honor code. Students aren't issued dorm keys because their doors aren't locked. (Sticky-fingered residents get shipped back to Brentwood.) Filthy rich alumni: Howard Hughes, *Our Town* author Thornton Wilder, and Bechtel CEO Riley P. Bechtel. $38,800 per year

THE FILTHY RICH · TION · ARY

ST. GROTTLESEX \ sānt grä-tᵊl-seks \ *n*

Common slang for an elite group of boarding schools founded in the mid-to-late-19th century catering to well-to-do Episcopalian boys. Borrowing liberally—and, often, shamelessly—from the English public school tradition (Harrow, Eton, Winchester, Rugby, et al.), they attempted to instill character and industry in America's fortunate sons. The "St." refers to St. Paul's, St. Mark's, and St. George's; the "Gro" to Groton; and the "-ttlesex" to Middlesex.

THE OLD COLLEGE TRY

Haute Spots for Higher Learning

FILTHY RICH KIDS TEND TO BOUNCE AROUND AFTER HIGH SCHOOL, RARELY ENROLLING IN any one college for any length of time. So the pressure isn't exactly on to pick the right one. Just close your eyes, point to one of the following, ask Daddy who he knows, and let the rest of your life unfold as it may.

BROWN

Providence, Rhode Island

LOOSEY-GOOSEY requirements (take whatever you want! no grades!), naked traditions (the Sexpowergod Party), highly "flexible" admissions standards, and celeb spawn galore make this the filthy richest college in the land. Alums: JFK Jr., Allegra Versace, Dustin Hoffman's kids, Mike Ovitz's son, Chris (dropped out), Billy Getty (dropped out), Princess Theodora, and Lady Gabriella Windsor

PRINCETON

Princeton, New Jersey

EATING CLUBS, JOCKS, "Gatsby parties," WASPy nerds: It's a perfect incubator for an increasingly rare breed of studied snob. The superiority complex will suck you in for life. Alums: Queen Noor, the sons and daughters of scores of very important people you've never heard of

SARAH LAWRENCE

Bronxville, New York

LIVING ON 41 HILLY acres surrounded by reality, the tiny student body is an artsy pastiche of misanthropic heirs and bi-curious heiresses just trying to make it through the day without running out of dope.

USC

Los Angeles, California

WHEN YOU'RE TOSSING a Frisbee in the California sunshine surrounded by glistening models, you'll thank Daddy for calling his friends on the board. Very rich-kid friendly. Alums: Shipping heir and professional kiteboarder Stavros Niarchos, New York socialite Lauren Davis, Hollywood nepotista Jason Reitman

YOU MIGHT ALSO LIKE . . .

- Bard College
- Bennington College
- Colorado College
- Georgetown University
- Hamilton College
- Hampshire College
- Harvard College*
- Pepperdine University
- Rollins College
- St. Lawrence University
- Texas A&M
- The Claremont Colleges
- Trinity College
- Tufts University
- Tulane University
- Vanderbilt University
- Vassar College
- Yale University*

**Minimum $2.5 million donation for substandard non-legacies.*

Rory Gates • 1835 73rd Avenue, N.E. • Medina, WA 98039

As The World 'Terns

Summer Gigs for Filthy Rich Go-Getters

Objective: Regardless of how involved you are in their day-to-day lives, it's imperative you ensure your kids aren't wasting their summers harassing strangers for Greenpeace. Let their less-connected peers drive ice-cream trucks and John Deere mowers—your kids should have sexy unpaid internships in fascinating locales with fabulous people you sat next to once at a dinner party. So don't be shy. Hooking up your fellow plutocrat's progeny with a cushy summer gig is the unspoken duty of every tycoon—a nouveau riche twist on the old boy's network. Next time someone asks you what your kids are doing on their summer vacations, any of the following name drops will do:

Summers

- **Fetching decaf espressos for Steven Spielberg on the set of his new made-for-TV epic in Budapest**
- **Helping Jeff Koons install a series of three-story-high ceramic sex toys in the courtyard of the *Fondazione Nazionale* in Venice**
- **Taking dictation from Henry Kissinger in Connecticut**
- **Assisting the assistant to the assistant to Bill Clinton in Harlem**
- **Caddying for Tiger Woods at Augusta, Brookline, and Pebble Beach**
- **Researching Tina Brown's next book in London**
- **Helping Francis Ford Coppola build a butterfly farm on his ecoreserve in Belize**
- **Ferrying Halliburton CEO David Lesar around the Dubai campus in an armored golf cart**
- **Working in the fashion closet at French *Vogue***

MONEY TROUBLES

The Burden of Great Wealth

INHERITING A LARGE SUM OF CASH IS A phenomenon as old as cash itself. But even the Filthy Rich have never experienced anything like the present deluge—more than $30 trillion will be passed on within the next 50 years. Financial advisors refer to it as the Great Wealth Transfer. Although it sounds exciting, there is a downside. There will be those who wonder, "Why me?" and then leave $65 million to the Church of Scientology. Others will be driven to despair by the discovery that no one wants to hear them whine.

To teach practical wealth management (and noblesse oblige), you might consider sending your kids to wealth camp. At UC-Irvine's three-day $5,000 Financial Skills Retreat, future tycoons are tutored in the essentials—how to manage stocks, bonds, and future fiancés. At the Robin Hood Foundation's weeklong philanthropy retreat in Manhattan, they can even experience how the other half lives by riding the subway. Maybe there's hope for them yet.

CLOSET RICH KIDS

They keep their wealth under wraps—cashmere wraps.

Frat-Pack funny guy Vince Vaughn's mom, Sharon Eileen DePalmo Vaughn, was ranked among the country's top rainmakers by *Bloomberg Wealth Manager*. Before he dissed Yale to pursue acting, Vaughn dreamed of playing professional water polo.

• Though he's open when asked about it, CNN anchor Anderson Cooper doesn't like to broadcast the fact that his mother is Gloria Vanderbilt. As a child, he was snapped by Diane Arbus for *Harper's Bazaar*.

• *Seinfeld* alum Julia Louis-Dreyfus is the daughter of Franco-American business titan William Louis-Dreyfus, who has an estimated $3.4 billion fortune, making him one of the world's richest men. Her cousin, Robert Louis-Dreyfus, is the former CEO of Adidas.

• Credited as Liesel Matthews in 1995's *A Little Princess*, she was born Liesel Pritzker, one of 12 surviving heirs to the Hyatt Hotels–owning Chicago dynasty. Her share is said to be worth around $500 million.

DIRECTORY

BABY CLOTHES

GIGGLE
Pint-sized everything.
102 Greenwich Avenue
Greenwich, CT 06830
Tel.: 203-622-6775
Giggle.com

98% ANGEL
A Malibu staple.
3806A Cross Creek Road
Malibu, CA 90265
Tel.: 310-317-8560
98angel.com

BONPOINT
Impeccable French tailoring.
1269 Madison Avenue
New York, NY 10128
Tel.: 212-722-7720
Bonpoint.com
Other locations:
Beverly Hills: 310-278-1161
Boston: 617-267-1717
Palm Beach: 561-659-2119
Paris: 33 01 49 27 94 82

FLORA AND HENRI
Beautiful clothes for the genetically blessed.
225 26th Street
Santa Monica, CA 90402
Tel.: 310-587-1188
FloraHenri.com
Other locations:
New York: 212-249-1695
Seattle: 206-749-9698

LA LAYETTE ET PLUS
Appointments, please.
170 East 61st Street
New York, NY 10065
Tel.: 212-688-7072
LaLayette.com

PETER ELLIOT FOR KIDS
Make sure Milo's the coolest dude in pre-K.
1070 Madison Avenue
New York, NY 10028
Tel.: 212-570-2300

PICCOLINO
Versace, Armani, and Trussard for 0-to-15-year-olds.
9606 Santa Monica Blvd., 100B
Beverly Hills, CA 90210
Tel.: 310-276-3116

PORTHAULT
The cutest terrycloth bathrobes.
18 East 69th Street
New York, NY 10021
Tel.: 212-688-1660
D-porthault.com
Other locations:
Dallas: 214-526-3545
Paris: 33 014 720 7525

SPRING FLOWERS
Burberry ensembles; La Perla bathing suits.
905 Madison Avenue
New York, NY 10021
Tel.: 212-717-8182
or
337 Worth Avenue
Palm Beach, FL 33480
Tel.: 561-832-0131
SpringFlowersChildren.com

KIDS' FURNISHINGS

BLOOM'S HIGHCHAIR
Ultra-modern "dining nest."
807 5th Street, #7
Santa Monica, CA 90403
Tel.: 310-980-1899
BloomBaby.com

NETTO COLLECTION
Sleek designs camouflage functionality.
Tel.: 866-996-3886
NettoCollection.com

NANNY AGENCIES

ENGLISH NANNY & GOVERNESS SCHOOL
37 South Franklin Street
Chagrin Falls, OH 44022
Tel.: 800-733-1984
Nanny-Governess.com

NANNIES INCORPORATED
Suite 512, Linen Hall
162-168 Regent Street
London W1B 5TF, UK
Tel.: 44 020 7038 3757
NanniesInc.com

NORTHWEST NANNIES INC.
11830 SW Kerr Parkway
Suite 330
Lake Oswego, OR 97035
Tel.: 503-245-5288
NWNanny.com

WILDERNESS CAMPS

COTTONWOOD DE TUCSON
4110 Sweet Water Drive
Tucson, AZ 85745
Tel.: 800-877-4520
CottonwoodDeTucson.com

NEW HORIZONS FOR YOUNG WOMEN
P.O. Box 186
Orrington, ME 04474
Tel.: 207-992-2424
DaughtersAtRisk.com

REDCLIFF ASCENT
757 South Main
Springville, UT 84663
Tel.: 800-898-1244
RedCliffAscent.com

BOARDING SCHOOLS

CHOATE ROSEMARY HALL
333 Christian Street
Wallingford, CT 06492
Tel.: 203-697-2000
Choate.edu

DEERFIELD ACADEMY
1 Albany Road
Deerfield, MA 01342
Tel.: 413-772-0241
Deerfield.edu

ST. GEORGE'S
P.O. Box 1910
Newport, RI 02840
Tel.: 401-847-7565
StGeorges.edu

GROTON
P.O. Box 991, Farmers Row
Groton, MA 01450
Tel.: 978-448-7510
Groton.org

HOTCHKISS
11 Interlaken Road
P.O. Box 800
Lakeville, CT 06039
Tel.: 860-435-2591
Hotchkiss.org

LAWRENCEVILLE
2500 Main Street
Lawrenceville, NJ 08648
Tel.: 800-735-2030
Lawrenceville.org

MIDDLESEX
1400 Lowell Road
Concord, MA 01742
Tel.: 978-287-4759
Mxschool.edu

MILTON ACADEMY
170 Centre Street
Milton, MA 02186
Tel.: 617-898-1798
Milton.edu

ST. MARK'S
25 Marlborough Road
Southborough, MA 01772
Tel.: 508-786-6000
StMarksSchool.org

ST. PAUL'S
325 Pleasant Street
Concord, NH 03301
Tel.: 603-229-4600
SPS.edu

PHILLIPS ACADEMY
180 Main Street
Andover, MA 01810
Tel.: 978-749-4000
Andover.edu

PHILLIPS EXETER ACADEMY
20 Main Street
Exeter, NH 03833
Tel.: 603-772-4311
Exeter.edu

MISS PORTER'S
60 Main Street
Farmington, CT 06032
Tel.: 860-409-3500
MissPorters.org

TAFT
110 Woodbury Road
Watertown, CT 06795
Tel.: 860-945-7777
TaftSchool.org

THACHER
5025 Thacher Road
Ojai, CA 93023
Tel.: 805-646-4377
Thacher.org

DAY SCHOOLS

ST. ALBANS
Mount St. Alban
Washington, DC 20016
Tel.: 202-537-6435
StAlbansSchool.org

BUCKLEY
3900 Stansbury Avenue
Sherman Oaks, CA 91423
Tel.: 818-783-1610
BuckleyLA.org

CHAPIN
100 East End Avenue
New York, NY 10028
Tel.: 212-744-2335
Chapin.edu

COLLEGIATE
260 West 78th Street
New York, NY 10024
Tel.: 212-812-8500
CollegiateSchool.org

CROSSROADS
1714 21st Street
Santa Monica, CA 90404
Tel.: 310-829-7391
Xrds.org

DALTON
108 East 89th Street
New York, NY 10128
Tel.: 212-423-5200
Dalton.org

FRANCIS W. PARKER
330 West Webster Avenue
Chicago, IL 60614
Tel.: 773-353-3000
FWParker.org

HARVARD-WESTLAKE
700 North Faring Road
Los Angeles, CA 90077
Tel.: 310-288-3200
HW.com

HOCKADAY
11600 Welch Road
Dallas, TX 75229
Tel.: 214-363-6311
Hockaday.org

ST. JOHN'S
2401 Claremont Lane
Houston, TX 77019
Tel.: 713-850-0222
Sjs.org

LAKESIDE SCHOOL
14050 1st Avenue NE
Seattle, WA 98125-3099
Tel.: 206-368-3605
LakesideSchool.org

LATIN SCHOOL
59 West North Blvd.
Chicago, IL 60610
Tel.: 312-582-6000
LatinSchool.org

ST. MARK'S SCHOOL
10600 Preston Road
Dallas, TX 75230
Tel.: 214-346-8000
SMTexas.org

MARY INSTITUTE AND ST. LOUIS COUNTRY DAY SCHOOL
101 North Warson Road
St. Louis, MO 63124
Tel.: 314-993-5100
MICDS.org

NATIONAL CATHEDRAL
Mount St. Alban
Washington, DC 20016
Tel.: 202-537-6300
NCS.cathedral.org

NOBLE AND GREENOUGH
10 Campus Drive
Dedham, MA 02026
Tel.: 781-326-3700
Nobles.edu

PINGRY
Martinsville Road, P.O. Box 366
Martinsville, NJ 08836
Tel.: 908-647-5555
Pingry.k12.NJ.us

SIDWELL FRIENDS
3825 Wisconsin Avenue NW
Washington, DC 20016
Tel.: 202-537-8100
Sidwell.edu

SPENCE
22 East 91st Street
New York, NY 10128
Tel.: 212-289-5940
SpenceSchool.org

EUROPEAN ED

ETON
Windsor SL4 6DW, UK
Tel.: 44 1753 671000
EtonCollege.com

INSTITUTE LE ROSEY
Château du Rosey
1180 Rolle, Switzerland
Tel.: 41 21 822 55 00
and Campus d'hiver
Chalet Rex
3780 Gstaad, Switzerland
Tel.: 41 33 748 06 00
Rosey.ch

CHAPTER TEN / SURVIVING AT THE TOP

AFFLICTIONS & PRETENSIONS

"Finding wealth an intolerable burden is the mark of an unstable mind."
—SENECA

Congratulations! You are now completely unrecognizable to everyone you grew up with. It's not just the vacant frown, leathery tan, or Maybach in the driveway. It's how you've changed on the inside. (The bodyguard's a nice touch, too.)

In light of your outstanding progress, it's only fair that you be properly acknowledged. You're no longer just another boring young jerk with a nine-figure bank balance. From this page forward and ever after, you're officially Filthy Rich, and have the borrowed tastes and cultivated eccentricities to prove it.

Of course, there's a strong likelihood you've also picked up some quirks along the way. A heretofore undiagnosed gluten allergy, perhaps? A mild case of adult-onset OCD? A teeny-tiny painkiller issue? As a Vertu-toting member of the capitalist conspiracy, it's important you know what you're up against and which symptoms to look for. To get yourself on the road to recovery, please refer to the DSM-FR Manual of Millionaire Mental Disorders excerpted on the following pages. While not currently sanctioned by the American Psychiatric Association, it's sure to be approved in the coming months.

Lest you assume all your problems are in your head, however, we'll also be addressing other common hazards, like divorce, kidnapping, and substance abuse. Once you've got those nailed, it's time to learn how to die.

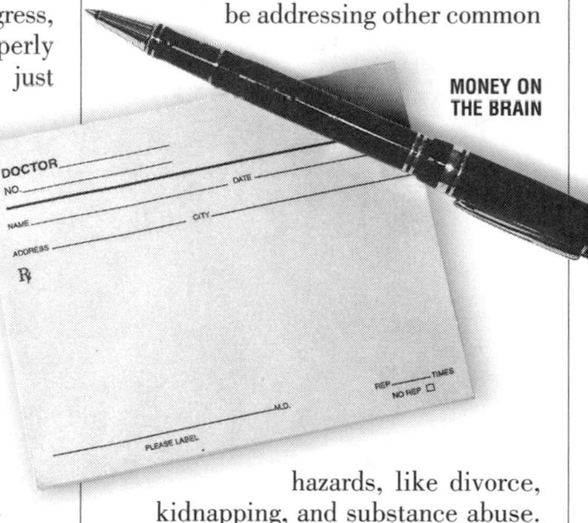

MONEY ON THE BRAIN

Unfortunately, you won't find much wriggle room there. With so many tycoons floating around, the devil doesn't bargain like he used to.

DIAGNOSTIC AND STATISTICAL MANUAL OF MILLIONAIRE MENTAL DISORDERS

FILTHY RICH EDITION

DSM–FR

First published in 1952, *The Diagnostic and Statistical Manual of Mental Disorders* (or DSM) is the Talmud of psychiatry—a definitive guide to everything that can possibly go wrong inside a human brain. To the consternation of the country's $600-an-hour shrinks, however, its most recent edition (DSM-IV) all but ignores the growing list of mental disorders unique to the Filthy Rich. Uncomfortable as it is to discuss, bottomless wealth can have quite a profoundly perverting effect on the mind. In an attempt to curtail your suffering, the following pages contain an early excerpt from the forthcoming first edition of the DSM-FR, for easy self-diagnosis.

Term	Examples of clinical situations
ACQUIRED INCOMPETENCE DISORDER (AID)	**DIAGNOSTIC FEATURES** When doted upon excessively by handlers, PAs, and household servants, highly functioning adults grow incrementally incapable of performing even the simplest of tasks (programming their cell phone's speed dial, operating a dishwasher, remembering *anyone's* name) without professional assistance. **ASSOCIATED FEATURES AND DISORDERS** Often misdiagnosed with spoiled bitch syndrome, AID sufferers undergo a retro-infantile softening of the skull and observable loss of motor skills. **SPECIFIC CULTURE AND GENDER FEATURES** Though AID is seen across all FR strata, it shows up most frequently in successful members of the entertainment and fashion industries. As a rule, the newer the money, the swifter the onset.
ACQUIRED SITUATIONAL NARCISSISM (ASN)	**DIAGNOSTIC FEATURES** Sometimes referred to as the "celebrity disease," ASN is defined by a delusional belief in one's own awesomeness, typically triggered by irrational and prolonged public adoration and excessive employee ass kissing. A substrain of clinical narcissism (CN), ASN can strike any public figure, at any time, well into adulthood. Those afflicted display the full range of unappealing traits on the egoism spectrum, from insufferable arrogance to obsessive self-pity. **ASSOCIATED FEATURES AND DISORDERS** The situational narcissist's intense love of self, lack of empathy, grandiosity, habit of laughing at his own jokes, and (in the case of Hollywood A-listers) faux-casual references to the Church of Scientology can suck the air out of any room. **SPECIFIC CULTURE AND GENDER FEATURES** Like '80s hair metal, biker gangs, LSD, and mass murder, ASN was first codified in California. Today, its sufferers include Fortune 500 CEOs, Wall Street rainmakers, music industry moguls, socialites—even celebrity chefs.

Term	Examples of clinical situations
CACOPHOBIA (from *kakos,* ancient Greek for "ugly")	**DIAGNOSTIC FEATURES** Harboring deep-seated fears of physical ugliness in both people and places, cacophobes use words like "ghastly" and "hideous" with alarming frequency. Sufferers have been known to cross the street to avoid passing a fat person. **ASSOCIATED FEATURES AND DISORDERS** Weaned on a Condé Nast–curated version of American life, cacophobes recoil in horror when confronted by the poorly designed, morbidly obese, Wal-Mart–outfitted reality. **SPECIFIC CULTURE AND GENDER FEATURES** Typically undereducated and overprivileged, cacophobes tend to work at *Vogue.*
ECDEMOMANIA (from *ekdemeos,* ancient Greek for "being away from home")	**DIAGNOSTIC FEATURES** A close second to alcoholism as the defining disease of the jet set, ecdemomania compels otherwise normal people to wander the globe in search of the next party. Its sufferers live in a state of permanent vacation, driven by a perpetual fear that someone, somewhere is having a better time than they are. **ASSOCIATED FEATURES AND DISORDERS** The ability to make ten minutes of small talk in seven different languages before repeating the same well-rehearsed stories; tanorexia (see p. 225). **SPECIFIC CULTURE AND GENDER FEATURES** Ecdemomaniacs can be male or female, and are often British, or wish they were. Lesser royals are especially prone.
EREMOPHOBIA (from *eraemia,* ancient Greek for "solitude")	**DIAGNOSTIC FEATURES** Eremophobes display an extreme and all-encompassing fear of loneliness. Rarely seen solo outside of the bathroom, they are terrified by the notion of spending an evening at home. **ASSOCIATED FEATURES AND DISORDERS** To facilitate his or her anti-loneliness agenda, the eremophobe surrounds him or herself with a "posse," and is generally overenthusiastic when it comes to drink and drugs. Friends come for the conversation and stay for the cocaine.

Term	Examples of clinical situations
	SPECIFIC CULTURE AND GENDER FEATURES Long associated with tragicomic funnymen like John Belushi and Chris Farley (whose last words, to a prostitute after a two-day coke binge, were, "Please don't leave me! Please don't leave me!"), eremophobia has recently reached epidemic proportions among Hollywood's younger set. But it isn't just the province of Lindsay Lohan types: Anyone with a rep for "attending the opening of an envelope" is likely afflicted.
ONIOMANIA (from *onios,* ancient Greek for "for sale")	**DIAGNOSTIC FEATURES** Commonly known as "shopaholism," oniomania is defined by an insatiable desire to buy things regardless of need. Diagnosing oniomania among the Filthy Rich is therefore quite difficult. Is Candy Spelling—whose Holmby Hills fortress boasts an "eBay room," a "gift wrap salon," and a "doll wing"—suffering from oniomania, or just exquisitely bad taste? If the doll wing were filled with Van Goghs instead of tacky figurines, would anyone bat an eye? **ASSOCIATED FEATURES AND DISORDERS** While oniomania is technically an impulse control disorder, any reasonably intelligent eight-year-old could tell you that an oniomaniac is simply trying to fill the gaping hole inside her heart with worldly baubles she doesn't need. Hell, the entire Louis Vuitton spring collection couldn't fill the bottomless chasm inside a power shopper like Cher. **SPECIFIC CULTURE AND GENDER FEATURES** In the U.S., oniomania is most readily observed in places where high-end shopping options are extensive: New York, L.A., Dallas, Boston, and Palm Beach. But thanks to the Web, anyone can get in on the credit-destroying action.
ORTHOREXIA (from *orthos* and *orexis,* ancient Greek for "correct" and "appetite")	**DIAGNOSTIC FEATURES** Bored by anorexia but grossed out by bulimia, today's weight-obsessed ladies have had shockingly few alternatives. Enter orthorexia, the status disease-of-the-moment, which takes the salad of genuine concern for healthful eating that's been tossing around the culture of late and drizzles it with evil. An orthorexic's list of what she won't put in her body is truly something to behold.

Term	Examples of clinical situations
	ASSOCIATED FEATURES AND DISORDERS There is no orthorexic rulebook, but generally sufferers err on the side of "can't eat that." Also, way too much planning: Being a strict macrobiotic vegan who never consumes wheat, starch, or gluten takes considerable forethought. **SPECIFIC CULTURE AND GENDER FEATURES** Found among anyone seeking the fat-burning power of an eating disorder, without the stigma. While women are more commonly afflicted, men are starting to catch on.
PENIAPHOBIA (from *penia,* ancient Greek for "poverty")	**DIAGNOSTIC FEATURES** An irrational fear of going broke is surprisingly common among those who came of age during the Great Depression or inherited their wealth. Late New York real estate tigress Leona Helmsley was a notorious peniaphobe: Beneath her De la Renta gowns and yards of diamond jewelry, the "Queen of Mean" wore $5 panties from Macy's. **ASSOCIATED FEATURES AND DISORDERS** Although peniaphobia is sometimes considered cute in the elderly, there is nothing less endearing than a cheap billionaire. **SPECIFIC CULTURE AND GENDER FEATURES** Despite its negative connotations, peniaphobia has proven to be an extremely effective survival mechanism for countless WASP dynasties, enabling their descendants to subsist just below filthy richness on interest alone while never generating a dime.
GERMAPHOBIA	**DIAGNOSTIC FEATURES** While not restricted to plutocrats per se, germaphobia, like type 2 diabetes, is rarely observed outside the first world (it's hard to fear germs when soap is a luxury). The typical germaphobe is an ambitious, anal retentive, and highly dominant personality. In the days before Purell Hand Sanitizer, he might have worn gloves indoors or washed his hands raw, or simply covered everything in Kleenex, as Howard Hughes did. Today, he keeps boxes of disposable "guest slippers" at both his home and office. **ASSOCIATED FEATURES AND DISORDERS** Acute smugness interrupted by nervous tics; heavy reliance on Valium; appalling hair.

Term	Examples of clinical situations
	SPECIFIC CULTURE AND GENDER FEATURES In general, germaphobes are male and shower before they have sex.
BODY DYSMORPHIC DISORDER (BDD)	**DIAGNOSTIC FEATURES** A mental disconnect between reality and what the sufferer sees when he or she looks in the mirror. Those with body dysmorphia often think they are heavier than they really are, or shorter than people tell them, or that their eyes are spaced too far apart, and that they look like Abe Vigoda. **ASSOCIATED FEATURES AND DISORDERS** In female celebrities, body dysmorphia can lead to agoraphobia (fear of going out in public). Better to be lonely than labeled a hatchet-faced fatty in the blogosphere. **SPECIFIC CULTURE AND GENDER FEATURES** Socialites, actresses, models, and prep school girls are particularly susceptible to BDD's destructive spell. Curiously, among males, it seems to have the opposite effect, allowing even the most pathetic Wall Street slob to believe he is somehow attractive. The world sees a jiggling gut, thinning hair, armpit stains, and a BlackBerry holster. He sees Adonis.
ACUTE PARANOIA	**DIAGNOSTIC FEATURES** The typical sufferer suspects, often with little or no basis, that others are trying to exploit him. Too bad he's always one step ahead of them! Reluctant to confide in anyone but his beleaguered consigliere (note: he has a consigliere), the acute paranoiac has a paper-thin skin, perceiving nefarious subtext in the most benign of Page Six mentions and obsequious birthday toasts. **ASSOCIATED FEATURES AND DISORDERS** Comorbid with acquired situational narcissism, it frequently compels the purchase of laser-sighted automatic weapons and bleeding-edge home security technology, including, but in no way limited to, pressure pads, heat sensors, underground escape passages, and lead-lined safe rooms. To buttress his own security detail (and smoke out suspected spies when needed), the acute paranoiac often maintains a house account with a blue-chip private security firm, such as Kroll, as well as back-channel relationships with one

Term	Examples of clinical situations
	or more disreputable private dicks in the Anthony Pellicano mold. Like the President, he insists that all employees refer to him only by his initials or code name ("Ice Man"). **SPECIFIC CULTURE AND GENDER FEATURES** Generally, an inflated sense of self-importance stemming from the afflicted's involvement in a controversial issue—Israel, the deunionization of Las Vegas, stiffing Suge Knight—coupled with one or more actual threats, however half-hearted, is enough to fuel a lifetime of acute paranoia. To be fair, in some reported cases, persons originally thought to be suffering from acute paronoia turned out to be right. (Most just turned out to be pricks.)
SEXUAL DEVIANCY	**DIAGNOSTIC FEATURES** Increased access to physically attractive sexual partners leads certain male moguls to "up the ante" and engage in ever-more elaborate and bizarre behaviors. With the means to indulge their fantasies daily and without restraint, they push boundaries further and further until, eventually, even the most hetero big shot gets to "gay." **ASSOCIATED FEATURES AND DISORDERS** Autoerotic asphyxiation, S&M, cross-dressing, group sex, and other extreme forms of stimulation are common. **SPECIFIC CULTURE AND GENDER FEATURES** Although sexual deviancy crosses all economic and social boundaries, the role of "been there, done that" boredom underpinning the privileged hedonist's journey to the freaky side sets him apart. Director Lee Tamahori's 2006 arrest for solicitation (while dressed as a woman) is a classic example, as is Eddie Murphy's legendary dalliances with a large-handed lady of the L.A. night. Palm Beach billionare Jeffrey Epstein's fondness for thrice-daily massages administered by local teens is yet another. Not that women are immune: Palm Beach doyenne Roxanne "Strumpet with the Trumpet" Pulitzer's legendary affair with a wind instrument (recounted in depth on p. 129), being the most charming example.

SECONDARY DISORDERS

ANGLOMANIA

DIAGNOSTIC FEATURES

Among the more common disorders, Anglomania has been afflicting the American ruling class since the country's inception. In recent years, it's claimed several revered female celebrities.

ASSOCIATED FEATURES AND DISORDERS

The casual use of Britishisms like "loo," followed by romantic involvement with an Englishman or woman, emigration, and the adoption of an unconvincing accent.

SPECIFIC CULTURE AND GENDER FEATURES

All manner of extreme snob can fall victim. If you climb high enough into the social stratosphere, eventually you reach the British aristocracy, which, supposedly, you cannot buy your way into. This drives filthy rich anglomaniacs insane.

FRANCOMANIA

DIAGNOSTIC FEATURES

A generalized obsession with France, often coupled with a rabid disdain for the French themselves.

ASSOCIATED FEATURES AND DISORDERS

The wearing of espadrilles; overuse of French phrases; *joie de vivre.*

SPECIFIC CULTURE AND GENDER FEATURES

More common in women than men, but only slightly. Epidemic among couture-loving Texas matrons, posh Persians, and other fans of gilt furniture. For additional case studies, see St. Barts between Christmas and New Year's.

PLUTOPHILIA

DIAGNOSTIC FEATURES

A judgment disorder, plutophilia leads otherwise decent people to forge friendships solely with other plutocrats, regardless of common interests or glaring character flaws.

ASSOCIATED FEATURES AND DISORDERS

A consistent ability to overlook astounding faults in one's dinner guests. Plutophiliacs often wonder why everyone they know ends up in jail.

SPECIFIC CULTURE AND GENDER FEATURES

The plutophiliac's obsession with having "successful" and "interesting" friends has a clouding effect on his or her morals, allowing the sufferer to befriend Arab dictators, Wall Street swindlers, et al.

RUSSOPHOBIA

DIAGNOSTIC FEATURES

The vague feeling of self-doubt and anxiety one feels following an encounter with a Russian oligarch. He's 39, he's worth $13 billion, and he could make you disappear.

ASSOCIATED FEATURES AND DISORDERS

The sinking feeling that some day your descendants will be working for his.

SPECIFIC CULTURE AND GENDER FEATURES

A rite of passage for newly minted males in St. Tropez, St. Barts, London, and Verbier in the French Alps.

TANOREXIA

DIAGNOSTIC FEATURES

A quasi-religious devotion to maintaining a year-round tan. The complexions of late-stage sufferers have the smooth patina and feel of a baseball glove.

ASSOCIATED FEATURES AND DISORDERS

Dandyism; extreme vanity; melanoma.

SPECIFIC CULTURE AND GENDER FEATURES

A certain type of man (and it's always a man) wants the world to always assume he just got back from Palm Beach.

THE LUSH LIFE

Where to Go When the Party's Over

AFTER YEARS OF OVER-INDULGENCE IN DRINK AND DRUGS, YOU WILL ONE DAY DECIDE you've had enough. Five to ten years after that day, you will start examining your rehab options. But where to turn? With so many high-priced treatment centers out there, it's harder than ever to find the right insta-cure. Thankfully you'll have the following guide to filthy rich rehabs, based on actual reviews from former patients. Let go and let God.

BETTY FORD

Rancho Mirage, California
BettyFordCenter.org

F 20 D 17 S 19 C $$

"ARRIVE WITH A CHECK, AND YOU GET lots of hugs," says one habitué, even if you "show up drenched in beer"; however, any complaints about the "sterile" "four-to-a-room" quarters—even if you're "Drew Barrymore or Billy Joel"—will draw a sharp reminder that the facility is a palace compared with the "naval hospital where Betty Ford got sober"; clients like Jay-Z are free to splash about in "the four-foot-deep Olympic pool" or play badminton "under certain controls"; inveterate shoppers rave about the selection of "popcorn and teddy bears in the gift shop."

CLIFFSIDE

Malibu, California
CliffsideMalibu.com

F 28 D 26 S 27 C $$$$

"YOU DEFINITELY GET YOUR $45,000-per-month's worth"; excursions include "the Getty Museum" and "shopping on Rodeo Drive"; for many, "the most exclusive treatment center on the planet" is worth checking into "for the mani-pedis alone"; unfortunately, capacity is "six clients at a time," so even "celebrities, athletes, and captains of industry" have to "fight for a bed"; all that exclusivity ensures "guests' names never make it into the tabloids" (well, aside from that report in the *Star* about Mel Gibson's son, Christian); notable luxuries include "on-site massages" and "absurdly high thread-count sheets."

CROSSROADS

Antigua
CrossroadsAntigua.org

F 19 D 25 S 22 C $$$$

"TWENTY FEET FROM THE WATER, right on the beach," its location is "second to none," say Crossroaders, even if "barrier fences to keep clients like Britney and Whitney from swan diving to their deaths" obscure the view somewhat; excursions to Half Moon Bay for "recovery work on the beach" help foster a "Club Med–like atmosphere," but "without the activities"; founder Eric Clapton "was down there the whole time I was," says one satisfied customer who still treasures the aging rocker's "lecture on self-esteem."

HAZELDEN
Center City, Minnesota
Hazelden.org

F 17 D 20 S 17 C $$$

"YALE, JAIL, PARK AVENUE, OR PARK bench"—everyone's treated the same at egalitarian Hazelden, one of the "few treatment places that actually work"; although, complains one guest, "what I had in common with Liza Minnelli is beyond me"; while "the coffee is actually caffeinated," the diversionary activities are so few even the "weekly Dairy Queen run in below-zero temperatures was eagerly anticipated"; graduates like "James Frey and Calvin Klein" receive a "little lapel pin in the shape of a camel."

PROMISES
Malibu, California
Promises.com

F 23 D 24 S 21 C $$$$

"NOTHING BEATS PULLING UP TO AN AA meeting in a luxury SUV," and guests of Promises—a list that's included "Ben Affleck, Matthew Perry, and Britney Spears"—do just that; the 22-bed villa-style facility offers "equine-assisted therapy" and "group meetings galore"; client favorites include "movie and popcorn" nights and the opportunity on weekends for "a hasty sexual encounter with a sober outsider" in one of the house bathrooms; the menu boasts high-end fare like "inch-thick steaks"—but you might be eating them with your fingers, since "new kids have to be vetted to use knives."

SIERRA TUCSON
Tucson, Arizona
SierraTucson.com

F 19 D 23 S 18 C $$$$

THE ULTIMATE IN "RANCH-STYLE RESORT rehabbing" also functions as a "level-one psychiatric facility," so "you can address underlying issues," while enjoying hiking, horseback riding, and "adventure therapy climbing" on Sierra's "160-acre campus"; even the "wives of rock stars" (including a "certain Starr named Ringo") must abide by the modest dress code—arriving in skimpy "junkie chic" attire will get you "sent into town for a new wardrobe."

RATINGS KEY

F FOOD
D DECOR
S SERVICE
C COST

0–9 POOR TO FAIR	20–25 VERY GOOD TO EXCELLENT	$—BUDGET ($499 OR LESS PER DAY)	$$$—EXPENSIVE ($750 TO $1,249 PER DAY)
10–15 FAIR TO GOOD	26–30 EXTRAORDINARY TO PERFECTION	$$—MODERATE ($500 TO $749 PER DAY)	$$$$—LUXURY ($1,250 AND UP PER DAY)
16–19 GOOD TO VERY GOOD			

STRANGER DANGER

Bound and Gagged for Being Filthy Rich

Sadly, there will always be certain degenerates unable to resist the lure of making a quick buck off the pain and suffering of the more fortunate. Be careful out there.

ADOLPH COORS III

NABBED: *1960*

The 44-year-old beer dynasty scion was accidentally murdered during a botched kidnapping attempt as he made his way to work at the family brewery in Morrison, Colorado. His killer, Joseph Corbett Jr., tried to ransom him nonetheless, delivering a note to Coors's wife demanding $500,000. His remains were found seven months later.

FRANK SINATRA JR.

NABBED: *1963*

Snagged at Harrah's casino in Lake Tahoe, Young Blue Eyes was released two days later, after his father paid a $240,000 ransom.

JOHN PAUL GETTY III

NABBED: *1973*

After John Paul Getty III's miserly grandfather refused to pay his $17 million ransom, suspecting the 16-year-old was in on it, his kidnappers cut off one of his ears and sent it to an Italian newspaper. Eventually the family got the boy back for the bargain price of $3.2 million (which John was required to repay at 4 percent interest). Traumatized, he later became addicted to heroin. A 1981 overdose triggered a stroke that left him paralyzed and legally blind. His son is the actor Balthazar Getty.

PATRICIA HEARST

NABBED: *1974*

Shortly after being seized by the Symbionese Liberation Army—a whacked-out black liberation group—19-year-old Patricia adopted the *nom de guerre* "Tania" and joined her

DADDY'S GIRL
Patricia Hearst

creepy captors on an interstate bank-robbing spree. Publishing scion Randolph Hearst was ordered to give $70 worth of food to every needy Californian. Realizing this would cost him over $400 million, he instead distributed $6 million worth of groceries to the homeless of San Francisco. The SLA judged the grub to be of "inferior quality," and refused to release his daughter. Patricia was arrested a year later and served two years for armed robbery.

MARCI KLEIN

NABBED: *1977*

Grabbed on her way to New York's Dalton School and returned after her father, überdesigner Calvin, dropped a $100,000 ransom in the lobby of the Pan Am building.

EDDIE LAMPERT

NABBED: *2003*

One of the world's most successful hedge fund managers was abducted from the parking garage of his Greenwich, Connecticut, office and held for two days in a motel bathroom before being released. When the assailants used his credit card to order pizza, he convinced them that a tracer had been activated and police were on their way.

HOW THE OTHER HALF LEAVES

RUPERT & ANNA MURDOCH
$1.7 BILLION

AFTER 32 YEARS AND THREE RUGRATS, Aussie press lord Rupert Murdoch amicably split from his wife in 1998. Then he forced her off the News Corp. board. Bad move. When the dust finally settled in June 1999, Anna had been awarded $1.7 billion in assets and $110 million cash. Seventeen days later, Rupe kept it classy by marrying one of his own employees, News Corp. exec Wendi Deng.

ADNAN & SORAYA KHASHOGGI
$873 MILLION

AFTER 21 YEARS AND COUNTLESS AFFAIRS, the jet-setting Khashoggis finally called it quits in 1982. At the height of Adnan's power, the irrepressible Saudi arms dealer/bon vivant/Iran-Contra middleman's fortune was pegged at $4 billion. Estimates vary on how much Soraya received, as her reported settlement was pegged to oil prices.

CRAIG & WENDY MCCAW
$460 MILLION

CELL PHONE PIONEER CRAIG McCAW MET his first wife, Wendy, when she tutored him at Stanford, and married her in 1974. By the mid-1990s, however, their relationship had cooled considerably. (Selling your startup for $12 billion, as Craig did in 1994, has a way of broadening your horizons.) At their 1995 divorce hearing, Wendy demanded $200,000 a month to support her considerably upgraded lifestyle. She ultimately netted $460 million, mostly in stock.

JACK WELCH & JANE BEASLEY
$180 MILLION

THE TOUGH-TALKING GE GURU MARRIED his second wife, Jane Beasley, in 1989. They divorced in 2003, a year after Jack admitted to an affair with Suzy Wetlaufer, an editor at the *Harvard Business Review* who'd been dispatched to profile him. As luck would have it, a "10-year clause" in the couple's prenup had nullified the agreement, allowing Beasley to cart off an estimated $180 million of Jack's scratch. He married Ms. Wetlaufer soon after and began a second career as a motivational book author.

NEIL DIAMOND & MARCIA MURPHEY $150 MILLION

THE HIRSUTE BALLADEER AND FUTURE ironic sex symbol married a TV production assistant just prior to releasing his first gold album, *Touching You, Touching Me,* in 1969. By the late '70s, he was raking in over $14 million annually. Murphey filed for divorce in 1994 after 25 years of marriage and two kids, and was subsequently awarded half of Diamond's fortune. Ever the gentleman, he later remarked that she had "earned every penny."

STEVEN SPIELBERG & AMY IRVING $100 MILLION

HARD AS OTHER COUPLES TRY, STEVE and Amy still hold the record for the most expensive breakup in Hollywood history. Never one to leave things to chance, Steve had, of course, made her sign a prenup. Unfortunately, it was written on a cocktail napkin. Irving successfully contested the gin-soaked pre*nap* on the grounds that she did not have a lawyer present when she signed it. A judge sympathized and awarded her half the director's fortune.

BILLION-DOLLAR BREAKUPS

When the Filthy Rich Split

Extrapolating from the divorce rate of the Forbes 400 (30 percent, compared to the national average of 50), soap opera writers have it all wrong: The Filthy Rich do not divorce at a higher rate than the rest of the country. They just do it bigger and bolder and brasher than everyone else, with armies of $1,000-an-hour lawyers, expert witnesses, and private investigators egging them on. They also do it repeatedly: At last count, there were 25 twice-divorced and 10 thrice-divorced tycoons on the fabled list. As usual, Revlon roué Ron Perelman is in a class all his own: With four ex-wives at press time, he is the most-married billionaire in America.

Of course, considering the manner in which today's plutocrats accumulate toys, it should come as no surprise when their capriciousness extends to spouses. Which is a circuitous way of saying: Thank God for the prenup! Properly executed, this magical contract will allow you to walk away from any marital entanglement with what you brought into it—minus years of your life, your mental health, and your dignity. It will be challenged (they always are), but you'll have a starting point for the decade-long court battle.

Where you get married is key, so make sure your attorney is versed in the local statutes. In L.A., for instance, if a union survives ten years, both parties are entitled to 50 percent if they split. As a result, scores of women get dumped just shy of the decade mark—or "Cruised," as it's called, in honor of discarded power wife Nicole Kidman.

YOU GOT CRUISED! Nicole Kidman

LAST LAUGHS

Inspired Wills of the Well-to-Do

WHEN COMPOSING YOUR LAST WILL AND TESTAMENT, YOU'LL NEVER MAKE EVERYONE happy. So why not have some fun?

- In 1910, bestselling *War and Peace* author **Leo Tolstoy** bequeathed his possessions to a tree stump. Seriously.

THANKS, LEO! The Stump

- When he kicked it in 1950, Irish playwright **George Bernard Shaw** bequeathed a portion of his wealth to whomever could invent a new English alphabet. He specified that it had to have at least 40 letters and be easier to use than our current one.

- When McDonald's widow **Joan Kroc** moved on to the drive-thru in the sky in 2003, she left $300 million to an obscure, nearly defunct magazine called *Poetry*.

- In 2007, billionairess **Leona Helmsley** left her beloved Maltese, Trouble, a $12 million trust fund. Two of her grandsons received $5 million apiece, contingent on their visiting the family mausoleum at least once a year (no fool she, Grandma stipulated that a guest book be installed so that her trustees could monitor their visits). Her other two grandchildren got nothing, "for reasons known to them."

A TOMB OF ONE'S OWN
The Importance of Planning Ahead

After devoting so much energy to stylish living, it would be a shame to skimp on the dying part. Mausoleums—those gaudy cemetery status symbols of yore—have recently made a comeback. And considering that, of all your homes, this is the one you'll be spending the most time in, dropping several million on one *before you're even dead* almost sounds like a sane idea. So make like a robber baron and call Frank Gehry today. You'll be in good company.

DONALD TRUMP
(1945–?)

The real estate kingpin hopes to build a massive family mausoleum near the first hole at the Trump National Golf Club in Bedminster, New Jersey. Presumably there will be room for all his wives.

TOM FORD
(1962–?)

The former Gucci guru isn't leaving the afterlife to chance: He's commissioned starchitect Tadao Ando to build a mausoleum on his Santa Fe estate, where Ford, his boyfriend, and their pets will reside in post-mortal fabulosity.

TIMES UP

Write Your Own Obit

AS SOMEONE WHO INSISTS ON ALWAYS HAVING THE LAST WORD, THE VERY IDEA OF SOME biased newspaper writing the summation of your life's achievements chills you to the core. What do they know, really? Aside from what they've read in *Fortune, Forbes, W*, *New York Social Diary*, the *Congressional Record*, and Page Six? The very idea of it is downright insulting. Although *The New York Times* does not accept outside submissions, it couldn't hurt to fax over a completed copy of the following fill-in-the-blank obituary. If you've read one, you've read 'em all. At least you'll know they have your net worth right.

________ (YOUR FULL NAME), who famously parlayed a $________ (NUMBER BETWEEN 1 AND 5,000) investment into one of the world's leading ________ (BASIC COMMODITY/TECHNOLOGY/RETAIL/MEDIA/REAL ESTATE/FINANCIAL) concerns, has died. He/she was ________ (NUMBER BETWEEN 50 AND 100).

Mr./Mrs. ________ (YOUR LAST NAME) passed away at his/her storied estate, ________ (PLANT SPECIES) Hill, following a ________ (BRIEF ILLNESS/TRAGIC BOATING ACCIDENT), according to a spokesperson for the ________ (YOUR FULL NAME) Charitable Trust, the nonprofit foundation Mr./Mrs. ________ (YOUR LAST NAME) established to fight ________ (UNIMPORTANT SOCIAL ISSUE) shortly after selling his/her firm to ________ (CORPORATE BEHEMOTH) 20 years ago.

Mr./Mrs. ________ (YOUR LAST NAME), who also owned the ________ (SECOND-TIER SPORTS FRANCHISE), and the beleaguered ________ (REGIONAL NEWSPAPER), is survived by his/her third wife/husband of ________ (LESS THAN 10) years, ________ (FIRST NAME ENDING IN VOWEL), and six children from his/her previous marriages. According to the September issue of *Forbes* magazine, he/she leaves behind a fortune estimated at over $________ (NUMBER BETWEEN 1 AND 25) billion.

Born into ____________ GREAT PRIVILEGE/A MIDDLE-CLASS HOME in ____________ GREENWICH, CONNECTICUT/THE MIDWEST, Mr./Mrs. ____________ YOUR LAST NAME was a man/woman of ____________ FEW/MANY words—a ____________ SUBDUED/LARGER-THAN-LIFE presence on the international ____________ EQUESTRIAN/SAILING/ART/POLO/FASHION circuit, renowned for his/her ____________ EXQUISITE SENSE OF STYLE/GENEROUS SPIRIT and distinctive collection of bespoke ____________ LUXURY FABRIC ____________ BODY PART wear. Mr./Mrs. ____________ YOUR LAST NAME and his/her spouse had, until very recently, been a fixture at charity events both in ____________ MAJOR CITY and ____________ ELITIST ENCLAVE, where their winter compound, ____________ SPANISH WORD de ____________ SPANISH WORD, played host to some of this century's biggest names. According to a recent profile in *W* magazine, their annual black-tie gala, the ____________ COLOR & ____________ COLOR Ball, drew luminaries like ____________ A-LIST ACTRESS, ____________ BRITISH ROYAL, Oscar de la Renta, and Moby. Last year's event, hosted by ____________ MIDDLE-AGED SUPERGROUP, raised over $7 million for ____________ UNCOMMON FORM OF CANCER research.

Shortly after ____________ GRADUATING FROM/DROPPING OUT OF ____________ IVY LEAGUE COLLEGE, Mr./Mrs. ____________ YOUR LAST NAME made his/her first big splash working for ____________ LEGENDARY DEFUNCT COMPANY, when he/she caught the eye of ____________ INDUSTRY titan, ____________ FAMOUS RICH PERSON. ____________ RESPECTED/FEARED within the industry, his/her reputation suffered a blow when his/her firm was investigated for ____________ FRAUD/ACCOUNTING IRREGULARITIES/BRIBERY/PAYOLA by the U.S. Attorneys' office. Although six of his/her close associates ultimately pled guilty and served lengthy federal prison terms,

criminal charges were never filed against Mr./Mrs. ______________
YOUR LAST NAME
after he/she agreed to pay an undisclosed sum in fines to the ______________. In a sly nod to the scandal, Mr./Mrs.
FTC/FCC/SEC/WORLD BANK
______________ christened his/her 530-foot superyacht—
YOUR LAST NAME
the first of its kind outfitted with a ______________—the
POPULAR RESTAURANT CHAIN
______________.
BAD LEGAL PUN

In addition to his/her philanthropic works, Mr./Mrs. ______________ served on the boards of ______________,
YOUR LAST NAME FORTUNE 500 COMPANY
______________, ______________, Memorial Sloan-
FORTUNE 500 COMPANY FORTUNE 500 COMPANY
Kettering Hospital, the Kennedy Center, and the Metropolitan Museum of Art, where he/she provided the funds for the first-ever exhibit of ______________th century antiquities from
NUMBER BETWEEN 10 AND 17
______________. As a member of both the
OBSCURE ASIAN COUNTRY
______________ and the Council on Foreign
TRILATERAL COMMISSION/BILDERBERG GROUP
Relations, Mr./Mrs. ______________ often played a considerable,
YOUR LAST NAME
if mostly unseen, role in shaping world affairs.

Although Mr./Mrs. ______________ donated to both
YOUR LAST NAME
Republicans and Democrats, he/she was a ______________ of
CLOSE CONFIDANTE/VOCAL CRITIC
President ______________. On the floor of the Senate this after-
INSERT FULL NAME
noon, House ______________ Leader ______________
MINORITY/MAJORITY INSERT NAME
noted Mr./Mrs. ______________'s passing, calling him/her a
YOUR LAST NAME
"______________ [whose] biography is proof positive
TRUE PATRIOT/WORTHY ADVERSARY
that ______________ is alive and well."
THE AMERICAN DREAM/SHAMELESS CORPORATE GREED

ACKNOWLEDGMENTS

Credit and/or blowback for the preceding work should be apportioned amongst the following: Carol and Walter Tennant, the exceptionally upstanding and lovely people who have aided, abetted, and inspired me since birth; Peter Workman, as wise and supportive a publisher as any author could hope for; Laura Yorke, a master packager and class traitor of the very best sort, without whom this project would not have happened; Susan Bolotin, my patient and exceedingly clever editor who gave me far more rope than I deserved; Sarah Horne, whose easy wit and shocking recall for filthy rich trivia continue to delight and appall; Marnie Hanel, a star pinch hitter, dexterous writer, and even better sport; Carol Mann, who pieced this project together, and made sure it stayed that way; Maer Roshan and the brilliant minds at *Radar* magazine, who suffered my extracurricular indulgences; Elisa Lipsky-Karasz, whose fateful phone call started this whole palaver; and Zoë Turnbull, the most alluring and talented accomplice a guy could ever ask for.

Others who provided words, concepts, anecdotes, insights, artwork, advice, diversions, usable jokes, and libelous inferences, include, in no particular order: Oliver Kramer, Adam Laukhuf, Julie Bloom, Austin Lysy, Julia Allison, Janette Beckman, Terry Allen Kramer, Nick Simunek, John Connolly, Sam Orlofsky, Lucy McIntyre, Chris Wilson, Steve Garbarino, Andrew Breitbart, Marshall Heyman, Harry Lodge, Steven Gaines; Erica, Justine, and Alyson Tennant; Paula Froelich, Annabel Davidson, Brad Fisher, Anthony Haden-Guest, Sam Forman, Spencer Morgan, Sloane Crosley, Willa Paskin, Sarah Cristobal, Joey Jalleo, Billy Farrell, Lynn Guertin, Bruce Hammond, Greg Littley, Beverly and Ben Turnbull, Dale Hrabi, Kimry Blackwelder, Jimmy Jellinek, Camilla Long, David Goldweitz, Margot Bush, Patricia Hearst, Campion Platt, Michael Haverland, Jay Jolly, Polina Aronova, Alex Kuczynski, and Morris. To Elliott and Coleman Snyder, the unsung heroes of this endeavor, a message from your mother: "May your true wealth come from inside."

Finally, among the many stars at Workman who helped guide this book through its long gestation, I'm particularly indebted to Randall Lotowycz, Francesca Messina, Tom Boyce, Brianna Yamashita, Amy Corley, Andrea Fleck, Justin Nisbet, Amy Lewis, Savannah Ashour, Aaron Clendening, Anne Kerman, Basia Zamorska, and Patrick Borelli.

Thanks a billion, all of you.

INDEX

A

B

C

D

E

I

J

K

L

M

N

S

T

U

CREDITS

PHOTOGRAPHY

FRONT MATTER: p. iv Janette Bekman, p. v (top) SuperStock/age fotostock, p. v (bottom) Personalized Pacifiers.

CHAPTER 1: p. 1 Food Collection/age fotostock, p. 2 (both spots) AP Images, p. 3 (left spot) AP Images, p. 3 (right spot) Patrick McMullan, pp. 4–15 (all spots) AP Images, p. 16 (left spot) Tim Grant/ Stringer/Getty Images, p. 16 (right spot) AP Images, pp. 17–18 (all spots) AP Images, p. 19 (top) Beauty Photo Studio/age fotostock, p. 19 (middle left) Photos.com, p. 19 (middle right) Dubrovskaya Maria/Shutterstock.com, p. 19 (bottom) Masterfile, p. 20 (top) Hulton Archive/Getty Images, p. 20 (bottom) AP Images, p. 21 (both) AP Images, p. 24 (mortarboard) Morgan Lane Photography/Shutterstock.com, p. 24 (all headshots) AP Images. All Plutocrat photography pp. 2–18 by Janette Beckman, except p. 10 and p. 17 by Jenna Bascom.

CHAPTER 2: p. 25 Photos.com, p. 28 Mali Azima/Between Inc., p. 29 Gene Peach, p. 30 Panoramic Images/Getty Images, p. 31 Tim Street–Porter/ Beateworks, Inc., p. 32 David Peevers/Lonely Planet Images, p. 33 Hulton Archive/ Getty Images, p. 36 Anthony Bolante/ Reuters, p. 38 (top) DEA/W. Buss/age fotostock, p. 38 (bottom) AlexShay .com, p. 39 Wayne Eastep/Getty Images, p. 40 James Aylott/Getty Images, p. 54 The Francis Frith Collection/age fotostock, p. 55 Widmann/age fotostock, p. 56 Nick Vedros/age fotostock, p. 57 AP Images, p. 58 Alberto Biscaro/ Masterfile, p. 59 J.K.E. Andanson/ Corbis Sygma

CHAPTER 3: p. 63 Kupka/age fotostock, p. 66 AP Images, p. 68 (all) AP Images

CHAPTER 4: p. 71 Hulton Archive/Getty Images, p. 74 (top) AP Images, p. 74 (bottom) Library of Congress Prints and Photographs, p. 75 (top) Library of Congress Prints and Photographs, p. 75 (bottom) Clipart.com, p. 76 (top) Mike Randolph/Masterfile, p. 76 (bottom) Bobby Deal/RealDealPhoto/ Shutterstock.com, p. 77 Edyta Pawlowska/Shutterstock.com, p. 78 Jupiter Images, p. 80 Masterfile, p. 83 Stephen Swintek/Getty Images, p. 84 demarcomedia/Shutterstock .com, p. 85 Thomas Northcut/Getty Images, p. 89 (all) AP Images, p. 90 (top) WireImage/Getty Images, p. 90 (bottom) Christie's Images LTD. 2008, p. 91 (left) WireImage/Getty Images, p. 91 (right) Dave Bennett/ Getty Images, p. 92 ElementalImaging/ Shutterstock.com, p. 92 Andy Piatt/ Shutterstock.com

CHAPTER 5: p. 95 Hulton Archive/ Getty Images, p. 97 SuperStock, Inc., pp. 98–103 (open book) Luminis/ Shutterstock.com, p. 98 (Post-it) Dorling Kindersley/Getty Images, p. 98 AP Images, pp. 99–102 (all) AP Images, p. 103 (top) AP Images, p. 103 (bottom) Courtesy MCH Swiss Exhibition (Basel/Zurich) Ltd, p. 104 Quayside/Shutterstock.com, p. 105 objectsforall/Shutterstock.com, p. 107 Ewa Walicka/Shutterstock.com, p. 109 Stephen Rudolph/Shutterstock.com, p. 110 AP Images, p. 111 George Green/ Shutterstock.com, p. 112 AP Images, p. 113 Alexandr Shebanov/Shutterstock .com, p. 117 Photos.com

CHAPTER 6: p. 123 Michel Renaudeau/age fotostock, pp. 126–127 Tyler Stableford/Getty Images, p. 130 Kindra Clineff/Getty Images, p. 132 sperrytopsider.com, p. 134 (left) Danilo Donadoni/age fotostock, p. 134 (right) Brannhage Bo/age fotostock, p. 135 (left) Wojtek Buss/age fotostock, p. 135 (right) Kord.com/age fotostock, p. 136 Austrophoto/age fotostock, p. 137 Mark van Aardt/Getty Images, p. 142 Courtesy Musha Cay at Copperfield Bay, p. 143 Andy Whale/Getty Images

CHAPTER 7: p. 149 Dirk Lindner/ zefa/Corbis, p. 150 (top) AP Images, p. 150 (bottom) Daimler AG, p. 151 (top) AP Images, p. 151 (middle left) AP Images, p. 151 (middle right) Neil Roy Johnson/Shutterstock.com, p. 151 (bottom) AP Images, pp. 152–155 (all) AP Images, p. 158 SuperStock/age fotostock, p. 159 Vova Pomortzeff/ Shutterstock.com, p. 160 Kurt Scholz/SuperStock Inc., p. 161 (top) U. S. Submarines, Inc., p. 161 (bottom) Eurocopterusa.com, p. 162 Getty Images, p. 163 Ocean Voyages, pp. 164–165 (all) AP Images, p. 166 (top) Gilles Martin–Raget/Wally, p. 166 (bottom) Onne van der Wal/ Hinckley, p. 167 (Post-it) Dorling Kindersley/Getty Images, p.167 (book) Luminis/Shutterstock.com, p. 167 AP Images

CHAPTER 8: p. 171 Time & Life Pictures/Getty Images, p. 172 (top) Photos.com, p. 172 (bottom) Simon Katzer/age fotostock, p. 173 (top) John Kelly/Getty Images, p. 173 (bottom) AP Images, p. 174 Lorenz/ Avelar/Jupiter Images, p. 176 (top) Keith Levit/Shutterstock.com, p. 176 (bottom) Jen Judge/Getty Images, p. 177 Asher Welstead/Shutterstock.com, p. 179 (all) AP Images, p. 180 Time & Life Pictures/Getty Images, p. 181 Getty Images, p. 182 RazoomGame/ Shutterstock.com, p. 184 Rod Beverley/Shutterstock.com, p. 185 Leonardo da Vinci/Getty Images, p. 186 John Coletti/age fotostock, pp. 187–189 (both) AP Images, p. 192 Mike McDonald/Shutterstock.com

CHAPTER 9: p. 195 James Steidl/Shutterstock.com, p. 197 (top) Personalized Pacifiers, p. 197 (bottom–woman) Clipart.com, p. 199 (top left) Time & Life Pictures/Getty Images, p. 199 (top right) AFP/Getty Images, p. 199 (bottom) Hulton Archive/Getty Images, p. 200 Hulton Archive/Getty Images, p. 201 Maclaren, p. 214 (both) AP Images

CHAPTER 10: p. 217 PhotoSpin, pp. 218–225 (notebook) Jenna Bascom, p. 227 PhotoCreate/ Shutterstock.com, p. 228 AP Images, p. 229 Time & Life Pictures/Getty Images, p. 230 WireImage/Getty Images, p. 231 Kshishtof/ Shutterstock.com.

AUTHOR BIO: p. 248 Nick Rhodes

ILLUSTRATIONS

CHAPTER 1: p. 22 Natasha Tibbott

CHAPTER 2: pp. 26–27, 34 Alan Kikuchi, pp. 44–48 Clare Mallison, pp. 50–53 James Williamson

CHAPTER 3: pp. 64, 66, 67 Andy Friedman

CHAPTER 4: pp. 72–73 Andy Friedman, p. 77 Natasha Tibbott, p. 82 Andy Friedman, pp. 86–89 Clare Mallison

CHAPTER 6: pp. 122–125 Alan Kikuchi, pgs. 138, 139 Andy Friedman, p. 140 Natasha Tibbott

CHAPTER 7: p. 153 Natasha Tibbott, p. 156 Clare Mallison

CHAPTER 8: p. 183 Andy Friedman

CHAPTER 9: pp. 196, 203 Andy Friedman, pp. 205, 207, 210 Michael Aron

Christopher Tennant has previously chronicled the foibles of the rich and infamous as an editor and writer at *New York* magazine, *Talk*, the *New York Post*'s Page Six column, and *Radar*, the pop culture magazine and website he cofounded in 2003. Born and raised in the leafy suburbs of Boston, he currently lives beyond his means in New York City.